Let There Be Pebble

LET THERE BE
PEBBLE

A MIDDLE-HANDICAPPER'S YEAR
IN AMERICA'S GARDEN OF GOLF

ZACHARY MICHAEL JACK

Anderson, S.C.
AND

University of Nebraska Press, Lincoln and London

Library of Congress Cataloging-
in-Publication Data
Jack, Zachary Michael, 1973–
Let there be Pebble: a middle-
handicapper's year in America's garden
of golf / Zachary Michael Jack.   p. cm.
ISBN 978-0-8032-3357-7 (cloth: alk. paper)
1. U.S. Open (Golf tournament) (2010:
Pebble Beach, Calif.) 2. Pebble Beach Golf
Links (Pebble Beach, Calif.)
3. Golf — United States I. Title.
GV970.3.U69J34 2011
796.35206'879476 — dc22   2010049044

Set in Minion Pro.

For Dad,
For the Grand Old Game,
For the Granddaddy of American Golf Courses

"Long John Silver never hated the sight of a Spanish galleon more than Pebble hates that of a guy walking up to it with a golf club in his hand and par on his mind. It'll broadside him, keelhaul him, throw him to the sharks. You almost can't bear to look."

JIM MURRAY, "Course Could Turn Him into Meatball," *Los Angeles Times*

CONTENTS

Let There Be Pebble

1

Then God Created the Heavens and Earth, and Carmel-by-the-Sea, and God Said, "Let There Be Pebble"

When I announced to my coworkers I would be taking a "professional leave" from teaching to spend a U.S. Open year on the storied fairways of Pebble Beach, they looked at me as if I'd taken leave of something else: my senses. They're intellectuals, teachers all, and not one of them an avid golfer.

I am going to Pebble for a year, and not just any year, but a year culminating in its hosting of the U.S. Open on the tenth anniversary of Tiger Woods's unprecedented 15-shot drubbing of the field in 2000, a year in which Pebble will host bigger, better professional men's golf events than at anytime in its celebrated history. I am going to live by, and tee it up on, the beautiful beast Dan Jenkins once dubbed "Double Bogey-by-the-Sea," the track about which Jim Murray once wrote, "It's not a golf course, it's a hellship." I, a former failed walk-on for my state university's golf team, will roll in the hay with the layout that eventual winner Jack Nicklaus described in 1972 as "scary" — and

1

that gave him nightmares so acute he confessed to waking up his wife for consolation.

I am going to Pebble, I suspect, as part and parcel of an early middle-age crisis. Not the Porsche-buying, romp-with-your-intern kind, though Pebble *is* the Porsche of golf—a brand ranked by the *Robb Report* as one of the top thirty of all-time, alongside Ferrari, Rolls Royce, Mercedes Benz, Sotheby's, and Louis Vuitton. No, my middle-age crisis, if that's what beast this be, is something far quieter and hinges on a simple, inarguable fact: I've reached the precise age of my father when his son, yours truly, first swung a pitching wedge.

There have been other clues, other intimations of sea change. This summer my pop saw fit to bestow upon me his old Tommy Armour irons, his ridiculous golf swing training aids, and his even more ridiculous Clorox-bleached shag balls. I would get more use out of them than he ever would, he said. After spending a life farming 500 acres and greenskeeping the greens-less pasture course we made on our farm and dubbed Foxbriar G.C., his knees and back are shot. I'd agree to this premature passing of the guard, I'd told him, if and only if I could take the sticks on loan, exercise them on the fabled fairways of Pebble, and maybe, just maybe baptize them in the blue-green waters of Carmel Bay.

I am not prepared to take my father's weapons, his lands, or his cattle. I am not ready to vanquish him as the Freudians would have me do. I am going to Pebble Beach because sons inevitably and sometimes joyfully shoulder their father's burdens. Two decades ago my pop and I had been within a frog's hair of entering the national father-son tournament contested on the fairways of that famous, faraway links. We came within a Ma Bell call and a Mastercard swipe of having grown men in wool vests and flat caps open for us the door to the famous lodge.

To reach the age of your father when he first introduced you to the game is one indicator of middleagedom, one milestone to knock some carpe diem into you. Another is seeing the golfers of your youth age right before your very eyes, finding yourself metaphorically winless at the age when they were collecting trophies hand over fist. My father's golfing heroes where always Jack Nicklaus and Tom Watson—Nicklaus, who famously said that if he had only one round left to play on earth, he'd play it at Pebble Beach. Dad liked Nicklaus for his mental toughness and unassailable integrity and Watson for his middlewestern ethic, speedy play, and boyish flair for the dramatic. By the time I came to the game both stars were on the wane. I had only my dad's accounts of their greatness to go on.

When I first picked up my dad's wedge, Watson had years earlier chipped in for birdie from left of the seventeenth green to beat Jack and win the '82 U.S. Open at Pebble. Two years later his career as a winner on the regular tour would be over, all but for a couple breakthroughs over the decade and a half that followed. Nicklaus would sneak in just one more magical major, the 1986 Masters, before his career as a competitive threat on the PGA circuit would be kaput, too.

Could it be the same Watson, then, a few more crow's-feet creasing the corners of his Firth of Forth eyes and a little less of that Tom Sawyer ginger, striding up the eighteenth fairway needing only par to win the 2009 British Open at Turnberry at the ripe old age of fifty-nine? Had I not been glued to the tube, I would have assumed the broadcast had gone into weather delay with ABC, anxious to avoid a ratings plunge, going back in the vaults to replay Watson's sublime 1977 Open triumph over Jack: the Duel in the Sun.

The 2009 time warp at Turnberry snapped me out of my early middle-age lethargy. The very summer that my dad surrenders his sticks—they of the grains-of-rice-in-a-rainmaker loose-metal-shaving shafts, he of the bowed and broken body—his golfing hero, Watson, strides up the home hole, all toothy grin, the world's biggest tournament all but in the bag.

Is this, then, how the golf gods do "bidness"—gifting one man with agelessness and abundant blessings and the other with a bum knee and a busted bank account? Or have both men reaped what they have sown, willing their life to be what it has become? Where does this leave me, a generation behind and every year golfing less and less, yielding to practical demands, divorcing myself from the purer, life-giving rumpus that characterized my many childhood rounds with my old man at our beloved Foxbriar G.C.?

Enter Pebble, the Camelot on Carmel Bay, where the same rituals played out every February at the National Pro-Am—Jack Lemmon trying his damndest to never make the cut, Bob Hope cracking his dated old-man jokes, Clint Eastwood grinning his wizened sex-symbol grin when the star-struck girls in the gallery invited him to make their day. The harbor seals at play, the shitty weather, the bagpipers piping in the milky twilight at Spanish Bay, the sailboats tacking in and out of Stillwater Cove—Pebble could be counted on to produce year after year that inimitable, quality-controlled brew.

Just as the men of my father's generation, the boomers, return with longing to the cars of their youth, I too am kicking it old school, going back to the old magic that sang a siren's song to a snowbound, golf-obsessed midwestern farm kid each February. Mine is no mere nostalgia, no mean attempt to recover faded glory, but a return to a place, a feeling, a word, *Pebble*, that sounds like comfort and healing and mystery all at once.

There is an even greater force pushing me toward what's begun to seem like destiny: an economical rental in Carmel-by-the-Sea, craigslist manna dropped in my lap in a town where "affordable housing" is an oxymoron. Only $950 per month for a sleeping room, a toilet, and a shower—no kitchen—mere blocks away from Pebble's tenth green. The last name of the purveyor of this blessed manger contains the word *angel*.

For I am your shepherd, and this is your Prostaff, and, behold, here is your course.

4

2

Dark Knights, Great Whites, Dear Young Watsons, Fuzzy Memories, and Felonious Meetings of Land and Sea

The first step I take onto the hallowed grounds of Pebble Beach Golf Links is an illegal one. At the least I have misdemeanored; at most I have sinned.

Though in a few short hours I will be prowling the grounds legit, for now I walk to the seaweedy end of Carmel Beach beneath the tenth fairway, and scramble up the cliff to the short grass of golfing heaven. Kelp-strung and felonious, I look like something the ocean dredged up, something wearing Rockports and polarized shades. I look like the first step in an alternate Darwinism . . . shapeless protoplasm yielding to the erect bipedal golfer.

I put my foot forward gingerly, just inside the hazard line, thinking of the scene in *Field of Dreams* where Shoeless Joe can't quite bring himself to set foot into foul territory lest he turn back into a mortal. I let the shoe drop, consummating, irrevocably, the love affair of a championship year alongside the breathtaking bay Robert Louis Stevenson

of *Treasure Island* fame called the "the most felicitous meeting of land
and sea in creation."

From now until the fat lady swings it's Pebble and me, toe to toe,
two to tango. One year and four big-time professional tournaments,
among them two pro-ams thick with celebs—the WalMart First Tee
Open, the Callaway Golf Pebble Beach Invitational, the AT&T National
Pro-Am, and the U.S. Open—all played on the number-one public
course and the top-ranked resort course in America. It's a sacred site
Sports Illustrated and CNN ranked in the Top 20 Sporting Venues of
the twentieth century, eight spots ahead of St. Andrews; a track dear
old Bing Crosby way back in 1950 called "the stiffest medal test in the
country"; a layout Tiger Woods lists first among his top-five: Pebble
Beach, St. Andrews, Carnoustie, Augusta National, and Shinnecock
Hills.

Confession: I am a Pebble Beach virgin. Not only have I not yet taken
a swing at the legendary Jack Neville, Douglas Grant–designed gem,
I've never before covered a tournament here. Weeks ago I'd sent my
editor at a golf publication I occasionally write for a one-inch-by-one-
inch mug; less than a week before the first tee shot would be struck at
the WalMart First Tee Open he e-mailed, "You're in. Do me proud."

Me . . . Pebble?! As John McEnroe used to holler at the chair ump,
"You cannot be serious!" But this is Carmel-by-the-Sea, the town
Clint Eastwood once mayored in the state that gave us Ronald Reagan.
Dreams? California does dreams.

Carmel-by-the-Sea, 1 mile square and a population just north of
four thousand, is a town that would make Eastwood's Dirty Harry
or Pale Rider want to spit nails. By Dirty Harry standards it's downright European. Practically no one's pumping out babies, the Census-
takers doing well to turn up fifty kiddies under the age of five. The
kids that do grow up here and graduate from Carmel High are, and
always have been, precocious. "Carmel children are just as talented
and original—and temperamental—as their parents," Carmel resident

and writer Daisy Bostick wrote in 1925. "Art is the air they breathe, the food they eat, the work they do, the studies they pursue." These days the same holds true, though it's a pity poor old Daisy B. didn't live to see reality TV, where, since 2005, Carmel's gifted and comely young have been finalists on *American Idol,* CBS's *Victoria's Secret Fashion Show,* and BRAVO's *Manhunt.*

"It smells like California, it looks like Paradise, and it *is* New York," Alma and Paul Eberle wrote of 1920s Carmel in the *New York Tribune.* Bostick likewise noted a "flavor of Italy" in what are, to this day, Euro-looking streets of languid belladonnas holding hands while strolling streets lined with rustic Dutch doors, steeply pitched Swiss roofs and tidy Bavarian window boxes; where purebreds and designer pooches rule the roost; and where Census bean-counters typically find nearly a third of the population isn't doing anything strenuous at all, occupation-wise, unless you count day-trading or espresso-drinking. The streets are filled with Jaguars and Beemers and the town is lousy with amateur golfers. The per capita income is twice that of the national average, and it's rife enough with old-school Republicanism to make even Dick Cheney's pacemaker hiccup.

Carmel-by-the-Sea is Pebble Beach's nearest city, its host, if you will, Pebble being something more of a neighborhood association or privately owned fiefdom under the jurisdiction of Monterey County than an actual honest-to-God town. Follow the money trail from the links, down 17-Mile Drive, to the gate that guards, at $10 a pop, the golfing sanctuary from the madding crowds, and you'll land in a town devoted to fantasy, rife with humble multimillion-dollar vacation bungalows, many of them 1920s Hansel and Gretel specimens of the "fairy tale" or "elfin" architecture of Hugh Comstock, "Carmel's Builder of Dreams," as well as modern, stone-and-glass visions like Frank Lloyd Wright's 1948 masterpiece, the Walker Residence, hard on Carmel Bay. The gingerbread cottages of Carmel-by-the-Sea's residential district go by names such as "Tinker Bell," "Nut Cracker," and "Snow White." Whimsical boutiques with such appellations as "Where the Sidewalks End," "The White Rabbit," and "Jane Austen at Home" dominate Ocean Avenue on its handsome descent to the sea.

It a city literally blessed, a pilgrim city of trans-golfing wonders heady enough to light even the most unrepentant spiritual hack's path to holiness. Pope John Paul II paid his respects here in 1987 to one of the most important and historic missions of Alta California, the San Carlos Borromeo de Carmel, a National Historic Landmark better known as the Carmel Mission, founded in 1771 by Father Junipero Serra. As if that blessedness weren't enough, at the foot of the mission ebb and flow the translucent, transhuman waters of the Monterey National Marine Sanctuary, a federally protected stretch of water larger than Yellowstone Park and home to the nation's largest kelp forest, not to mention, at more than 12,000 feet deep, one of North America's largest and deepest underwater canyons. Stack vertically Pebble Beach's own natural wonder — the par-5 eighteenth — eight times over, making it, in effect, a giant dipstick, and you still wouldn't get to the bottom of one of the most miraculously diverse marine environments on the planet.

Carmel's an enchanted village in the forest, to be sure, and it damn well wants to stay that way. Roads here brake for trees, swerving around them as if the D.O.T. was staffed by druids. Ancient Spanish moss–laden live oaks lean precipitously over narrow, sidewalk- and curb-free streets. "Lanes wind through stately groves of pine along the old Serra trails, footpaths dodge in and out among the bushes, and the motorist finds himself frequently slipping into low gear to climb an unexpected alpine stump or to plow his way to a sand dune," Daisy Bostick opined. "The people of Carmel . . . are not moved to pity even by the innocent tourist returning crestfallen to the hotel, after a block of painful stumbling over humps and hollows in thin-soled, French-heeled agony."

To this day a permit is required to wear high heels, not because the burg's down-to-earth but because it's a city meant to be freely and unself-consciously walked, a city devoted to environmental rather than fiscal conservation (not to mention fearful of a lawsuit over its tree root–swelled or altogether absent sidewalks). Maligning or molesting a tree meets with grievous penalty; tags on newly planted pines on the lower end of Ocean Avenue threaten citation under municipal codes, warning prospective arboreal pervs what fate will befall them if they "remove, prune, or damage this tree." The legalese continues, "If you question this tree's location or health, contact the city forester. DO NOT TAKE ACTION ON YOUR OWN!"

Tree-hugging residents don't receive mail at a street address here—too antisocial, too much carbon-emitting hustle and bustle. At the height of the summer tourist season much of the town goes silent and deadly black after 9 p.m., streetlights being likewise verboten due to light pollution. You can choose from a half-dozen coffee shops within the central business district, but you won't find a Starbucks unless you're prepared to go slumming at the Safeway across Highway 1—the traditional dividing line between the original, historic Carmel-by-the-Sea and the rest of Carmel and Carmel Valley. Contemporary Carmel-by-the-Sea's a passionate patron of the arts but it won't exactly roll out the red carpet for anyone more risqué than Amy or David Sedaris.

In Carmel even crimes of passion are mostly of the petty variety: windows jimmied open in 50 percent occupancy second homes, the occasional mountain lion with criminal tendencies gobbling up a registered Pekinese out in Carmel Valley, high-brow crank calls like this one from the Carmel Police Log: "A male Carmel Valley resident, age sixty, who is the regional director of the United States Golf Association, reported that an unknown subject left several messages on his voicemail making statements including, 'Golf is for (wimps).'" Other recent faves of the blotter include "Two Russian turtles reported missing" and "unknown suspect stole dog water bowl." In Carmel, crime is, with a few notable exceptions, funny. When Clint Eastwood coaxed his rabid non-golfer pal Robin Williams to Monterey for a Make-a-Wish Foundation benefit, Williams tweaked the high-brow crowd, "Right now people are breaking into your homes saying, *These people have some really nice stuff.*"

It's a his-and-hers burg where, humorist Lewis Grizzard wrote on the occasion of Eastwood's election to the office of mayor in 1986, "Men wear their shirts with the top two buttons unfastened so nobody will miss the fact they have a couple hundred thousand dollars worth of gold hanging around their well-tanned necks. They also play a lot of golf. While they are doing that, women shop for brass ducks and get face lifts."

This is a presidential town playing princely host to its still-wealthier neighbor, Pebble Beach, where, in the last fifty years, only Lyndon B. Johnson, Jimmy Carter, and George W. Bush have failed to set wingtip at the hallowed resorts. This is not a town of bumper-sticker party affiliations, though a few vestigial Obama-Biden stickers decorate Subarus out at Point Lobos State Reserve, where the granola-lovin', tree-huggin', lib-dems plot coup d'état. My favorite resident bumper sticker thus far in otherwise straightlaced Carmel pictures a mud flaps–styled nude accompanied by this Carmel traffic–inspired caption: "If you're going to ride my ass, at least pull my hair."

It's a proud town, and a beguiling one. In a 1967 *San Francisco Chronicle* feature, a former city official once said, "Carmel is like the unwilling virgin. The more she resists, the more people are attracted to her." "It has," Shirlie Stoddard once wrote in *Game & Gossip*, "an indefinable, almost insidious charm." Paradoxically, Carmel's a virgin that's also a mature, well-seasoned control freak. In addition to requiring a permit for high heels, Carmel-by-the-Sea has at times banned or tried to ban, in chronological order, electricity, cars, short-term renters, obnoxious t-shirts, Frisbee in the park, and, in a story that made the newswires in 1986, an "almost total ban on the sale of ice cream cones" that took a Dirty Harry smackdown to reverse.

It is (or rather was) a town of reactionary bohemian artists and thespians like Perry Newberry, erstwhile *Carmel Pine Cone* editor, who long ago issued the rallying cry, "Carmel is for all art and against progress." Newberry's "platform" in his successful bid for city trustee in 1926 began, "Believing that 9,999 towns out of 10,000 is just what

Carmel shouldn't have, I am a candidate for trustee ... DON'T VOTE
FOR PERRY NEWBERRY: If you hope to see Carmel become a city. If
you want its growth boosted. If you desire its commercial success. If
streetlamps on its corners mean happiness to you. If concrete pave-
ments represent your civic ambitions. If you think a glass factory is of
greater importance than a sand dune, or a millionaire than an artist,
or a mansion than a little brown cottage. If you truly want Carmel
to become a boosting, hustling wide-awake lively metropolis. DON'T
VOTE FOR PERRY NEWBERRY."

Before it was the golf capital of America, if not the world, Carmel-
by-the-Sea held sway as one of the nation's most important artist
colonies, a veritable "Seacoast of Bohemia," as the title of a local history published in 1966 put it. At the beginning of the century writers
as world-renowned as Ambrose Bierce, Sinclair Lewis, Jack London,
and Robert Louis Stevenson sojourned in or near the idyllic, unpaved
fantasy island, where the living was affordably laissez-faire. Lots that
now sell in the millions could be had for as little as $50. Poet George
Sterling, first among the prominent Bay Area bohemians to make these
piney hills his manifest destiny, wrote, "At Carmel-by-the-Sea, I will
be able to live naturally and quietly ... I wish to be a lone pioneer—to
find out for myself whether or not one can exist on little money and
less 'society.'" In letters to literary pals Sterling had so talked up the
"the Carmel group of literary people" and the "anarchist freeland" they
had created that buddy Ambrose Bierce wrote in reply, "I am serious in
wishing a place in Carmel as a port of refuge from the storms of age"
and as a balm for "two gouty finger joints as a result of the other kind
of life." In her autobiography writer Mary Austin recalled moving from
crowded San Francisco to sensual Carmel, with its "strange wild beach
... the dunes all white and silvery, the glittering chaparral." Austin's
rapturous rendition of the area's coastal beauty found visual expres-
sion in the landscape paintings of Carmel resident Francis McComas,
who in the early 1900s coined the oft-misattributed phrase "greatest
meeting of land and sea" about nearby Point Lobos. McComas paved

the way for future generations of fantasy-minded *artistes* to set up shop in this fairy-tale incarnate, including "America's most collected living artist" and Disney-obsessed "painter of light" Thomas Kinkade, whose Garden Gallery exists in a fit-for-a-hobbit nook just off Ocean Avenue.

The enchantment-by-the-sea put stars in the eyes of far more than painters and writers, however, and by the 1930s this precious, passionate hamlet of poets, painters, dramatists, and scholars had succumbed to the very intrusions its founding artists and intellectuals most feared. Poet-intellectual Robinson Jeffers had moved to the remote, treeless headland of Carmel Point in 1913, but by the 1930s the still-standing cottage (Tor House) and the tower (Hawk Tower) he fashioned of his own hands atop a knoll on Ocean View Avenue—where Carmel's first golf course once stood—had already begun to be encroached upon. Jeffers, an advocate of "inhumanism" and a thoroughgoing contrarian who once famously wrote he'd rather kill a man than a hawk, took the occasion of his 1938 poem "Carmel Point" to confront his once-pleasant Bohemia with its new identity, calling it "this beautiful place defaced with a crop of suburban houses" and bitterly lamenting that the unrepentant "spoiler" had slouched toward his Eden.

When I, in my 200,000-mile Toyota Echo, roll up to the gates of Shangri-la, the guys at the Carmel gatehouse guarding 17-Mile Drive exchange a look that says, "We got us a live one here, Jose." I get up the gall to say I've moved to Carmel, and the security dude interrupts my spiel with a cheerful "Good."

"Good"? Not, "Ya right, you're moving to Carmel. Now turn that piece of shit around!"

Just these two uniformed officers, this one tollgate, and the small matter of zero ready cash separate me from my first real encounter with the holy of holies, the sanctum sanctorum, founder S.F.B. Morse's 1919 pipe dream. "I'm a journalist," I stutter.

The guy's suddenly knit eyebrows tell me I don't look the part. In fact, I look more like David Feherty, Beelzebub, or the swarthy guy the TSA pulls off a 747 at Dulles than a dude about to cover the whitest, tightest sport this side of curling. Still, he gives the Echo that final, border security–ish once-over, looks back at the line of vehicles building behind me, and waves me through. "Jeest tell the people you write for to give you a gate pass, okay?"

I'm off on the yellow brick road to Pebble, past the smiling Smoky the Bear sign at the entrance to the Del Monte Forest warning me fire danger is high, past the deer grazing the third fairway off Palmero Way, past The Tap Room, which *Golf Digest* rated as one of the 50 Best 19th Holes in all of golfdom, past The Shops at Pebble Beach orbiting tightly around the putting green, past the Cinderella Rolex clock, right up to the goddamn Lodge itself. I'm expecting security guards, bells and whistles, golf marms running after me, shouting with mounting hysteria, "Excuse me . . . Sir!"

Instead, I roll right past the Lodge and almost out the back gate, overclubbing. I swerve down a side road at the last instant, figuring that if I've done the 2,100-mile, Brigham Young–esque overland trek to set foot in the temple, the least I can do is keep my drive inbounds. I park my prairie schooner not more than a sand wedge from the Pacific itself . . . a mere hundred yards behind the eighteenth green.

I make a beeline for the course, for the sacred ground that has brought me 2,000 miles through pasture golf courses and salt flats and burning deserts and mountain passes and High Sierra pines. A weird, maritime layer of fog has unfurled in a white scrim across the Carmel Highlands, appearing white and rain-laden one minute, bright with an eye toward clearing the next. I stroll down the eighteenth hole, turning druid long enough to scope out the famous transplanted cypress tree guarding the approach.

Farther down the fairway a series of anonymous hacks scar the most dramatic finishing hole in golf. Watching the massacre-in-progress shivers me timbers—like watching your twelve-year-old daughter practice putting mascara on Gisele Bündchen. Approaching the cocktail hour, the practice-round traffic has slowed to a trickle and, by the time I've reached the majestic eighteenth tee on its sea-spray promontory, I, too, am considering heading back to the house.

It's then, out of the corner of my eye, that I spy a kerfuffle on the seventeenth tee: a big, hairy microphone angling downward, a very large man shouldering a very large television camera, an intern carrying one of those humongo light reflectors, and a small covey of amateurs huddling around what must be the center of all the fuss.

The golf scrum parts to reveal the unmistakably ageless, Dick Clark–like figure of Gary Player. His sharp South African accent, the voice of a schoolmaster about to rap your knuckles, cuts through the fierce winds. The camera zooms as Player gets down on his knees, sets his hands on his amateur playing partner's grip, and guides him through a revised impact position to a nice full finish.

"There now. That's how I want you to finish," he purrs, "perfectly balanced." He springs up from his prone position with surprising agility for a man born in 1935, a man with twenty grandchildren, bounding down the tee, all five-foot-seven of him. "Let's 'ave that swea-tah," he calls back over his shoulder to his caddy as the Golf Channel crew follows in hot pursuit.

On the short grass Player continues to profess as each of his partners tries his hand at the slippery downhill putt. He debriefs each on the proper stroke — you must keep the "putt-ah 'ead" moving through the ball, rhythmic and true. The South African bats cleanup, and though his ball finishes outside the amateurs' marks, he has walked his talk, executing a slow, controlled stroke with twice as much silk as the weekenders had spun.

"Okay, Gary," David Marr, Golf Channel impresario-announcer interjects once everyone's putted out, "we're going to do a spot on the famous 1-iron that Jack Nicklaus hit here in the '72 U.S. Open." Player nods as if this is an old card trick he's done a thousand times. He swings into position with the ease of a TV anchorman, adjusts his collar, puts a smile on his face, and, as the camera rolls, says, "Remembah the 1-iron Jack hit 'ere that struck the pin and finished just a few feet away?" Marr nods his approval; his man is perfectly on script. "Well now, Jack felt a gust of wind and altered his swing on the way down to hit that shot. Imagine the skill it took to do that." Player licks his lips, grins his impish grin. The camera comes down from the shoulder and the crew jovially backslaps. "Mister One-Take! Good work, Gary."

While his playing partners face the most daunting tee shots of their lives, Player is backed up against the split-rail fence behind the eighteenth tee and made to do a half dozen additional reps: "This is Gary Play-ah, and you're watching the WalMart First Tee Open at Pebble Beach." He's no longer Mr. One-Take but he's still damn good. He strides up to the tee, pulls out a driver that looks almost as tall as he is, and spanks a low draw that splits the two fairway cypresses.

The team plays Player's poke, naturally, but they do not use his second shot, which ends up a couple dozen yards shorter than the best of his three playing partners'. He marches up to his ball and, almost without stopping, lobs an easy wedge back-left of the pin. "I'll play this one, and you play that one," he says.

As the entourage moves to the green, Player strides the fairway with all the vim and vigor of a Viagra ad. I ask his caddy if I can have a few brief words with the legend after the round. "Probably, if you ask him," he says. Then, after a pause, "I don't know why he makes the time for you guys." A few hours into the bona fide world of big-time Pebble golf journalism and I'm already getting the media slight. It almost feels good to be so reviled.

After Player misses his downhill birdie bid on the last, he stops to take a picture with each amateur in his foursome, smiling beautifully as each man in turn wraps an arm around his smallish frame and hovers it there in the small of his back. Next comes a Kodak moment with a couple of the First Tee junior contestants who've gathered around the green to press the flesh of the six-time Major champion.

I ambush the Hall of Famer on his way back toward the Lodge. "Mr. Player," I ask—he is South African, I figure he'll appreciate the boarding school formality—"do you have time for a quick question?"

His eyes narrow, take me in, then fall to the ground to signal assent. "Come on, then!" he says, all postcolonial pep.

"Tell me what appeals to you most about this place?"

He stops in his tracks, swings around to freeze me in his gaze, the same that, along with his penchant for wearing sun-absorbing black outfits, earned him the nickname "The Dark Knight." A pregnant pause. "Pebble," he says, "is a heritage. It's a place where peace prevails." I'm so close the lines around his eyes read like a map of Johannesburg. "You know, I'm an environmentalist, and people all over the world complain about traffic and hustle and bustle . . . That doesn't happen here."

There are more voices clamoring for his attention now, and an officious-looking man directing the group to the Lodge. I've done what I set out to do. I've lost my Pebble virginity utterly, legally, in one day. I've rapped briefly with one of golf's legendary Big Three—a star the magnitude of Palmer and Nicklaus.

Ya, Pebble does dreams.

Tom Watson walks into the Pebble Beach media room at 2:00 p.m., a full half hour before his scheduled appearance. When he arrives the room breaks into spontaneous applause. Someone in the press corps hollers, hooligan-style, "Tom-ME!" Watson acknowledges the crowd of scribblers with the same magnanimity he did the gobsmacked crowds at Turnberry.

Watson is paired with seventeen-year-old Gianna Misenhelter from his hometown of Kansas City, Missouri, and he's stoked. Our dear Mr. Watson is, as always, upbeat, energetic, quick-witted, and puckish with his sun-brightened cheeks and Tom Sawyer looks. If ours was a job interview, he'd be a lock. He's offered food, drink, everything but personal attendants and palmetto leaves, all of which he politely declines, telling the press he's already had two chocolate chip cookies with forty chocolate chips each, but who's counting. Someone in the room quips that Gary Player's weakness is ice cream. Watson nods sagely. "Don't let his fitness thing fool you," he says.

Phil Stambaugh, media official for the PGA Tour, asks Watson to sign a flag from the British Open, where Old/Young Tom shocked the world first by contending and then by having the tournament in his grasp coming up eighteen, then by leaving a crucial par putt woefully short and getting pummeled by Stuart Cink in the resulting playoff.

"We had some of our guys working over there get this for us," Stambaugh explains, sounding a little bit like the CIA guy in a James Bond flick. "We're gonna get Stuart to sign it, too." Stambaugh asks whether Watson has seen the write-up in the *San Francisco Chronicle*, wherein Ron Croichick refers to Watson's popularity after finishing runner-up as "a mix between Tiger Woods and Mick Jagger," and quotes the president of the Champions Tour, Mike Stevens, as saying, "Tom was an absolute rock star over there."

Watson is an absolute rock star here, too, as he settles in front of the mike, having won back-to-back titles at Pebble in 1977 and 1978 at the forerunner to the AT&T National Pro-Am, the Bing Crosby National Pro-Am, and, by dint of his famous chip-in on seventeen, the 1982 U.S. Open.

Watson and Pebble go way back, all the way to Stanford University when, contrary to popular rumor, Watson did not ditch class to tee it up on the Monterey Peninsula. Instead he'd drive down in the wee hours on Saturday mornings when the starter, Ray Parga, would let him on for free. In 1967 Watson would have had to pay about $15 for the privilege of playing Pebble, a privilege that now runs just shy of $500.

"I would be first off," Watson tells us. "I'd get around in about three hours, and I'd play-act: 'I've got to finish the last three holes even par to win the U.S. Open.' I never did. 'Against Jack Nicklaus.' I never did. Then I did!" Watson, by his own recollection, never shot better than 75 on the iconic links until he turned pro. The first time he broke par here was at the 1972 Crosby, where he had seventeen straight pars before birdieing eighteen for a personal-best 71.

Watson calls Pebble one of his "favorite courses in the world" and a textbook case for how a golf course ought to play. "It's one of those courses that if you're playing pretty well it's pretty receptive. It's inviting. You can hit a good shot, you get rewarded, and now you have a shot . . . and now you have a birdie chance . . . When you're playing U.S. Opens you're always fighting for pars," he adds. "But you are going to have a number of birdie chances here. That's what I like about the golf course. It still holds up."

Asked about the far-reaching changes made to the course in preparation for its hosting of the 2010 Open, Watson is sober: "I looked at those back tees at nine and ten and actually hit one from thirteen. Number nine's going to be a 3-shot hole for this guy! I think I can deal with ten and thirteen, but to try and hit that tiny green with water on the right and the big, deep bunker in front with a 2-hybrid in hand . . . that's a hard shot."

"Overall, I like the changes. They've narrowed up six, narrowed up four. Added the three tees. Pebble is the type of course that you love to play because you know you have certain shots you have to play. If I play those holes [nine and twelve] well, I'm going to be successful. Those are the two that give me the most problem. Fourteen, the third shot, has also been kind of a problem," Watson says of a hole Jeff Sluman will later tell me is the "most difficult 3-shot par 5 in golf."

Known for playing his best in adverse weather, Watson waxes nostalgic about the rigor of the past Open setups at Pebble: "The greens in '72 were as hard a surface, as firm a surface, as I've ever played, including the British Open." Watson shot 76, 4 over par, in the last round at Pebble that year and somehow leapfrogged more than thirty of his fellow competitors. "I came in and watched Jack hit an absolutely perfect 4-iron at number twelve . . . only Jack could have hit it. He hit it straight up in the air. It landed perfectly over the bunker, took one hop to the back of the green, another hop to the downslope . . . That green was impossible."

"In '92, when Tom Kite won, what happened? Sunday round. Same thing. They didn't predict the sun to come out. They predicted low skies and cool and damp. No, it got windy and dry and those greens were again like rock."

You get the feeling Watson, golfer, architect, psychology graduate, could lecture endlessly and authoritatively on nuances of the greens at Pebble. Every green, he tells us, is twenty-eight yards deep. "Jack Neville just said, 'It's gonna be twenty-eight deep; that's the proper distance,'" Watson says, conjuring Pebble's visionary course co-designer and five-time winner of the California State Am in the 1910s and 1920s. "You've got to put a ball on a hard surface and, from the front edge, you've got twenty-eight yards to stop it."

As press time draws to a close I ask Watson to talk about Pebble as a model for his own courses. "I admire this golf course and the way it plays," he tells me. "When you hit a good golf shot here it invites you. That's the way golf should be. If you hit a risky shot then the next shot should be an easier shot. It shouldn't always be a landmine here and here and here. There needs to be a risk-reward. That's in general what this course does."

As Young Tom exits the pressroom he's still carrying on about what makes Pebble different. Most courses, he says, conjuring the name Pete Dye, say, "No, no, no." The seduction of Pebble Beach, he says, smiling, is that it says, "C'mere."

Almost from the moment Our Father in Heaven, Samuel Finley Brown (S.F.B. to you and me) Morse cut the ribbon—or, more accurately, planted the ceremonial cherry tree—for the Lodge and links at Pebble Beach on the Washington Birthday weekend of 1919, golfers have been fawning over it. The February 24, 1919, *San Francisco Chronicle* carried a picture of R. R. Flint of Sacramento administering the "golfer's oath," the text of which ran as a banner headline across the width of the paper: "We Pledge Ourselves by Our Faith in the Cherry Tree to Turn in Honest Score Cards." Covering the opening soiree, the *Chronicle's* Hay Chapman quoted English visitor William Tucker as saying, "I do not know of any course anywhere that can excel Pebble Beach from a golfing point." Tucker's comment was oddly prescient — sort of like picking out a babe from the maternity ward and declaring it to be a future president. The *Pebble Beach Scorecard* quotes another of the day's correspondents, Lady Teazle, as she gushed, "The Lodge is set six miles deep in the oak and pine forest, the very ultra of exclusiveness in the way of a fashionable retreat."

After seeing it in the 1926 Pebble Beach Open, the world's best golfers found themselves on the same page, literally, regarding the merits of the new course. Morse's magazine *Game & Gossip* quoted 1928 U.S. Open champ Johnny Farrell as saying, "The course is on par with our best championship courses in the East, and the surroundings are the most beautiful I have ever seen." Ditto for 1924 U.S. Open winner Cyril Walker, who enthused, "The course is a wonderful test of golf, fit, in my estimation, to hold any national championship." Leo Diegel, who would beat Bobby Jones to win back-to-back PGA Championships in 1928 and 1929, sang the links' praise at length: "Pebble Beach is the most beautiful course I have ever played. . . . A number of professionals are visiting California for the first time, and are absolutely sold. They even talk about staying out here for the year round. . . . Some of the holes, such as the eighth, tee shot at the tenth, the fourteenth, seventeenth, and eighteenth are holes that cannot be equaled anywhere."

Reading the hot-and-bothered recitations of rusty-dusty Major champions of yore prompts me to chase down the major championship winners among the Champion's Tour legends teeing it up at the WalMart Open this week. I want to find out if the guys from my father's generation are still as bullish on Pebble.

The usually taciturn, totally Texas Tom Thumb of golf, Tom Kite, drops the word "love" when I ask him about the course where he won the 1992 U.S. Open, adding, "And I've got some good history here. It's a beautiful place." Lanny Wadkins, who beat Gene "The Machine" Littler in a playoff for the PGA Championship in the 1977 drought year at Pebble, likewise recollects great memories here, calling Pebble his favorite, and saying, "I wouldn't want to be anywhere else." Five-time

Pebble champ and winner of two Major championships in 1998, Mark O'Meara gushes, "If you could win any tournament, you'd like to win one at Pebble. There's no prettier place in the world than this." California boy Scott Simpson, a U.S. Open winner at San Francisco's Olympic Club, looks me in the eye to say, "It's my favorite golf course in the world . . . the best, most beautiful course I've ever played, being able to play right around the coast with the greens sitting right on the edges." Former Open champ and Crosby Clambake mainstay Jerry Pate calls S.F.B. Morse's brainchild-of-a-course "first-class" and "timeless." Two-time Open winner and forty-year Pebble veteran Andy North says that, between Carmel-by-the-Sea and the links at Pebble, "the whole scene is almost surreal," adding, "the golf course is always different. And it's always interesting."

Even the Major champs oft-befuddled by Pebble have a kind word to say about her, including the ever-grumpy Masters champ and ageless Walrus, Craig Stadler, who calls it "one of [his] favorites"; PGA winner Hal Sutton shoves my shoulder to explain how the formidable course "feels like it's always pushing on you . . . like you're always a little bit off-balance"; The Great White Shark, Greg Norman, two times the British Open champ and a man who, like Nick Price, has never played particularly well here, prefaces his comments by informing me that "there are probably twelve phenomenal holes and six average holes," and concludes by saying, "Across the board, one of the best land-meeting-sea golf courses in the world."

Saving the best for last, I wait around like a Nervous Nellie for Ben Crenshaw who, after completing an exasperating round in which his usually masterful putting stroke utterly fails him, asks me to walk with him as he gathers his thoughts. We walk from the back of eighteen to the practice green, and lingering there, Crenshaw tells me about his emotional connection to these sacred acres, calling it "the unique and beautiful place . . . a wonderful piece of art." Looking me unswervingly in the eye, the two-time Masters champs confesses, "It's amazing to me the foresight of Samuel Morse to put the course where he did . . .

There's no question it's one of the great landscapes in the world in golf ... The nature of the holes and how they play is a stroke of genius."

Amen, Brother Ben, Amen.

Approaching a pro coming off the Pebble Beach practice tee, or any driving range for that matter, can be dicey—a bit like trying to talk to a linebacker fresh from the field with his blood still up—most of them, that is, except Frank Urban Zoeller. Fuzzy. The pride of New Albany, Indiana, and, like me, a stranger in a strange land out here on the Left Coast, though he won here in '86 and finished second to Sluman in the 2008 WalMart First Tee Open. He loves this place.

For Zoeller the driving range isn't an office so much as a living room. "I'm working too hard," he says, all Rodney Dangerfield, turning to his daughter Gretchen, a former member of the College of Charleston women's golf team and a good player in her own right. She'll be playing alongside her old man this week. "I gotta go back to the hotel room," he tells us.

Fuzz's influence on golf far exceeds his number of PGA Tour victories (ten) in part because, among them, he managed to defeat Watson and Ed Sneed in a playoff for the 1979 Masters and polished off Norman in the famous white towel-waving incident at the 1984 U.S. Open at Winged Foot. In short, Fuzzy does Majors. So what does he think about the changes made in Pebble for the 2010 U.S. Open? "Tell you what," he says, "those new bunkers will make the guys pucker. They force you to play closer to the water on number four and number six."

I ask Fuzz if he remembers his first time playing Pebble. "1975? Naw, I don't remember anything about it."

Except the year, I want to add, but don't.

Did he dream about the course as a kid back in Hoosierland? "Fuck no," Fuzz says. "I'm a midwesterner. I didn't even know this placed existed."

3

Bill Murray's Cinderella Story
Meets Slu-Dog Millionaire's

During the Friday round of the WalMart First Tee Open, I sniff out the man who, according to surveys, trumps Elvis and Marilyn Monroe as wished-for golf partners among most demographics. I find him texting furiously post-round as he staggers across Pebble's third fairway, a man in his own world, or at least in his own Private Idaho.

You can't miss "Billy," as his friends call Bill Murray, even when he appears all witness protection in frayed, faded denim, deck shoes that look as if they've been stewing in bilge, and larger-than-life, gender-bending shades. For Murray, disguise is a well-practiced yet improvisatory art, and today he's sporting something very similar to the "oversized tennis hat" and "post-cataract-removal sunglasses" he once donned to, in his words, "dress down" for the Masters. He's as costume-friendly as Peter Sellers and about as easy to pick out of a crowd, too, with his six-foot-plus slump-shouldered frame and Frankenstein gate.

"Is that Andy Bean or [Mark] Wiebe?" he asks me, squinting. We've drifted seaward together from the third green to seventeenth tee.

"Wiebe," I say, examining the tell-tale Humpty Dumpty waistline and trademark follow through. "They look similar from a distance, don't they?"

"Ya," he mumbles, his whirligig mind spinning onto other things. We watch the first of several amateurs in the Wiebe group tee off; Murray winces after one especially tortured pass. "God, that's ugly." He shivers. "This guy here," he whispers, "is kind of a bigwig . . . chairman of the First Tee or something. I've never seen him, though." His tone resembles Carl Spackler's slack-jawed mock-announcer's voice in *Caddyshack*. The man in question, I'll later learn, is Geoff Couch, chairman of the First Tee of Monterey County and a scratch golfer.

"Your pal Jeff Sluman says you're a genius," I tell him, as the Wiebe-Couch groups moves off toward the seaside green, leaving us in a public silence, a vacuum comedians abhor.

"Ya, well, what does he know?"

"You miss Chicago?" It's a dumb question, I realize, as both of us stare at a Pacific so blue it makes Lake Michigan look like a cesspool. Even if Murray's IQ is higher and his handicap lower than mine, we've both called Sweet Home Chicago home. He gets serious for a quick, Zen sec. "You try never to miss anyplace," he says. "If you're missing someplace, you're not where you are, you know?"

He's drifting away from me now, the ever-elusive Murray is. It must be hell to be married to such a darkly comic genius . . . one minute you have their attention, the next they're in la-la land. I try to reel him in using the usual celeb tack—ask him about him. "How's your game, Bill? What're you working on?"

"I'm working with a lady . . . She's got me all loosened up."

I'm tempted to ask just what kind of lady this is, whether he's talking loose in the physical, metaphysical, or moral sense. Are we talking mentor, masseuse, or madame?

"Good loose or bad loose?"

"*Wiiiild* loose." He shakes out the heebie-jeebies. "I'm all over the place. I'm playing with Slu tomorrow," he says, turning to face me for the first time in our two-guys-leaning-over-the-fence conversation. "Come out and see for yourself."

I take Billy up on his personal invite, catching up with the Slu-Murray group the following day on the par-4 eighth, the cliffside gem where the second shot must carry the ocean inlet. Murray sacrifices his approach iron shot to the water gods, then opts to sit the rest of the hole out, sunning himself on the grassy hill facing Carmel Bay while haranguing his partners, including first-round leader Sluman, who's fighting gamely to stay at level par.

"Are these good enough seats?" he asks a crowd cozied up close enough to touch the pros. "I suppose now you'll want wine."

Murray lives for afternoons like this. So much so, in fact, that the former Wilmette, Illinois, caddy opens his bestselling memoir *Cinderella Story* with a surprisingly poetic evocation of a "breeze being flavored by one of the fireplaces in the hotels rooms of The Lodge at Pebble Beach." As down-to-earth as this working-class son of Chicagoland is, he doesn't mind the royal treatment. "For one week," he writes, "I'm on the Princess Cruise of amateur golf, playing the greatest stand of courses in pro golfdom in front of galleries larger than those at the Little League World Series at Williamsport, having more fun than I will have for the rest of the year."

"Unlike just about everyone else in the tournament," Tommy Smothers writes of his friend and fellow jokester, "the more Bill communes with the gallery, the better he seems to play." Smothers goes on to describe a night at Pebble's Club XIX when Murray and co-conspirators Sluman and Scott Simpson actually picked Smothers up in his chair, pharaoh-like, and paraded him around the bar. Murray has coined a special term for such a warm recollection: a "Monterey red wine remembrance."

He's also the first to admit the rosé sometimes interferes with rosier golfing prospects. "After a few years, I'd become frustrated with cooler golf," he laments in *Cinderella Story.* "Me and the cooler would be fine until the thirteenth hole when the wayward shots begin to come in rapid succession. Sufficiently coolered, I would be unable to reverse this trend, and a storm cloud of hubris and juice-induced wagers would drown me till round's end."

By celebrity standards Murray's transgressions, if it's even fair to call them that, seem quaint. Only occasionally does his joie de vivre get the better of him. But when it does it usually involves golf, and it always makes news. In 2007 *People* magazine reported with something like relish, "Perhaps more than the herring was pickled at Stockholm's Café Opera when Bill Murray left after 3:00 a.m.—in a golf cart." Murray was given a little talking to by the Stockholm police, but the Swedish pigs opted not to arrest.

On the course, Murray's antics have sometimes seemed sinful in the eyes of uptight golfing execs. On the Monterey Peninsula he's most famous, or infamous, for pulling an elderly woman out of the gallery at the AT&T, dancing with her in a bunker, then throwing her playfully into the sand. That, and he once shouted at slow-playing former vice president Dan Quayle to "Hurry up!" "That," Gary Van Sickle reported in *Sports Illustrated,* "brought the wrath of then–PGA Tour commissioner Deane Beman, who blasted Murray's behavior as 'inappropriate' and 'detrimental' to the tournament." In the aftermath Murray famously compared the tour to a "Nazi state" and called Beman "just another screwhead too big for his britches."

In an interview with *Golf* magazine's Cameron Morfit, PGA Tour pro Bart Bryant recalls the splash Murray made in his early years at Pebble. "On the second hole at Spyglass, there was this seventy-year-old lady wearing a skirt, and Bill was holding her ankles and she was holding Bill's ankles and they were walking down the fairway. I think the powers that be told Bill to dial it back a bit after that."

Forever partial to silver foxes, Murray once hit his ball in the rough on the sixteenth hole at Pebble. When a woman in the gallery provocatively stretched out in front of it, "Murray promptly pounced on her, gyrating spasmodically." When they were through with the charade, writes Van Sickle, Murray asked her if she was okay and the woman reportedly said, "I am now."

Beside the eighth green now, Murray is flat-out on his back, facing a beatific Pacific. For his day in the sun he's sporting a mess-with-your-gender-norms getup consisting of a Cadillac / Pepto / It's-a-girl pink sweater vest, baby blue cotton long sleeve, yard-sale plaid pants, and red, black, and white spikes that look like first-generation Air Jordans.

On nine Sluman tees first, smoking his drive coolly down the middle, while off to the side Murray stops in front of an adorable little blonde and her proud father. The girlchild pipes up, sweet as can be, "Mr. Murray, would you like to use my lucky tee?"

He cocks his head, taking in this Shirley Temple.

"Would you like to live in my garage?"

The girl laughs nervously and looks at Dad, whose grin falters.

"Just for a couple of years . . . I've got clothes," Murray hastens to add. "And lots of helmets."

Billy puts the girl's lucky peg in the ground, commences his baseball-swing warm-up routine, and proceeds to split the fairway.

Robert Boerner is in Murray's gallery with me for the Saturday round with Jeff Sluman. Boerner worked for the Pebble Beach Company for sixteen years, starting at the Chevron station at Pebble and working his way up to director of rooms at both The Lodge and The Inn at Spanish Bay. A friend of Billy's and the innkeeper at the comedian's preferred haunt while he's on the Peninsula, the Pacific Gardens Inn in nearby Pacific Grove, Boerner tells me that the biggest prank Murray plays is being himself. "He comes to breakfast wearing a robe with his hair sticking up," Boerner says, recounting a real-life scene like the one in *Groundhog Day*. "One of the funniest things was this guest who was checking out the other day. I was at the desk. The guy was English. He said, 'You know you have a gentleman around here who simply acts and looks like Bill Murray, but I can tell it wasn't Bill Murray because Bill has much more hair.'"

Murray has, at various times, written unsolicited letters on behalf of Boerner's eleven-year-old son (in an attempt to spring him from school) and for Boerner himself, in support of whom Murray once wrote to Boerner's superiors at the Pebble Beach Company, "Robert was a swell dude. He should be given complete control of the place."

Boerner's at a loss for words to describe his most famous guest's golf game. "His is a golf game that's just waiting to break out of its shell," he tells me, flashing a smile before turning serious for a sec. "I won't say he's all business when he comes to town, but he works hard. He takes what time he has and he spreads himself real thin . . . For Bill to come back and play really well here . . . he might consider that selfish. He's gonna go to the hospice, and you can't do that if you're going to the driving range all the time . . . The best thing about Bill is he just rolls along. He doesn't have an entourage . . . He's completely opposite what you think a big movie star should be, but he could have all that . . . I don't even think he had a cell phone until not long ago . . . Really, he's a genius. He's very quick. Very well-read. It's hard to pull one over on him, although I've tried."

"He's a loyal kind of friend," adds Boerner, who likewise counts among his best friends the late great John Denver. "Billy could stay wherever he wants . . . I tell him, 'Billy, if you find a nice-looking girl, take her to The Lodge, man. Actually take her to Casa Palmero and really do it up.' He pooh-poohs it all."

I ask Boerner, a man who's checked in thousands of golfers at the front desk at The Lodge and The Inn at Spanish Bay, to tell me, beyond the obvious, what makes Pebble such an irresistible draw, even for a star of the magnitude of Murray. "The history behind Pebble and the mystique that surrounds it makes it a place that everybody who's part of golf wants to experience. It's an adjective. It's a verb. It's a noun. It's golf."

The rest of Murray's Saturday round is a comedy of errors, as he alternates almost unbelievably well-struck shots that cause the crowd to ooh and ahh with heinous, inexplicable misses. Along the way he steals sandwiches from the gallery while occasionally pulling off flop-shot recoveries that would make Phil Mickelson jealous. His partner, Sluman, turns in a disappointing 1-over-par 73 that puts him nearly half a dozen shots back going into the final round.

I meet Bill and Co. again in front of the scorer's trailer behind eighteen green. A local reporter asks Murray if he and his team have made the coveted cut. "We'll be playing at the Bayonet," he quips, meaning the public course at Ford Ord that passes for cheap golf here. "We didn't even make the Del Monte cut. They're sending us further up the Peninsula to work on our game." Del Monte Golf Course is the lesser course over which the three-round WalMart First Tee Open is contested, and inevitably the ugly stepsister to Pebble's Cinderella, though it's the oldest course in California and predates Pebble by a couple of decades.

"Your swing looked good today, Bill. You were long, loose, just like you said yesterday," I console him. "You looked like Harry Vardon out there with that loosey-goosey overswing."

"I was a little bit like Mrs. Harry Vardon—alternately kind and irrational."

"So what do you like best about Pebble?" I ask him.

"I like the atmosphere . . . the physical sense of the place." He turns to admire the bay.

"I saw you waving to people in the houses on the back nine. I figured the least they could do was bring you a glass of champagne."

"I'm on a first-name basis with almost everyone. You see, they're all my friends." He waves at the crowd awaiting his autograph, and they wave back, clueless but on cue. "Ya, if I'm waving to the houses, I usually know them. But some of them are just inebriated people."

Jeff Sluman—all five-foot-seven-inches and 140 pounds of him—is one of the more appealing figures on the Champions Tour, and not just because I am taller than he is. I adore Slu because he chooses to make his home in Hinsdale, Illinois, in the Chicago burbs, and hails from Rochester, New York—two towns that aren't exactly Jupiter Island, Florida. Third reason I dig this unlikely winner of the 1988 PGA Championship at Oak Tree: he's as serious on the course as he is witty off it. In as classic an example of the odd couple as exists in professional golf, he counts among his best friends one Bill Murray.

Murray's known for rubbing people one way or another, mostly to love but sometimes to hate, while Sluman might as well have his own sitcom called *Everybody Loves Sluman*. All his George Bailey karma, in addition to the more than half a million dollars he's raised for the City of Hope and other Chicago-area charities, has put Sluman in excellent stead among his peers, who he represents as a player-director for the Champions Tour. To give you an idea of just the kind and caliber of "props" Slu gets, consider this: Jack Nicklaus twice named him captain's assistant for the President's Cup.

But the real thing that makes the WalMart First Tee Open defending champ stand out at Pebble is his track record on the course he loves more than any in the world, a record that, by weekend's end, will be rivaled only by the likes of Jack Nicklaus, Tom Watson, Tom Kite, Hale Irwin, and Mark O'Meara. He won here once before, in 2008, blowing out Fuzzy and Craig Stadler by 5 shots in the widest margin in tournament history. Just as frequently, he's knocked on the door at Pebble, losing in a playoff to O'Meara in the 1992 AT&T Pebble Beach National Pro-Am and finishing runner-up to Tom Kite at the 1992 U.S. Open. In summation: Slu Dog Does Pebble; Slu Dog Digs Murray.

A longtime friend of Billy's, Slu understands well his amigo's idiosyncrasies on and off the course, having known him for fifteen years and having guested on Murray's set in Rome for *The Life Aquatic*. "Frankly," Slu tells me in an after-hours session on the Pebble putting green, "it's not always just ha ha ha. We have a lot of serious conversations . . . It's scary how intelligent he is. He studied at the Sorbonne. He's a brilliant guy," my interviewee says, adding, "I've been very fortunate to have him as a friend."

Sluman, Murray's longtime Pro-Am partner, first came to Pebble in 1983 and, in his own words, "fell in love with it." He remembers watching Nicklaus win both the Bing Crosby National Pro-Am and the 1972 Open at Pebble, remembers Jack saying if he had one round left to play in his earthly existence he'd make sure to book a tee time in Sam Morseland. Slu's affinity for the classic layout, though, isn't due to a rocking debut. He actually turned in an amateurish 45 for his first-ever competitive nine here, making a 10 — an X in hacker parlance — on eighteen after a tenth-tee start. But he came roaring back with a 29 on the front, and the rest, as they say, is history. Since that first round, Sluman has been hooked by the course's unmatched variety.

"At the end of a round here a guy will say, 'Well, I knocked it on in two here. Hit a driver and 7-iron there.' But then some of us would have hit a driver and 3-wood on the same hole earlier in the day. You're just facing so many different conditions," Slu enthuses. "Then you look at the scenery, and you say to yourself they could never build a course like this now because all of the homes would be on the water."

What about the Pebble naysayers, I ask him, the ones who say it's overrated, overhyped, overpriced?

"Some people maybe don't think it's the greatest course in the world. Some people say, 'Well, it wouldn't be much of a course if it didn't have the ocean on it.' Duh. So what's your point? Augusta wouldn't have been a great course if it didn't have Bobby Jones."

And what about the folks, and there are plenty, who believe Pebble gets too much play, that conditions suffer? Sluman tells me he's seen the course get brown and fast, especially in the Majors, but by design, and he has no beef with it. "That's the problem with American golf. Everybody thinks the course is great if it's green and lush. And truly that's not the way most golf courses are. It's not like the golf course rests like it does in the Midwest or Northeast," he adds. "This is basically a public golf course. They can't shut it down like a private and say, 'Well, look, we're gonna give it a month to rest and punch the greens while we're at it . . .' If there's no golf, you can't get the revenue for the rooms. They do have a business to run."

"This would be the place I would play if I had one round left. I like the fact that any type of player can play well here. Every type of player has won on this golf course. It favors a guy who really understands how to play . . . a shotmaker . . . a strategic thinker. If you're here long enough you'll have to play every shot. Under all type of wind and rain and sleet."

I prompt the 2008 champ for his favorite holes but he's hard-pressed to choose. "Eight is the favorite hole in the world. It takes two well-hit shots, discipline, and accuracy to play. Sometimes you hit and say 'I've done all I can; the rest is up to the gods of golf.' Seven is a classic hole. Fourteen is the hardest 3-shot par 5 in the world. Of course eighteen you come into all that history . . . Overall I don't think there's an awkward shot out there. Maybe the second shot on six coming up that hill, especially when that tree was there at that corner."

What about the Monterey Peninsula as a golfing mecca, with Pebble as its foremost shrine? Yes, Sluman, a wine aficionado, says, and double yes: "You've got Carmel. Then you can run up to the Napa Valley or San Francisco. There's just so much around here. If you really like warm weather you drive 5 miles and it's ninety degrees. If you love golf, there's so much around here to do. It's spectacular."

And if imitation is the sincerest form of flattery, would Slu borrow any plays from the Jack Neville–Douglas Grant playbook when he begins designing courses of his own? He's interested in the golf architecture biz, and already co-owns, with golfer Dudley Hart, Lakeshore Golf Course in Rochester, New York, the course he cut his teeth on growing up. "I wish I could copy everything. Neville and Grant hit a home run. They've rarely had to do anything but push a few tees back. The golf course is defended by the small greens and the winds and strategic bunkers. Really they hit the whole deal," Sluman says, draining another money ten-footer.

Tomorrow Slu's karmic annuity will pay big-time dividends, as he'll ace the 178-yard, par-3 fifth, firing a 68 to come from 6 shots back, leapfrogging O'Meara and "Boss of the Moss" California native Loren Roberts, to defeat journeyman pro Gene Jones by 2.

As his buddy Slu plays his way up eighteen clinging to a 2-shot lead, Murray will rematerialize, this time carrying a glass of red wine. He'll taunt the upscale Pebble Beachers sunning themselves on the decks of their multimillion-dollar abodes, shouting at them over the hedges, "Your lawns are looking great, ladies." Meanwhile, he'll exhort a gaggle of teenage girls in jean shorts to scream "Wildcat!" at the top of their pubescent lungs. Wildcat, Slu will later tell me, is one of many ironic nicknames Murray has tagged him with, sort of like calling the big guy in the office "tiny."

Cheerleading finis, Murray will disappear once more, the chameleon of Carmel Bay, to resurface when the glasses are raised in the Wildcat's honor. On a gusty day when the average score will balloon to nearly 75 in a preview of likely U.S. Open conditions, Slu will wear a huge smile to his press conference after his second win at Pebble in as many years, a victory that will propel him into the top five on the official money list and, maybe, just maybe, inaugurate a new, more flattering moniker: Slu-Dog Millionaire.

4

Shivas Irons, the Great White Whale, and Golf in the Kingdom of Pebble

It takes me nearly a month to finagle a face-to-face with the bestselling golf fiction writer of all-time, Michael Murphy. I hadn't intended to search him out until one day on the Carmel Beach, as I reread the dog-eared copy of *Golf in the Kingdom* that my dad had given to me as a teen, I'd found myself unexpectedly in tears. With pencil in hand as I read, I absentmindedly scrawled in the margins *Dad . . . my partner . . . dying*. I'd taken my fearful, subconscious doodling as reason enough to attempt to close another circle that involved my father, Pebble Beach, Michael Murphy, and me.

After much back and forth with Murphy's personal assistant, I happily agree to meet the golf guru at the prearranged location: Horizons Restaurant in Sausalito, a fishing village turned upscale shopper's port of call at the north end of Golden Gate. Our rendezvous has all the makings of a bad blind date. First, I don't know Horizons from a hole-in-the-wall; for all I know I could get stuck with a $200 tab for some

Bud Lights and lobster bisque. Second, none of the few published interviews with the golfer-philosopher-bestselling author I've seen have featured his mug, so add a pinch of platonic intrigue to the mix. And then there's the romantic setting: the blue-water Sausalito Bay lapping at the pilings beneath me, Alcatraz humped in the distance, and, beyond, the misty San Francisco skyline.

"Is there a man here named Murphy?" I ask the hostess at what turns out to be something like a chic Long John Silver's with valet parking. The maître d' is a shapely young brunette fresh from some faded copy of *Cosmo*. He's a writer," I add. "I was supposed to meet him here."

"There's a man around the corner sitting alone," she says hopefully.

"How old?"

"Sixty, maybe. Wait here."

A matchmaker's smile plays across her lips when she returns. "He says come on over."

Murphy stands to greet me. He's wearing a black synthetic short-sleeve, the pec-hugging kind stud golfers wear these days, and a beat-up pair of blue jeans. If a classics professor, a dazed spiritual wanderer, and Clint Eastwood had a ménage-a-trois, their lovechild stands before me. Murphy actually looks a smidge like Eastwood, but then every man of blazing eye and sweet soul-wound old enough to collect Social Security looks a bit like Dirty Harry to me. Murphy seems mildly disappointed, like he was expecting a reporter from *Golf Digest*, Barbara Wa-Wa, or some perky little intern from the USGA. After we shake hands and sit, he wants my life story—in Reader's Digest form. His next appointment is at 2:30.

In a few minutes he knows more about my past than many of my friends do, though I do not tell him of my dad's alcoholism, the recent sale of the land upon which we'd built or blessed Foxbriar G.C., nor of my pop's surrendering of his sticks prior to my coming here. Five more minutes and I've given away the proverbial farm, telling him the story of the pasture course Dad and I built and producing my childhood golf course design sketches from a pocket folder, including my two full-color redesigns of Pebble. "How old were you when you did those?" he asks, incredulous. "Twelve? Incredible. So colorful!"

When I'm done with my spiel about why I've come—to pick his brain on the subject of a true golfing mecca—he says, "Very enterprising," which I take to mean, "How'd this guy get past my personal assistant?" After we've ordered drinks—iced tea for him, an Arnold Palmer for me—he begins to tell me his own story, a story that sounds, in its retelling, like the villain's in a James Bond flick but for that fact that Murphy is one of golf's good guys.

He was born to a Basque mother and an Irish father in 1930 in Monterey County—a stone's throw from where I've moved for this U.S. Open year. He doesn't play golf much anymore—it's gotten too distance-obsessed for his Byron Nelson–styled, accuracy-built swing—but way back when, while on the Salinas High golf team, he was consistently shooting in the mid 70s and his talented younger brother, two years his junior, a few shots better. Murphy once teed it up against future U.S. Open champ Ken Venturi in the finals of the Northern California Golf Association junior tournament. And in those sweet salad days he routinely played Pebble.

"One day we were playing behind Bob Hope and Bing Crosby," he recalls. "I'll never forget that day. I was in high school. My brother was 14 and I was 16 maybe, but he was still very short. So, on the tenth hole, which is the long one, he sank a 2-wood for an eagle 2, and he rolled it in past Hope and Crosby on the green.

"So Hope and Crosby started to take notice of us. And they were good. I mean, they both shot in the 70s. So finally they let us through on the seventeenth hole because we were pushing too hard. They stood and watched my brother and applauded as we came through for those prodigious shots he was hitting."

When he pauses to swirl his iced tea I tell Murphy—not mere flattery—that I think *Golf in the Kingdom* may be the best novel on sport ever written, that it feels almost flawless, one of those golden eggs that drops into the lap of the unsuspecting scribbler who barely knows what to do with it. I produce my own dog-eared copy, the one my father kept on his bookshelf and that I'd brought with me to the Left Coast as a talisman, the one in which I wrote *Dad dying* on that teary afternoon on Carmel Beach when I'd resolved to seek Murphy. "It's well-loved," I say, pointing to its Velveteen Rabbit edges.

"That's an early one," Murphy says, picking it up from the table. "I can tell from the cover. But not as old as some." He regards the book almost longingly, as if a long-estranged parent reunited with a distant child or lover with a beloved, giving it a look that says, "Lots of water under the bridge, eh, partner?"

He tells me the volume, first published in 1972, came quickly—seven months from start to finish. It was barely off the drawing board when it was contracted by Viking, who was already partnering with the spiritual center Murphy cofounded with Richard Price, the Esalen Institute, to publish groundbreaking psychological studies. Murphy was barely into his forties and he'd accidentally penned what would become the bestselling golf fiction of all time—a million copies and still counting—and counted as a fave by the likes of John Updike and Tom Watson, a book Clint Eastwood liked so much he bought the film rights. A book Murphy never intended to write.

"John [Updike] wrote me when the book first came out," Murphy recalls, smiling at the recollection, "and told me I was like some no-name slugger who steps to the plate and hits one out of the park on his first try." The nearly four decades that have elapsed since have all but fallen down the rabbit hole to hear Murphy, something of a Rip Van Winkle, tell it. He's actually seventy-nine, nearly twenty years older than our winsome hostess had him pegged for. And he's still virile, still fully alive . . . that Eastwood thing again.

In between the publication of *Golf in the Kingdom* and this, our Cali lite lunch of butter salad and roasted potatoes, there have been many more books—three more works of fiction and a handful of mostly serious nonfiction on human performance and what Murphy calls "transformative practice." Clearly he's far from a one-book author or a one-hit wonder, yet his reputation has been built on that initial walk-off home run and the worldwide movement it created, including the formation of the Shivas Irons Society, a nonprofit organization with members in fifty states and twenty countries.

He's good-humored about the twist of fate. "It's been one of my privileges to take confessions from golfers—'Father Murphy'—telling me about their latest epiphanies on the golf courses," he says wryly, almost ruefully. "Now I'm the world's leading authority on mystical and occult experiences on golf courses because of this book and thirty-seven years of listening to stories."

So, I ask my lunchmate, getting down to business, what are the characteristics of a golfing mecca? Father Murphy falls silent for a momentum, considering. "That's actually a provocative question," he asks, apparently a bit surprised I'm not just throwing him batting practice. "I have to put that in the plural, *meccas*. Golf courses are the world's largest gardens. Never has the human race invested so much time, energy, money, architectural wit, designer's know-how, or technical expertise on the flora and fauna of particular regions, and much else, to design these 25,000 150- to 250-acre places. And some of them are truly enchanted—Pebble Beach, for example—and, for very different reasons, St. Andrews."

"But," he cautions, "I'd be very careful about being prescriptive. I imagined one golf course in *The Kingdom of Shivas Irons* . . . In imagining that course I came up with a number of dimensions . . . first the element of illusion, which has been made conscious by some golf course architects like Robert Trent Jones Jr. . . . . . The art of illusion exists to challenge the golfer but also to enchant, to offer a prismatic view. No human will ever play the same golf shot. Even if you stand in exactly the same place, the wind will be different, the texture of the grass, the heaviness of the air, the placement of the pin, the season, everything. You'll never have the same shot twice."

Murphy leans in, his voice hitting a John McCain–esque high note when he gets exercised: "Certain courses, take Pebble Beach, are just naturally endowed, like a supremely beautiful woman. They were not made that way by make-up or by physical training, although that can enhance their beauty. There's a magnificence in their looks when they turn to the camera. Great beauties who are beautiful from the front, the side, from all angles. Or let's say a beautiful male. A beautiful anything."

"Those courses have great bones, like Pebble. To bring out the prismatic nature of the land and of your perceptions and thus of your emotions and thus of your overall experience and the complexity and the fun of the game you're going to have there . . . that, you know, leads a golfer into falling in love."

I perk up at the mention of love, like a college kid in anatomy class when the prof moves to sex. *Golf in the Kingdom* pays homage to Plato's *Symposium*, in which the key players indulge in a night of wine-fueled debate about the nature of eros. Murphy is first and foremost a philosopher, a term that quite literally means "lover of wisdom."

"When you fall in love with someone, man or woman," Murphy continues, "and look at their face, it becomes psychedelic, this face that moves and changes, just as lovers fall into one another's eyes. And that's the prismatic thing . . . Often for golfers it's the enchantment of the game that leads them into seeing for the first time . . . they fall in love with life. They fall in love with the beauty of this garden . . . And that evokes in them, even in someone who never meditates, and who is not of any religious persuasion, love. All this comes into play in the making of a golfing mecca."

"So is Pebble Beach the center of a larger mecca, the Monterey Peninsula?" I ask. In a way, by his logic I am asking if he is still capable of falling, and falling hard, for golf in his own home kingdom.

"The Monterey Peninsula for me still would rank in the top five in the world. Of course, Scotland as a whole . . . the Kingdom of Fife . . . But you're never going to top the Monterey Peninsula to have Pebble and Cypress and Spyglass. There are five incredible layouts and two that are on virtually any list of the top ten. They have to be. I don't care what anyone says. They once asked Jack Nicklaus, 'What course do you want to die on?' And he said, 'I'd like to play my last round at Pebble and be buried at St. Andrews.' It made me love him more when I heard that."

Murphy's sentiments about Pebble, and about the worldwide golfing mecca that is the Monterey Peninsula, echo the convictions of his closely autobiographical character Michael in *Golf in the Kingdom*. "Nothing in England or Scotland could rival Pebble Beach for sheer grandeur," Michael protests to his Scottish dinnermates in the book, adding that the famous California golf course could certainly "produce some wonderful states of mind."

"Must all great courses have the quality of a haunt?" I ask. "I mean, are they haunted by the spirits of those who have gone before?"

"I subscribe strongly the theories of F.W.H. Myers, the great pioneer of psychical research . . . He felt that all hauntings were caused by what he called *phantasmogenetic centers* . . . that is, a portion of space that has been powerfully influenced typically by a human spirit, for example, a negative ghost in these old haunted houses, someone who held a murderous rage for a long period of time, or extraordinary grief, or extraordinary fear, and shaped a portion of space."

What about the sacred space of a golf course?

"Certainly St. Andrews the Old Course would carry such an imprint from so many great golfers," Murphy replies. "I don't know if you could call it a phantasmogenetic center created by a particular person—let's say Old Tom Morris, I mean, he'd be your first candidate—but, rather, by the incredible devotion of all the golfers in the world, and the Royal and Ancient, it becomes, willy nilly, a Vatican. As the Greeks used to say, every culture has an *umbilicus*. Mecca is the umbilicus of the world of Islam. Delphi was the umbilicus of the Greek world."

And what about the poor schmucks who tee it up, so to speak, at the oracle and feel nothing in their bones? What about the duffer who's dumb to the magic?

"Before you feel a haunting you have to bring something to it," Murphy reiterates. "And it's conceivable to me that certain golf shots are so terrifying they could cause a haunting . . . let's say, to carry the inlet of the ocean on the eighth hole at Pebble Beach. If you get too close, it's straight down 200 feet and you fall to your death. And there your ball is right up there at the edge, as occasionally it was when I was playing there. Are you going let it all out with a club? What if you fall forward? So you tend to fall back if it's within a foot or two of the cliff. So, yes, such hauntings are possible. I would say it's transactional. It depends on what you bring. Some people go to St. Andrews and they can't see it. They're stunted people. Now, we're all stunted, but some are more stunted than others." Murphy chuckles at his own needless equivocation, adding, "If they can't feel it at St. Andrews they should reincarnate as a dog and work their way back up."

"Is Pebble haunted?"

"It's immensely *evocative*," Murphy says, treading carefully. "I've walked that course when there's been a broad cigar-shape of a cloud with gorgeous green underneath and the brilliant blue sky above . . . You'd see emerald green, then this silver, gold-tinged cloud, then beautiful blue sky beyond. The beauty is so staggering, and the views so different, every time you play it.

"I've played it so often. I saw Ben Hogan play there. Nicklaus in the '72 Open . . . I saw Lanny Wadkins win the PGA there. I've seen so many great events . . . That course is so luminous and prismatic. I wouldn't call it haunted. I would call it enchanted."

Listening to Murphy discourse, I realize I'm needy when it comes to older men. I want them to dish the ugly truths and hard-won wisdoms resident in those hoary heads. I want them to tell me what love is, how to navigate it, as if love were itself a perilous golf course where local knowledge proves key. "So what about the quality of bad charm?" I ask him. I'm thinking back to my last lover, Jacqueline, one of those wreck-you-on-the-rocks beauties who counted the daily compliments she received at work and celebrated at the office what she called NPFs—No Panty Fridays. I'm coy in my query, or at least I think I am. "Think about Odysseus. Think about your own relationships over the years." I'm goading him and, to my delight, he's taking.

"Circe, you mean? Every golf course has a Circe in it. All men are turned into pigs by golf courses."

"You can meet a great beauty . . . you've probably met some," I add, eyeing him carefully, "who are empty and who are, in a way, dangerous. They're enchantresses, right? And you end up getting turned into a pig. You lose years of your life, like Odysseus."

"Of course you always have to ask how much of it was them and how much of it was you." Murphy raises a frosty eyebrow at me.

"What about charm, when it's bad charm?"

"When it comes to golf, it's all that way. There's not a golf course on the planet that hasn't driven men to prayer. Nothing can drive you to prayer faster than a broken heart. There's no quicker path to have concourse with an angel than a broken heart after a broken love affair. Same with a golf course. Golf naturally drives people to prayer. It's so *fiendishly* frustrating."

Murphy pauses in advance of his summary argument. "So the most beautiful and innocuous course is a witch, every one of them . . . really. It's a *dangerous game*." His voice reaches that high note again. "I think every golf course should have a big skull and crossbones right on the first tee: *Beware ye who enter here*."

"But there must be a distinction between a Bette Davis . . . a darker attraction in a woman, a golf course, whatever," I prompt him, probing the wound.

"I had that kind of relationship with Spyglass Hill. I can't play Spyglass. I—cannot—play—Spyglass," Murphy repeats, emphasizing each word like it's an incantation and an anti-affirmation all in one. "It's a bitch of a bitch. A monstrous bitch." He smiles. "But I can play Pebble Beach. Why? You know, I don't think I ever broke 75 or 76 on Pebble, but from the white tees that's a good score. And it was fun. I think I once shot 34 on the front nine. Spyglass . . . forget it. I can't do it. It's the same game . . . Others guys play Spyglass and shoot a 68 and they're in love. And they've just had a great roll in the hay. So it's relative to your game."

So does wisdom lie in playing Pebble more often, because it fits your eye?

"As you become a man of experience, since we're on this metaphor, you learn to dance with the girls you can dance with. So I just don't like to play certain golf courses. I don't go back there. Now, some courses are just so scroungy and ugly, it's like going out to dance with the ugliest girl at the ball . . . I don't like to play those courses."

"There's no fascination," I say, egging him on.

"Poorly made golf courses and poorly kept."

"The spirit is poor, you mean," I say, trying to steer us back to kosher territory. But Father Murphy's on a roll, bless 'im.

"It's the lady who hasn't bathed in weeks. She just smells wrong. Something feels bad. Something smells bad. It *is* bad."

"So," he continues, "you've got yourself a good metaphor here. If you're a great Latin lover you can take on any course. Tiger Woods has never played a course he couldn't play. But his eye still fits certain courses. He's won seven times at Firestone. Six times at Bay Hill."

"And Mark O'Meara has won five of his sixteen at Pebble."

"There you have it."

I can't resist. "Going back to your earlier comparison, about an enchanting golf course being like a beautiful woman: What kind of woman would Pebble Beach be?"

Murphy thinks long and hard. "Pebble Beach is a woman with a kind of beauty that has so many aspects . . . of course, a tremendous figure, obviously someone like Ava Gardner, Jean Harlot, with this figure to die for, and this face . . . it would not be Doris Day. It would not be Audrey Hepburn. This would be a classically handsome woman and beautiful but alluring in a more feminine way."

"Lauren Bacall?" I throw out one of my faves.

"Lauren Bacall had an edge of the masculine beauty. There was an awful lot of Roman profile in Lauren Bacall."

Murphy's already racing ahead to his next candidates. "Pebble Beach is even too big for Hedy Lamarr. Hedy Lamarr would be Pasatiempo Golf Club. For a roll in the hay that you would never forget, that would be Hedy Lamarr. Oh, *Ecstasy*."

I raise an eyebrow, and he hastens to explain. "When I was growing up there was a movie called *Ecstasy*. Oh my god, I never saw it, but one heard about it."

I can't help but laugh. "That's what they all say."

"I think she was shown nude, but you didn't really see anything. It was a kind of contour." He snaps out of whatever erotic reverie the conversation has induced. "I'll have to think about this awhile. I can't find a woman beautiful enough to match Pebble. I go in the direction of Jean Harlow, Ava Gardner or, well, Sigourney Weaver is in that direction in her prime. She had that statuesque beauty to die for and nothing off-putting. Providing but big and strong. None of them match up."

"So, back to your earlier point, enlightenment and maturity exist in choosing the golf course you dance with or the woman you dance with?" The schoolboy in me makes an attempt to sum up the lesson, but Murphy isn't having it, not just yet.

"Now you can choose like brave men do to play with a woman who is beyond your capacity, but at some point you're . . . "

I complete the syllogism: "going to be turned into a pig."

"Going to be turned into a pig." He smiles, pleased that I've grasped his Socratic intention.

"Has any of the magic gone from the contemporary game?" I ask Father Murphy, who, post–*Golf in the Kingdom*, began to turn his attention to distance running as his sport of choice, his own personal laboratory for the human potential movement.

"Absolutely. Oh my God, yes!" he replies. "When I could play Pebble Beach for five dollars. I'll never be able to do that again. Everything about it was so enchanted. There was more magic in it for me."

I'm prepared to let these words serve as Father Murphy's homily, but no sooner have they left his mouth than a hubbub happens out in the bay. Murphy turns in the direction of the noise, to see a fishing boat with two dudes working hard at the stern, their pole bent. All the diners on the patio are enraptured, oohing and ahhing empathetically as if they're watching successive contenders lip out birdie putts that might have won them the tournament.

"Probably a sting ray," Murphy mumbles. "They really fight, those sting rays. Tremendous fighters." He sighs, turning back to the table. "I never could fish or hunt. Everyone fished and cleaned the fish down at Esalen when I was a kid. I didn't like to clean them. Anyway . . . Well, gee, it's been a delight."

And, with that, Father Murphy, scribe of the bestselling golf fiction of all-time, stands to go. I rise with him, offering him my hand. He promises me another interview if I'm ever in the area, implying that more and greater truths await. I assure him I'll gladly pick up the tab in exchange for his time, and he puts up no fight. Then, just like that, he is gone — shazam, like his alter-ego, Shivas Irons, who disappears at will into the cobblestoned Scottish night.

As I am doing the difficult math of what constitutes a fair tip in chichi Sausalito, a roar goes up from the tables around me, and I turn, half expecting to see Murphy levitating or sawing our handsome hostess in half. Instead, one of the two long-suffering fisherman outside pumps his fist while the other hauls in a sleekly beautiful, perfectly fleshy stingray, its underbelly glistening like a whetstone. The patio crowd breaks into applause and, out on the bay, the fisherman with the lucky reel doffs his cap.

I shake my head at the weird literary import of the events outside the window . . . the Great White Whale . . . the Old Man and the Sea . . . the Fisher King, all symbolic of the quest itself and, suddenly, here before my very eyes, the very instant after the golfing Elvis has left the building, comes the miracle catch.

I hear the surf crash to port, swirling in my ear-hole, the plaintive cry of gulls, the whistling of the wind on a pissy, dishwater day when the moody Pacific looks as though it, not Hatteras, should be called the "graveyard of ships."

I know it deep in my seaman's bones, in my salty dog's wizened gaze, and I know it in my Mastercard bill: I am playing my first round at "Pebble Beach," except at 90 percent off rack—$50 rather than $500. I am at the "the poor man's Pebble Beach," as it's called here: the municipal golf course more lately called Pacific Grove Golf Links on Asilomar Boulevard—P.G. for short and fo shizzle. Named a *Golf Digest* "Best Deals in Golf," it's a few miles up-Peninsula from its pricier namesake, with a seaside back nine likewise designed by Pebble co-designer Jack Neville and a front nine drawn up by Chandler Egan, who renovated Pebble in 1928 after the famed Alister Mackenzie rebuilt the eighth and thirteenth greens a couple of years before. S.F.B. Morse, the Duke of Del Monte and father of Pebble Beach, owned this land, too, and in the Depression agreed to part with it in exchange for a ten-dollar gold coin and a promise that the City of Pacific Grove would maintain it as a public golf course.

I am looking for my wayward pearl on the sixteenth—a short par 4 nicknamed the "lighthouse"—that's routed through the dunes not more than a wedge away from today's pewter gray Monterey Bay. I am doing recon in a roped-off ESA, or "Ecologically Sensitive Area," where, according to the many posted signs, I dare not tread. I've been in Cali long enough to know golf course ESAs are often only quaint cover-ups for sleeper cells of that terrorist scourge known as ice plant, which I feel no remorse in busting. Like snow back home, the Ice Man, as I've come to call the whole chilly species, is beautiful from afar and a bitch up close.

I'm muzzled from sounding my barbaric yalp, though, prevented from hollering "A LITTLE HELP OVER HERE!" because today I am playing with one Steve Cohen, erstwhile food service manager at the Esalen Institute, amateur gestalt psychologist, and, more relevant to my current predicament, president and grand poobah of the Shivas Irons Society, a society devoted to the mystically literate, albeit fictional mad Scottish golf pro created by Michael Murphy. During the many moments when I convince myself I've fallen into the hands of some no-name cult, I remind myself of the names of the various Tour pros who are or have been SIS members: John Cook, Peter Jacobsen, Scott McCarron, Mike Reid, Kirk Triplett, D. A. Wiebring, LPGA Hall-of-Famer Carol Mann, and, weirdly, comedian Tommy Smothers.

At the moment I hate the otherwise likeable Steve Cohen. He is the object of several sailor's oaths that have escaped from my blowhole for he has, by near-papal decree, declared this to be a hole of Zen silence — a Shivas Irons–inspired gag he sometimes pulls out of his bag when at the helm of a globetrotting, philosophy-laden golf outing.

After I'd "celebrated" a lipped-out birdie putt on the thirteenth with the flailing of arms and a few choice fricatives, he'd asked if any of us would object to playing a hole, or holes, during which no one spoke, as in no "Ahoy! Cap'n Cohen" or "Ice plant off starboard bow." Joseph and Mary, as I'll call them, likewise members of the society and our playing partners for the day, consented straightaway. Me? I'm an All-American farm boy. There's about as much Zen in my soil as there is in Warren Buffett's. So I'd stopped right there on the path, looked the SIS prez square in the eye, and said,

"Okay."

I hadn't really meant it, though, and now want to call take-backs. I suspected that Cohen had floated the scheme as a kind of antidote to my earlier "demonstrations." "You open to trying a little experiment?" he'd asked. It's one thing when you hear those words from your sweetie at the Marriot, but quite another thing when you hear them, still smarting from your missed birdie putt, from the mouth of a gray-bearded senior citizen who once described himself to writer Mark Soltau as an "overweight Jewish intellectual" and who Jim Achenbach of *GolfWeek* once pegged as "a former hippie with nests of hair and a vocabulary straight from the dens of protest."

I honestly can't remember the last time I'd willingly agreed to a tee-time prior to 9:00 a.m., but, in interviewing the gruffly sweet Cohen the day before, I'd all but insinuated myself into his foursome, so I had to deliver. Here I am, with my dad's rainmaker Tommy Armours, the first to arrive at the $50 P.G. Muni so socked in by fog we can't see the flag on the first hole, a short, straightaway par 3 — "Little Tombstone" they call it — that you could par with a hangover (a hypothesis I happen to be testing this not-so-fair morn).

The front nine at P.G. is, especially in today's miasma, eminently forgettable. Designed by back-to-back turn-of-the-century U.S. Amateur champ Egan in the early 1930s and later mucked around with in the 1960s, it's routed inland through tall pines and cypresses in the timeless, dogleg-less Way of the Muni. It's crowded, too, enveloped by once ho-hum now hot-to-trot real estate and spooked by San Carlos Cemetery cozying up to holes one and two. The continuous encroachment means yard after yard of high netting protecting the house-poor homeowners in their half-mil domiciles from my Ti-Tech golf ball which, having been zipped in tight for the better part of my twenty-one-hundred-mile trip here, is aching to do a little property damage.

Joseph, as coincidence would have it, is an Iowa farm boy like me whose old man sold a farm that became his whistle stop's only golf course. He lives near Puget Sound, which he loves. He doesn't say what's brought him downcoast for the long weekend — I assume it's playing golf with other members of the society, but it could be an illicit drug run for all I know. You've got to watch those Iowa farm boys.

Mary's story is harder to suss out. She's a regular society member and travels on many of the inspiring, not-inexpensive outings, including the group's upcoming trip to the upstart West Coast golfing resort Bandon Dunes, on the south Oregon coast. She and I both plan on attending the Pebble Beach horse show this afternoon: she because she knows horses, and I because I want to witness the incongruity of noble creatures taking noble creature–sized dumps on the sacred ground that is the Pebble Beach Equestrian Center just beyond the driving range. What I'll end up hearing at the horse show is more profanity than I ever thought possible from she-trainers screaming bloody murder as their prepubescent charges attempt to pilot thoroughbreds over thigh-high jumps. I'll end up seeing horse trailers and people "tents" that would put many a middle American home to shame, lots of tears (these are teenage girls), and, yes, lots of horseshit, only some of it issuing from the animals.

Back on the muni the real horseshit has yet to fly, as the four of us hack up the poor man's Pebble like bloodthirsty pirates. As I settle into a round of atrophied swipes that make up my moth-eaten golf game, I realize there's very little distinguishing our foursome from any other, apart from a few choice oddities. To wit: Among us, there's an anomalous, oft-verbalized interest in "having fun" that's a bit of a giveaway, as everyone knows your normal red-blooded corporate hack would rather better his handicap than prolong his life in enlightened mirth. There's also a disproportionate attention to The Rules of Golf. Already in one round I've seen more provisional balls played and two-foot putts holed out than I have in a year of casual kick-ins back home. Today, too, my vocalizations are more vociferous than usual, signaling both the advent of my mating season and a perverse reaction to our round's anomalous decorum. "Hey," I want to say, "I'm the polite and retiring one. I'm the Iowan here, okay?" After a few holes of this—of Mary's consistent ball-striking and affirmations, of Joseph's cheery demeanor and overall agrarian pleasantness—I've become in my own delusional mind the bad boy, the fourth child in a family who's already blessed with three perfect angels. As such I am all but obliged to misbehave.

The front side at the P.G. Muni turns out to be so much ho-hum exposition. We continue to play "ready golf," whoever's good to go teeing off, honors be damned. Ahead of us waits the back nine, Jack Neville's other hard-on-the-sea masterpiece.

On eleven, aptly named "Seaward" and the first hole to offer a truly close-up view of the Pacific, I overnuke my wedge approach on the less-than-300-yard hole, watching it bury in the berm behind the green. We find it plugged on the 45-degree downslope, 10 feet above a tiny green running away from me, necessitating the assumption of the classically uncomfortably downhill stance where you're right leg feels like it's a peg sawed off at the knee, your severely choked down club feels stubby as a golf pencil, and your overstressed left knee feels like you're aching to tear an ACL. Adding what had been my five-minute search for my plugged pearl to the five additional minutes and four swipes it has taken me to get my ball in the hole, and I feel obliged to apologize.

"We hate you for playing poorly and slowly," Cohen remarks, in a monotone that sounds like one of those canned Alcoholics Anonymous responses. The jibe lingers like a bad fog. Inside, I'm awash in spleen. After an uncomfortable silence that lasts all the way to the twelfth tee, Cohen initiates his grinning *rapprochement*. "Just kidding," he says. "Seriously, don't apologize. Slow down. Breathe deep."

Still, instead of feeling my existential load lightened by this attempt at levity, I just feel twice alienated. Apparently I'm not the only one warring with himself, as Joseph's controlled game has likewise begun to fray in the fog and wind. In the alternate world of Shivas Irons, a "bad" shot, like a mucked-up relationship, is often just one that the golfer didn't "commit to." At one point on the so-called Neville Nine, Joseph chastises himself for "breaking his promise to himself" not to overswing, and his mechanical, self-immolating tone resembles a recovering addict's.

I dig deeply our humble foursome of thinking golfers, but there is a bit of the annoying born-again, promise-keeping quality to these Shivas Irons acolytes. Several times Joseph comes over to tell me how beautiful the course is, and that's true—the gnarled, gnarly cypresses, the calico dunes, the wild deer browsing the ESAs. Today's foursome's aesthetic awareness is cloyingly unsettling but at the same time it's utterly refreshing. It's weirdly disconcerting to hear others mouth the kind of spontaneous aesthetic appreciations I used to unwittingly let slip back in high school, where I'd played number one on the golf team. Once, on the last hole of an important match, I'd commented from the tee that the fairway of the dogleg par 4—laying verdant green against the cornhusk brown of unwatered autumnal rough—looked like an "emerald isle," and I never lived it down. Artsy appreciation is an athletic breach, sort of like a center turning to his quarterback on a final drive and saying, "Gee, ain't this field pretty?"

Our little group of penitents, of seekers and aesthetes, seems to have upped its collective game for Neville's seaward holes which, I've got to admit, do inspire. Cohen's confidence as the leader of our motley crew has grown with each passing shot. Somehow he's found a rhythmic talisman for his short punchy swing, and though it's still not Michelangelo, he's got it grooved.

Cohen's born-in-the-Bronx gruffness sometimes escapes from his blowhole as refreshing honesty, sometimes as lukewarm antipathy. When poor Mary pushes her approach into the waiting arms of one of those goddamn ice plant commies on fifteen, Cohen says, "Whoops"—not "Such bad luck" or "You was robbed." Meanwhile, the ice plant holds Mary's ball like a POW, taunting her, adding to the indignity of her plight in the way only the Iceman can.

After Mary plays a nifty recovery from the ice plant cometh, and I hit a miraculous punch shot from beneath a tree only to have my 10-foot birdie do a cellophane bridge, Cohen turns to ask that sexy little question of his: "You open to trying a little experiment?"

That's how I find myself alone, trying to sustain a late-round recovery, looking desperately for my pearl in the spinach, as the sirens howl and the banshees wail from the bottom of Davy Jones's Locker, threatening to wash away my attempted comeback like some poor kid's sand castle. Selectively disregarding the signs threatening ecological peril, I deliver a mighty blow with a 6-iron to the noxious species, thrilling at the plant's shrill cry—a lobster's on the boil—as it releases its stranglehold.

While the sea gods rage and my inner-admirals spout unspeakable epitaphs, we play the rest of our silent hole, a silence that quickly becomes as goofy as the who-can-go-the-longest-without-speaking game you used to play as a kid, only there's no giggling allowed. As

Cohen putts out, a raucous pair of crows caw in the cypress beside the green and Mary smirks at me. We're communicating, Mary and I, we're just not talking.

Our voiceless hole completed, Cohen speaks first. "What did you think?"

"At first it felt punitive," I admit, "and sort of arbitrary. But I settled into it. It's true, you do hear the ocean better, the birds." My response is mostly honest . . . at least as honest as the dictates of the host-hosted relationship allow. After extracting my Ti-tech from the loathsome Iceman and playing back to the fairway, I did come to enjoy the experiment for experiment's sake.

"And you hear yourself better, too," Cohen says. "The society has played whole rounds that way. The idea is to relieve the golfer of the burden of speaking obligatorily. No 'goods shots' if it really wasn't a good shot."

Come to think of it, I did feel more camaraderie in the hole just past than anytime before it — my nonverbals with Mary being a prime example — and I did appreciate the freedoms inherent in being an uncommunicative, self-obsessed bastard.

Unexpectedly, the Zen effect carries over to the next hole and the hole after. After three total holes of it, I'm digging this mutinous, mute golf more than the willful chumminess and bland chatter of the front nine. I feel more companioned in the vacuum — like I'm in the company of fellow pilgrims, quiet before our Titleists.

Cohen is playing the best golf of the four of us, working that choked-off piston move of his into a serviceable rhythm. Joseph and I continue up and down, left and right, high and low. Mary's steady as she goes.

When we're through, no one adds up their numbers, at least not publicly. Among society members, an immediate tally is as verboten as counting your change in front of the store clerk. Caps are ceremoniously doffed and hands are ritually shook. Mary gives me a big bear hug. Together, we spend what's left of our afterglow in sincere praise of the poor man's Pebble Beach, which turns out to be a peach.

Maybe it's the Jekyll/Hyde, inland/ocean, Egan/Neville schizo of the Pacific Grove Links, or the weird, wistful fog, or the fact that we teed off at what seemed like the butt-crack of dawn, but chatting amiably with my SIS peeps, I feel as if I've lived two days, not one. Energy-wise I feel as if I could easily play another eighteen. Spirit-wise I am practically Holy Ghost. Maybe this Shivas Irons Society is onto something.

I'm secretly hoping that my Zen chops have sufficiently impressed Mary that she will invite me to tomorrow's round at Monterey Peninsula Country Club or, if not, maybe to the horse show.

Alas, as I pack my old man's sticks into the trunk, I suspect I've been allowed a one-time only glimpse, a single toke. Maybe Shivas is waiting for my membership check. Maybe he's waiting to see how long I'll stay in Monterey. Maybe there's some cult membership rite I've yet to complete, like seeing how many golf Topflites I can fit in my cheeks or if I can raise a Nike Noodle with my manhood. Or maybe—and this is what scares me the most—maybe I'm just not Shivas Irons material.

Maybe I'm just too fucking polite.

In-between bits of sweet potato fries at a double entendre of a coffee shop, Uncommon Grounds, adjacent to the "International Headquarters" of the Shivas Irons Society in Sand City, California, Cohen gives me the backstory of his unique, Carmel-based 501C-3. "The society was launched during the 1992 U.S. Open on a Friday night . . . The world golf press was there. Everybody showed up, including members of the Pebble Beach Company. We signed the incorporation papers that night, and it just took off."

Roughly four years earlier Michael Murphy, the cofounder of Esalen and the creator of the fictional character Shivas Irons, had suggested a workshop at Esalen on his book, *Golf in the Kingdom*, one that took advantage of Cohen's growing skills in gestalt. "That day was one of those days that you point to when life takes a new turn," Cohen tells me, still wide-eyed, many years later, at the accident of fate.

It was like John, Paul, and George meeting on Penny Lane—in the mystic California golf sense anyway. Cohen's brainchild had clout from the get-go, and star backers, including author of *Extraordinary Golf* and former Santa Barbara University golf coach Fred Shoemaker, Murphy's friend, and then-president of the USGA, Grant Spaeth, and Doug Ferm, then-publisher of *Golf Digest*, who, at the time, was so smitten with *Golf in the Kingdom* that he'd begin editorial meetings with recitations from its pages. "By the time he [Ferm] left," Cohen confesses, chuckling, "people on his staff hated the book."

All that remained to seal the deal was the staging of a Monterey Peninsula–styled brouhaha—something quirky, something epic, something clambakey. Something where golf balls could be ceremonially struck, kilts could be donned, whiskey could be drunk, and feel-good checks could be written. Enter the Shivas Irons Games of the Links. Enter the most iconic golf course on the Left Coast of the United States of America: Pebble.

The games kicked off in August of 1993, with rounds on both the famed links and at Spanish Bay. Well over a hundred golfers showed for the event, which had found cosponsors in the Pebble Beach Company and *Golf Digest*, ensuring it "tremendous national coverage," according to Cohen. "We were on the deck at Spanish Bay and we started hearing bagpipes," Cohen remembers. "And coming up over the hill is a full pipe and drum core playing 'Scotland the Brave.' It ends with a big roll of the drum, and people go crazy." Cohen, a non-golfer just a few years before, was getting an unprecedented, almost princely initiation into the game on its most storied courses, including moonlight golf at Spyglass Hill and sunrise rounds at Pebble Beach.

"I used to go out before revenue," Cohen says, meaning the uber-early tee times before the paying guests join the assault. Cohen's debut on the granddaddy of Peninsula courses proved to be something less than storybook. Picture this: It's the inaugural Games of the Links, and new prez of the society is tasked with the golf equivalent of throwing out the first pitch. He's standing on the first tee of the most famous public golf course in America. He's wearing plus fours. A crowd looks on. "I miss the ball. I absolutely miss the ball I'm so nervous. I turn around and catch Fred Shoemaker's eye and start to laugh. I walk over and whisper, 'I'm gonna make believe that this just didn't happen.' Everybody thought I did it on purpose."

Since that presidential whiff, Cohen's played the be-all, end-all links some two dozen times. "It's so beautiful," he gushes. "I've played it in good conditions. I've played it in the winter when it's wet. You're never out of touch with the history there."

Cohen tells me the best description he ever heard of the course's charms came from former USGA president Sandy Tatum, the man largely responsible for convincing dubious colleagues in the early 1970s that the far-flung and mostly unirrigated course was U.S. Open material. Tatum, who first played Pebble in 1936 and later recalled, for John Strege of *Golf Digest*, that he thought he'd "died and gone to heaven," has often spoken of his lifelong love affair with Pebble's "mystical element." Cohen recalls, "He talked about the first hole and how you don't have a real sense yet where you're going. It's a relatively easy hole and it welcomes you, though the green is tricky enough. Then you come down to the second hole, which is really a very easy par 5. You're still just starting to get ready. Then you come to the third hole, and you turn and have your first view of the ocean. You're starting to get a taste."

"On the opposite end, you come to the fourteenth hole, and you stand on the tee, and you look out, and you know you're about to play the second-greatest par 5 in the world, and you do it with the absolute knowledge that in forty minutes you're going to be playing the greatest par 5 in the world. I get chills just hearing it myself," Cohen says.

Still, the Pebble superlatives don't come as easily as they once did for Cohen who, for his day job, has the privilege of leading Shivas Irons golf outings at some of the most dramatic yet down-to-earth tracks in the world. "I'd say it's way overrated," he says of Pebble, adding that it wouldn't get the laurels it does if it "wasn't for the history and the view and several holes, which are absolutely outstanding."

Which holes, for him, make the "outstanding" mark? "The seventh and eighth. And you've got to include the sixth. I still manage to slice it into the ocean or pull it into the sand every time. You have this big vista and you know what's coming next." And what does he say to new members of the society who wonder whether a trip to the Monterey mecca is worth it? "You need to do it once. That's what I tell people."

After having unleashed his banana ball on the world's best tracks, Cohen's no longer convinced a half grand in greens fees is money well-spent. "I would never pay $500. I was comped out there. I played one time with guys who had waited two years. And they got out there and the greens were punched. Nobody told them. They gave them $50 back or something. But they had made this whole trip and planned it for two years. That's not right. Most elite courses won't do that."

Cohen isn't down on Pebble, he's just not as enamored with it as he once was. Other equally fetching courses with the same seemingly inimitable mix of sea, weather, roll, and tumble have caught his fancy, including Bandon Dunes on the Oregon coast and, inland, Ballyneal Golf Club in the remote sandhills of Colorado. But Pebble still feels seminal to him because to it some of his best, most poignant memories are attached. "There was a night when I left Esalen, and I had fully committed to the future of the Shivas Irons Society," Cohen recollects. "Fred Shoemaker invites me to meet him out at Pebble Beach. He says, 'Let's take a walk.' It's dusk. We walk along the sixth hole down toward seven . . . and when we get closer all my friends have gathered to kind of provide for me a moment of transition. After I hit a ball to the seventh green . . . they read poetry to me."

The baristas behind the chrome-swirl bar at Uncommon Grounds have, by now, amped up the industrial rock I'd earlier asked them to turn down, but I'm not leaving until Cohen riddles me this: If I met the prophet Shivas on some sacred, moonless night at Pebble, what would he have to say to a golfer like me? "You already know it," Cohen intones, rabbi-like. "You've already got the swing. Don't look outside yourself . . . You're not your handicap. You're not even your personality. You're just who you are. The more you embrace that, the easier golf gets."

I leave the coffee shop confused, infused with too much caffeine and the feeling I used to get in college when I knew I'd power-napped through an important lecture I could never again reconstruct, never get the notes for. What I feel now feels like the times in my life I've encountered something I'm just too stupid to comprehend, like calculus or Ikea assembly instructions. *I'm not my personality.* I repeat Cohen's mantra as I throw my notebook into the car, flirting with their promise. *I'm not my golf game.*

Initially the idea seems as obtuse as Derrida, but, once considered, the liberties boggle, promising freedoms Bill Murray–esque in their proportions. You mean I can wrestle an old gal down to the ground and make mock love to her—literally stealing a page from Billy's playbook? You mean that early wrist flip that's been causing my weak push-slice the last six months is as divorced from me as Tiger from Elin, K-Fed from Britney? You mean between my oversized ears I already hold the secret of the golfing universe, or at least *my* golfing universe?

Shivas me irons!

5

Hitting the Books at Pebble's
School of Hard Rocks

"Your swing's good enough to be a five."

"I haven't put much effort into it lately," I say, aw-shucks-ing. I feel like a cougar whose pool boy just mistook her for twenty-nine.

"A lot of guys are like that, until they make up their minds to chase the dream." My golf guru smiles the wry smile of someone well-acquainted with the dark recesses of the golfer's lizard brain.

I hit the next few pearls with renewed vigor, feeling my five-handicap oats. "You're cutting across the ball," my instructor declares, serious as a clinician. "You probably fought a hook when you were younger, didn't you?"

"My whole life," I admit, praise Jesus.

"All the good players do." He comes in close, and I know from previous long-repressed traumatic experience what's coming next . . . the laying on of hands, the stick where before there was only carrot. "I'm going to try to put you in a different position," he says.

Translation: Bend over and cough.

Walking Carmel's Ocean Avenue, you wouldn't know you were at ground zero of American golf. Sure, the t-shirt shops have the usual golfer's stock of obnoxious, double entendre sloganeering, and the sports memorabilia galleries have a few autographed pics of Tiger and Jack mixed in with snapshots of Derek Jeter and Barry Bonds and Steve Young and Jerry Rice. But beyond that, you could be in Sausalito or Mendocino or even Santa Barbara, not Golf Town, USA.

In fact, the only serious sign of links I found on Ocean Avenue upon my arrival turned out to be a small, black-and-white golf bag tucked nondescriptly in a display window in one of the few for-rent storefronts. The bag was of the older, single shoulder strap, heavy-duty leather variety favored by pros in the days before anyone cared about slump-backed caddies. Directly above the pocket usually reserved for spare tees and ball markers appeared the pro's name in jaunty cursive: *Doug Acton.* Leaned up against the bag was a sign listing a website and some digits for a "former touring pro."

Weeks later I surf to the site and find a homepage pic of Acton. He's wearing a wine-colored collarless golf shirt, a golf bag slung across his right shoulder, and a big grin. The website banner proclaims "Personal Pro" in display type, but at first glance this guy looks more like he should be my caddy. For anyone who knows Pebble, it's clear the shot's been snapped on the eighteenth hole, with a snatch of the seawall showing in the lower left-hand corner and Arch Rock and Stillwater Cove in the background. The photo seems trapped in the no-man's-land between self-engineered tourist shot and poor publicity take. The site's headline: "Is golf an ART or a SCIENCE?"

"As a gifted teacher and shotmaker," Acton's personal introduction reads, "my combination of verbal and visual skills has always planted me on the ART side of things. With all the data now available through technology, SCIENCE has become an undeniable piece of learning and improving the game of golf."

I admire the chutzpah—the guy poses the biggest metaphysical question in all of golfdom then has the nerve to come down on both sides of the fence. I click on the "About Douglas Acton" link. The resume's more than legit—thirty-seven years in golf, including a stint on the Asian Tour, and director of instruction at a handful of golf centers up and down the California coast. Any certified PGA pro quirky enough to own up to a name change, as Acton does in his bio—to say nothing of the trick of casting his Babe Ruth and Little League coaching experience as a possible hook to lure visiting golfers—is definitely worth a visit.

So I walk the five blocks to Acton's studio on Mission Street, sitting down on one of the barstools arranged around a high table. A minute later Acton runs in, out of breath. He's handsomer and more fit than the website photo, so much so that I wonder for a second if it's the same guy. He introduces himself, asking if I want an espresso or a Pellegrino. We chat idly for a few minutes, before he suggests it'd be easier to explain what he's up to if he could hook me up to his diagnostic equipment and watch me take a few passes in his indoor studio. That's when I begin making lame excuses about wanting to interview him first, failing to mention that I'd like to keep my twenty-year streak of instructionless golf virginally intact. In reply he hands me a Callaway 6-iron, as if to say, "Dude, let's see it."

I take a few rusty swings, making decent contact, and, predictably when I miss, missing thin and left. An awkward silence common to both golf lessons and first dates falls between us, while Acton's JVC Video Systems and Golf Achiever launch monitor gags on my data. My swing speed tops out at an anemic 80 mph, my clubface open four to five degrees on every pass. My best 6-iron strokes manage an elfin 165-yard carry.

That's when I start sensing bend-over-and-cough in the offing. He puts me back on my heels, turning my right hand so far "under the shaft" that I feel as if my palm is pointing skyward. "You're gonna feel like you can't even hit the ball from here," he says, taking the edge off with a little family doc–style narration. He strengthens my left-hand grip and, for good measure, shifts my weight over to my left side. "The golf swing's a race," he points out. "You wouldn't start a race from your back foot, would you? Now hit a few for me from that position."

He folds his arms across his chest, index finger over his lips in the classic teacher pose. I glance nervously over my shoulder at my yoda, the man who once described himself to *Carmel* magazine as "a golf savant," and then at the huge plate glass window to my right. It'd easily Bluebook for more than my car, and it's totally in my shanking range. Acton watches me thin a few more swings and then steps back in my business, this time from the front, reaching across to grab the club by the shaft. "This is how I want you to release the club," he says, moving the club inside out, like I'm hitting a topspin forehand. "That's the move you're trying to make."

I rehearse the action a few times, finding it as foreign as Gérard Depardieu. It feels indecent, actually, this spanking motion, the kind of thing that could get you arrested if seen in silhouette through Venetian blinds. "Here's what I mean," he says, pointing to the image of yours truly on the big-screen TV mounted on the wall behind us. "See how your right hand is on top of the club as you come into the ball rather than under the shaft? From there all you can do is get in your own way and block it. No wonder you're all scrunched up at impact."

There, on the swivel screen, in living color for all Carmel-by-the-Sea to see, is an image of my father at impact, as if time-warped from the 1980s—a variant of his over-the-top move that seared its way into my memory after we watched it too many times on our camcorder. Same retracted, impotent impact position. Same high handsy finish. Same threadbare light blue golf shirt. I realize, to my horror, that not only have I taken two steps toward becoming my father's golf swing, but that I've also unwittingly worn his hand-me-down golf shirt to my interview-cum lesson.

The revelation is stomach-turning and comforting all at once.

Acton and I compare my pathetic move to the slow-motion explosion of a young wiry Tiger Woods teeing off in the late 1990s, then to an image of Acton himself who, while his swing is more the knee-driven,

Reverse-C norm of the Johnny Miller era, nonetheless hits all the right positions. The evidence is indisputable: I may have a pretty swing but it's masking a closet hack.

"That's what I do here in the studio," Action says, yanking the metaphoric bag of cocaine after he's given me the first sniff. "If you really want to chase the dream, I tell people to see me every few weeks. Otherwise they're wasting their money, because every time I see them I'm fixing the same problem."

Chasing the dream. Moving to the putting green to continue our sample lesson, I'm tempted to throw myself at my mentor's feet, tempted to cry out unto my lord, "Yea, let me be reborn!" But it's the end of our lesson, the end of the trial period, the end of the hookup, the last pull on the hookah. If I want to chase the dream from here I'll have to pay through the nose for it.

Like many Carmel transplants, Acton has chosen to locate here on account of a golden memory. In the seventies he qualified for the California Amateur and drove down to Pebble, where he slept in his car and, on warmer nights, on the beach. He showered illicitly in the same Pebble locker room where today's superstars have permanently reserved lockers. Pebble was like that back then: an icon, but an eminently penetrable one.

Action ended up making it all the way to the semis, cementing countless feel-good memories. "I just fell in love with the whole place. It was beautiful. It was challenging. At that point and time, the community was tremendously nice to me. It wasn't that much to play the golf courses . . . I used to play Pebble in the morning and Cypress in the afternoon. I came down here for three weeks. Met a gal. Stayed with her. I was twenty-one . . . twenty . . ." He trails off, lost in the amber glow of youth and Carmel clambakes, the powerful opiate of romance, golf, and escapism that still gets people high here.

Hoping to recapture the old mojo, Acton found himself drawn back to the Peninsula when a trial move to Virginia didn't pan out. "I came down to Carmel one day for lunch, and I saw this storefront . . . I was trying to figure out where I wanted to live for the rest of my life." He pauses. "I'd saved a little bit of money, and I thought I would bet on me.

"Moving here has reconnected me with Pebble Beach and Spyglass Hill . . . the golf courses I learned to play golf on. Now I teach somebody at Pebble who lets me go out and play, and it's like happy days are here again. It's re-inspired me to play golf."

Upon his return, Acton played the famed links for the first time in almost twenty-five years and he's still jazzed about it. "I stuck it within 8 feet on the eighth hole. I hit it inside 10 feet all day. The only green I missed was the twelfth. Memories were just *filling* me . . . God, it was a blast. The ball never left the flagstick. My eyes were just trained to where I hit it twenty-five years ago. It was like I was a kid again."

Drawing on that kind of juice, it's easy to see why Acton followed the breadcrumb trail back to the Peninsula. Looking at him now, the effect of the reunion on his physiology is striking. He's dropped ten pounds, easy, since the barely six-month-old website picture. He looks five years younger. On the Internet he looked borderline goofy; today he's trending toward distinguished. I think of all the people I've met in town or seen from afar, and realize that most of them look ten to fifteen years younger than their biological age. Sure, some of that fountain of youth can be chalked up to plastic surgery and skin treatments and personal trainers and at-home spas, but some of it must be attributable to the healing powers of the place itself, a place my landlady swears has more oxygen in the air than anywhere.

"It was a lifestyle choice," Acton confesses. "I'm out on Carmel Beach at six o'clock every morning. I spend an hour on the beach. I go home and I do my stretches. I'm more physically fit and healthier than I've been in a long time . . . I've had a year off for good behavior on my own back from Virginia . . . I've got three boys who live in Marin County and a daughter who lives in Santa Monica. Personally, it's been huge. Financially it's a big risk. A huge risk."

And therein lies the rub. The tease of Carmel-by-the-Sea is difficult to afford, especially as a latter-day entrepreneur. You may look better, feel better, love better . . . hell, you may *be* better, but the fairy tale lasts only as long as you can keep the gingerbread roof over your head. Acton understands that hard math but to him it's a gamble worth taking.

"Monterey is different because you have such a diverse crowd. You have people who can't play a lick but they're here to play Pebble Beach for the only time in their life . . . I get some of that business model now: 'I played Spanish Bay yesterday. I sucked. I gotta play Pebble tomorrow. Do you have an half hour?' Then I get an email back saying, 'I played 20 shots better. I loved Pebble. Thanks so much.'"

If Acton's going to make it here, he realizes he's got to walk his talk. "Part of how I moved to Carmel I guess is because I'm the product. That means I better stay in shape. I better hit balls. It's a life challenge that I'm going to have to do."

For now my PGA Personal Pro is bronzed, happy, and chock-full of romantic prospects. Not coincidentally, he's also hitting the ball as far as he did when he was twenty-five. "I'm on the beach every day beneath the tenth hole at Pebble," he confesses. "I climb up on the rocks, have a glass of something, watch the sunset, and remember."

On my way back home in the Carmel gloaming after my unsolicited lesson with Acton, I wonder if there's a word for a golf swing that enters you, unbidden, as my old man's just did. It's my father I'm thinking of now, he who was only a few years older than I am now when he decided to "chase the dream," semi-retiring from farming to build, from his own blood sweat and tears, Foxbriar G.C. Most every morning in those drought years, in-between backbreaking jobs on the farm, he'd hit balls in the scant shade offered by our aluminum-sided shed. I'd awake to the thwack of irons, and cursing, and see him there, his Marlboro burning on the ground, working out some unseen kink in his swing.

All the way up Mountain View my ears are burning, and so are my hands, my legs, my wrists. My PGA Personal Pro has opened up Pandora's Box, the big bag of golfing demons I'd heretofore assiduously packed away. His impromptu lesson has loosed the jinni, begged the question: Am I man enough to chase the dream, to put Humpty Dumpty back together again?

I have dreamt of my father often in my months by the sea, anxious, exasperated dreams full of fist-pounding helplessness. I've wakened in the middle of the night, cold-sweating, as the stars sizzle above in the Monterey Pines. Somehow the oxygen-rich air here has set off a chain of internal combustions and trenchant haunts — the Big Bang of my departure to this place, the auction of the farm ground back home in Iowa in the fall — while I'd chatted leisurely with my childhood heroes, men like Tom Watson and Fuzzy Zoeller, on the greener pastures of Pebble. Across the miles my father is speaking to me, and he has chosen golf as the vehicle of his visitation.

Going to school, as the saying goes, is what good golfers are supposed to do, eagle-eyeing the green for some clue as to the mysteries topographical, kinetic, and spiritual of the correct line to where the sun don't shine. In fact, golf's the only major sport that encourages you toward nerdiness. In the course of a round, the duffer gets *schooled, goes to school, reads the break, calculates his yardage, tallies his score.* Hell, he does everything but dust the chalkboard. Golf history — consider the ancient university/theological town of St. Andrews, the oldest in Northern Europe — makes the point emphatically: a mecca, in the strictest sense of the word, cannot simply be a place of doing — racing cars, playing golf, screwing nymphs — it must also be a place of learning. After all, Christendom has a name for the other place, the hellhole sans contemplation.

I didn't expect to find much in the way of bookishness at Pebble Beach — Deano, Hope, and Bing not exactly known for turning down a night on the town for a good read. I, too, had arrived in Carmel-by-the-Sea long lapsed in the formal learning department. I was proud to say I had not had a proper golf lesson in two decades, a streak only slightly longer than my consecutive years of avoiding the dentist (five). My instructional drought, I realize, reaches all the way back to the winter my father took me for a once-in-a-lifetime trip to study at the feet of the legendary Jim Flick at Desert Mountain in Arizona.

The three-day crash course turned out to be more crash than course, the irascible but brilliant Flick subjecting his two wide-eyed Iowa charges to every draconian drill short of water boarding. He'd get so exercised at some gaff Dad and I would commit that strings of spittle would escape his mouth and land on our cheeks, juice that would have to wait to be tactfully removed back at the hotel room. In those three days of boot camp I had my fill of hitting pills from my knees, blindfolded, and backward, and I haven't darkened the door of a PGA professional since.

My evolving worldview of golf instructors makes the dentist analogy apt. A few grand and some anesthetic later, you leave root canal-ed, crowned, or crucified, and no better off, existentially speaking, than when you arrived. But the prospect of playing Pebble carrying a rusty game is intimidation sufficient to make any golfer hit the books and hit them hard. Who wants to be desperately searching for their A-game when they're facing the approach shot across the ravine at number eight?

So I drift inexorably toward Laird Small, a *Golf Digest* Top 50 Teachers in America pick and Peninsula native who's the closest thing at Pebble to a golfing guru. I meet Small on a foggy morning at the grill at Spyglass Hill, site of the Pebble Beach Golf Academy. Turns out Pebble's blessed with one of the top golf schools in the country, not to mention dozens of freelance, itinerant pros not unlike Shivas Irons—divining stars talking out of their asses and deciphering the weird calculus of golf swings. They're Einsteins, only with better hair. Small himself is handsome as a Kennedy.

"Because of the history of the place," Small begins once we've trekked uphill from the Spy grill, coffees in hand, to a drywall and faux-wood office, "and the variety and diversity of the golf courses, people want to make pilgrimage. It's become a religious experience for golfers . . . a spiritual experience. There's a kind of a love affair with this place."

"Can playing a golf course like Pebble be transformative? Absolutely." In the same breath, Small has reiterated my question and answered it. The author of *Play Golf the Pebble Beach Way* leans back in his desk chair. "People have always come here to play the game . . . They're drawn to this place."

To Small's way of thinking, Pebble, precisely because of its difficulty and drama, makes a big beautiful green screen on which players project their fears, an immensely revealing film for coach and player alike to break down. For an astute instructor it's like surgically opening up a man's brain pan to watch his most integral dreams and nightmares play out in the kind of saturated Technicolor only great horrors, romances, and golf courses can elicit. "Pebble throws you off balance in subtle ways," he explains. "That's what the magic is."

"One of my focuses has been, Can we have Pebble be a place where students learn how to play the game?" he continues. "A lot of players spend time on the driving range but that's not really learning how to play. The golf course has barriers—water hazards, bunkers, uphill lies. And it has boundaries, and freedoms . . . Most players get stuck on the barriers, and don't see the freedoms."

I take a minute to mull over my interviewee's words, the clock on the wall ticking so loudly in the nondescript office I feel like I'm on a game show. Meanwhile, the master-teacher masters on: "Manuel De La Torre once said that people approach golf differently than shopping. When you go shopping, you say, 'I want this, I want that.' When they go to the golf course they say, '"I don't want to hit it here, or there.' They've turned it around."

"So," I ask, getting my feet back under me, "you're telling me that a high handicapper could come here and, without even taking a lesson from Laird Small, Pebble itself could improve his game . . . by virtue of its beauty, its balance, its whatever?"

"I think so, if the player can . . . let go of their attachments to outcome. What happens to a lot of players out here, by accident, is their round will be shot early, and they just give up emotionally. They stop trying and their game comes around. If they'd do that early on, they'd play a lot better." He pauses. "The golf course can be transformative. Golf can be a window into how you are, and if you can be astute enough to stand in observation of what's happening, that can lead things to happen."

All good in theory, I tell him, falling back to the role of provocateur I'd played in college. But what about Laird Small? What has being a master-teacher at Pebble, a maestro, taught the prof?

"That golf is fun," Small muses. "That golf is a game . . . A lot of times we have projections of things . . ."

I cut him off mid-sentence when I hear the dreaded first-person plural. It's the end-around *we* politicians and teachers hide behind when they mean either *you* or *I*. I call him on it.

"Okay," Small says, shifting in his chair. "I'll change the tack. It's *me*. *I* find that when *I* play, *I* do better when *I* let go. *I* do better . . . Pebble has helped me be more present with my students, with my family, with my boss in realizing that when I go see him, I am in his environment, which is like being on the first hole at Pebble for the first time, and you're nervous, saying, 'Why am I here?' It's just a projection of my own making. Realizing that I can handle it . . . I can do anything in life I choose . . . It's freed me up . . . I'm more artistic. I'm more creative. I'm more present to the environment. My intention is more on the target. I'm way better . . . I'm paying attention to my intention, and I'm doing that in everything I do. All of a sudden I'm more dynamic in everything, not just golf."

I feel as if I'm listening to an infomercial testimonial or a born-again sermon, and yet my months in Pebble Beach have already partially borne out Small's truth. It's not that I'm any sexier, or more virile, or more talented—far from it—but I do feel different. Maybe Pebble's like getting a good drunk on, the kind that brings out the best traits in some people and the worst in others but, either way, amplifies.

The 2003 PGA Teacher of the Year is committed to helping all pilgrims achieve their goal, their spiritual high. He's helped PGA Tour pro Kirk Triplett, Oprah, Orel Hershiser, PGA Tour commissioner Tim Finchem, Coach Bill Walsh, and Dr. J., to name an illustrious few, find their intention, and now he wants to know about mine. I thought I'd come for a relatively painless bullshit session. Now I realize I'm in the hotseat—on the couch—pouring my golfing guts out.

"My goal," I stammer, "if I even articulate it to myself is . . ."—Socrates leans across the table expectantly—". . . is the pleasure of the swing, seeing the ball in flight. The thrill of the aesthetics of it."

I realize how goddamn precious that sounds, but it's true.

"Your goal is tied to the spirit of the game. Some people's goals are tied around beating the game. That's a whole different mind-set. You really have an awareness of the club then, how it's swinging."

"Oh, I don't know about that," I admit, suspecting I've probably got the club awareness of a Neanderthal.

"A big difference for you then becomes the awareness issue . . . your dance with the club."

Did fate decree all my inadequacies should be dredged up in a single unsolicited inquisition? So I can't break par. So I can't dance. So why don't you kill me?

"What's the object of the game?" Small persists. He's moving in for the kill, the bullfighter with his dagger. "To play, right?"

"Sure." I say.

"And any game you play you want to get a win, right?"

"Not necessarily."

I've pissed him off.

"Tell me what game you don't want to get a win in."

I've got a lump in my throat the size of a Titleist, the same lump I'd get back in college when a prof would call on me. "If you were taking your wife out on the dance floor," I manage, "you're not going out there to get a win. You're going out there for pleasure, for freedom, for romance."

I've landed a punch. But Small's already notched my score in his column. "So if I have that attitude, wouldn't that be a win? Maybe just the act of dancing would be a win. A win can be defined in many different ways. But the object of any given game is to win."

"By your own standards," I add.

"*You* determine what that win is."

"For me there's a difference between pragmatics and aesthetics," I say, floating a non sequiter.

The Great Oz furrows his brow.

"I'll give you an example," I say. "The shot I play best is a punch, always has been. But it's an ugly swing. It's faster, shorter, choppier. The ball doesn't have that great arc, so I don't play it as often as I should."

"You should play it all the time," my guru-du-jour observes.

"I hold back because I think, *God, I'm playing with these people, and I'd at least like them to think I have a nice swing . . .* "

My interrogator frowns. "So you're thinking about what other people think of you instead of hitting your ball and playing?"

I've touched a chord, clearly, and my Socrates is riffing on it. "A friend of mine, Fred Shoemaker, shared this story with me. It's the first tee at Pebble. A guy's really nervous. So he shares his anxiety with his group. He says, 'I'm really just going to try to go out there and make a full swing.' What's interesting is what people say. They say they're a little nervous, too, and they commiserate. The guy goes up to the first tee, hits it, and his partners say, 'Hey that was a really free swing. Way to go!' They compliment him on the freedom of his swing, not where the ball went."

And now the maestro returns in one well-orchestrated stroke to his original argument: "So for some people hitting a punch shot might be a win. We want to get more wins. The more wins, the more confident we feel." He chuckles. "A win for me dancing with my wife would be to not step on her feet."

The core conflict—whether it feels good versus how well it serves—is still there for me; Small's magic bullet hasn't yet penetrated. "I can take a 5-iron and swing very easy and knock it 160 yards," I continue. "That's safe. That's controlled. That's pragmatic. But lots of times I don't want to do that. I want to take my J. B. Holmes, John Daly grip-it-and-rip-it swing. That's the struggle. What's more pragmatically effective versus what's more liberating."

"People always go toward what's more liberating," my Bodhisattva says. "That's why they hit driver. That's why they practice their long game when they go to course . . . The more pragmatic approach would be to practice their chipping, their pitching, their putting, and limit their time on the driving range. But what do people always do? They go to the range."

"I think for you who love the game," my interviewee continues, locating me, golf's single-celled organism, in his microscope again, "I think you're going to want to have the freedom of hitting the shot that's called for, whether it calls for being free or hitting a punch shot. I think you feel it's less of a win when you have to protect it."

It's less of a win when you have to protect it. Small's psychoanalysis strikes the sweet spot, hits it in ways my few ex-girlfriends would amen.

"Bob Rotella was scheduled to be on one of the hijacked plans going from Boston to Washington DC on 9-11," Small says, trying a new tack with me, his special needs learner. "His plane was pulled back at the end of the runway. He ended up telling the story to the PGA Tour players the following week. He said, 'Guys, if you knew this was your last round of golf, how would you play it? If there's a tight tee shot — trouble left and right — would you take your driver out or would you lay-up and play safe?' They all said, 'We'd go for it.' Then he asked, 'Now you've got to hit a shot to a green where the pin is tucked back behind a bunker. Would you play to the fat side of the green or hit to the flagstick?' They said, 'We'd hit for the flagstick.' Then he said, 'If it didn't come out the way you wanted it to, would you beat yourself up for it?' Of course the answer was no."

"Let go," Small summarizes. "Go play and see what happens . . . The ball fits. Take the first hole at Pebble. If you could put one ball from one end of the fairway to the other, right next to one another, tons of golf balls, maybe hundreds or thousands, would fit end to end. So the ball fits. Let go, but don't beat yourself up if it doesn't come out."

We conclude our interview sharing stories of the people we know who've drifted away from the game even as golf has become more popular than ever, especially among juniors. It seems every thinking man's golfer I've encountered since coming to Carmel-by-the-Sea and Pebble Beach has backslid, held the Royal and Ancient game at arm's length like it's a Hepatitis risk. I'm thinking of someone like Michael Murphy, who I know Small knows. I admit that I myself have already begun to stray, and I'm resolved to get right with the best medicine I know: Pebble.

"I saw my dad quit playing," I confess. "I see myself, by and by, playing less all the time. Some of it's just logistical—I'm getting busier, my friends are getting busier. And some of it is just a force of age that you have to fight against."

Socrates grows reflective. "The question to ask is, What can bring your intention back to the game? What're your true reasons for playing? If it's for the love of the game, you're going to be out there no matter what. Could you be doing other things with your time? Sure. But this is pretty powerful stuff."

I fill Small in on the remote sand-green course I'd played in Nebraska en route to Pebble, how I'd felt more alive and engaged on that deserted cow track than I had recently on any groomed, irrigated course. He nods sympathetically. "It comes down to play. To rejuvenation. *Recreation*. Re-creating yourself via the game."

"It's not that I don't want to play," I assure him. "It's that you get out of the habit of pure play. You have to be more intentional about playing."

"Intention can be pretty soft, but it can be strong," Small says, springboarding. "The question is whether your intention is stronger than what's going to rise up to meet that intention? It's like bullfighters.

Their intention is strong and the bull knows it. Look at Tiger Woods. His intention is just so much stronger than everyone else's."

It's an interesting psychological case study, one I've witnessed in person covering professional golf—how Tiger can suck during the first round, almost as if he's trying to handicap himself, then turn on the afterburners for the weekend. Or how Mickelson will slap it around like he's playing hockey, then pull an amazing, one-in-a-million recovery out of his ass once a shot finally grabs his attention. Small knows the phenomenon well. "Carol Mann told me an interesting story once. She had this streak going years ago when she was the number one player in the world. She was just crushing everyone. She was winning the Open by like 10 shots . . . She got so darned bored by the fifteenth hole that she intentionally hit it out of bounds just to try to create some kind of excitement."

I raise my eyebrows at this, a pro not just thinking about self-sabotage, but actually pulling the trigger. "We try," Small says, wrapping our interview, "to get to the point where golf becomes boring."

The magical Monterey Peninsula has attracted not just Small, but a larger golferati—a motley crew of conspiracy theorists, doctors, quacks, gurus, bodhisattvas, each with a unique piece of esoteric truth. In this peculiarly oxygen-rich air, beside this preternaturally fathomless ocean, learned truths bubble up and vent, issue forth like a secret fraternal handshake or an apocryphal Bible slipped into your filthy pilgrim hands.

6

How to Lose Your Pebble Virginity
in Eighteen So-Not-Easy Holes

By November I have walked Pebble, I have covered Pebble, I have talked Pebble, and, yes, I have even dreamed Pebble. But, alas and alack, I have not played Pebble.

Booking face time with the buxom beauty of American golf is about as easy as grooving your forehand with Maria Sharipova. First, you can't typically book a tee time unless you've also booked one of the resort's high-end beds. The law of supply and demand and the theory of global warming both point to the same bummer conclusion: if you're not staying, you're almost certainly not playing until well-nigh Yuletide. Or, more accurately, if you're not hanging your hat here you won't unsleeve your Titleist until after you've stuffed your Thanksgiving bird.

However, today, after many moons, a change of season, an election, and a fall back to standard daylight time, I have engaged the Borg, which more precisely means I am submitting my credit card for ritual swiping by a professorial-looking gent at the Pebble Beach pro shop who sounds as if he might be affecting the slightest of British accents. I entertain second thoughts—none of them too serious—about the chunk of change I'm laying down for the privilege, finding handy-dandy rationalizations in the words of the pros I'd interviewed earlier in the fall on the subject of Pebble's pricelessness.

I'd asked Jim Thorpe, one of the Tour's first African American members, if he thought the half grand was worth it, and he'd said, "Absolutely. No question. It's worth it just to stand out there on the point." When I'd kicked the question around with Champions Tour pro Andy Bean, bitching that I could fly to Europe for the price of the greens fees, his southern drawl had dropped to a whisper and he'd said, "Hey, it's five hundred bucks. That's a lot of money to me, and they've got 'em from 6:15 to 2:30, man, God bless 'em." Still, Bean had said the course was in the best shape he'd ever seen it, and that I should definitely bite the bullet. I'd asked Robert Boerner, the former director of rooms at both The Lodge and at The Inn at Spanish Bay, and he'd offered me his summary judgment: "It's about bragging rights . . . If you're a baseball fan, how many times can you play a game at Yankee Stadium? If you're a football fan, who's going to let you on at Candlestick to play as a Forty-Niner? As a basketball fan, they won't even let me near the Staples Center. But, as a golfer, for five hundred bucks I can go out there and spend four or five hours playing a round of golf on everything I grew up watching . . . I always looked at the $500 as an investment in a memory you're going to carry around for the rest of your life."

Such dollars-and-nonsense enabling, in the case of Pebble, is weirdly inflationary. Reading back through the old literature, one finds Pebble has somehow always been "worth it," no matter the going rate. A case in point is Tod Leonard's 2010 playing of the she-beast as a U.S. Open preview for the *San Diego Union-Tribune*, despite the "wallet-thumping $495, or $27.50 per hole, or about $100 an hour" price tag. Predictably, Leonard came away, like the legions before him, deeming it totally worth it. One June swoon day thirty years earlier during the Tom Watson Open year of 1982, *Golf Digest*'s Peter Andrews did likewise, citing the then ball-dropping sum of $50 to $70 for greens fees and cart, and still he came away reporting, "And no one I spoke to thought it was anything but a bargain."

As I apply my John Hancock to the Mastercard receipt, I console myself that what former Fed chair Alan Greenspan might reasonably call my "irrational exuberance" has qualified me for entrance into a fraternity of equally irrational members expert in flimsy justification. Thus, I take special care in keeping out-of-sight, out-of-mind my carbon copy of today's damages, Jeeves behind the desk informing me I will be playing with one "Mrs. S."

You mean I've come all this way to play with . . . *a girl?*

I'm pissed, but it's a banner day and I'm determined to look on the bright side. What if Mrs. S. turns out to be a well-heeled Pebble Beach society gal who insists on a post-round highball and subsequently offers me her financial backing? What if Mrs. S. is keen to marry off her winsome daughter who just moved back home to 17-Mile Drive after divorcing her no-good Silicon Valley hubby. Or what if the old gal's better half, the venerable Mr. S., wishes to generously salary, feed, and water a house writer whose sole job it will be to produce a daily ode to his long-suffering wife while simultaneously escorting his grief-stricken daughter through nine holes at Pebble Beach in the morning, Kubler-Ross's Six Stages of Grief in the afternoon, and the seventy-seven positions of the *Kama Sutra* at night.

As I warm up to the idea on the range, I surreptitiously attempt to pick out Mrs. S. from among the likely suspects while simultaneously beating enough balls to guarantee the need for Tommy John surgery. The game of Guess Who continues until the Cinderella Rolex clock nears noon and I have to vamoose.

Mrs. S. turns out to be Mr. S.—given name Chris—a tidy, four-eyed, white-collar type from Cambridge, Massachusetts, with a shaved head and a fusty Germanic disposition. Our third, Rick, is a well-tanned, dark-haired, love-handled Ray Romano look-alike wearing wraparound sunglasses and black warm-up pants that swish whenever he takes a step. Both of my playing companions are laying their heads on Pebble Beach Co. beds. Chris is playing the Granddaddy for the first time while Rick's playing for the second day straight.

Our fourth is a caddie—actually Chris's caddie—the goateed Derrick, let's call him, his eyes masked behind dark sunglasses, his hair stuffed beneath a knit cap like some Aspen ski bum's. Chris has never played with a caddy, he tells me.

Standing on number one tee, I'm thinking of Laird Small's parable about the guy who admits to his mates that he's nervous, declaring his intention to make the freest swing possible. I consider a similar ploy to pacify my starting-block butterflies. Instead, goateed Derrick throws a tee up in the air to determine who'll take the first swipe, and Chris gets pegged. A second toss, pointing vaguely in Rick's direction, leaves me to bat clean-up.

The weather for our once-in-a-lifetime proves less than Chamber of Commerce. After several days of cloudless skies and temps in the mid to upper seventies, the day dawns blustery and cold. By our nooner start time the wind's whipping up whitecaps out at Carmel Point, the telltale sign to the locals to keep little Suzie from wading out in the riptide. The direction of today's zephyrs, I realize with growing dread, is the same as the impossible final round of the '72 U.S. Open.

Call me Flying Lady if you must, but with the advice of Pebble's head pro, Chuck Dunbar, rolling around in my head (he once told *Pebble Beach Magazine* that on the first hole "the clubhead is pulled off by an inch or so . . . because of shear nerves"), I opt to hit a 3-iron off the tee.

Once we're headed up the fairway, Rick pulls in alongside to tell me he's got two words for me: *Five hours.* "I'm telling you, it was awful," he bitches and moans, all Rodney Dangerfield in his recitation of yesterday's round. "I had a caddy and we played behind a foursome," he pauses for effect, "of *French women*. Dude, it was brutal."

We're standing in the right-hand rough, where my tee ball has gone to die. Behind a medium-sized cypress and 165 yards distant, I'm hearing the voice of Small again, reminding me how hole number one offers a case study in Pebble's subtleties. It pays to be conservative off the tee, he'd told me, but if you do, your mid-iron approach won't hold. Pebble's already presented me with exactly the kind of two-roads-diverged-in-a-yellow-wood dilemma designers Jack Neville and Douglas Grant drew into the plans. Blocked by the tree, I can either pitch out at a 45-degree angle back to the short grass or I can try to hit a slightly drawn, totally heroic 6-iron, skirt the tree, and hope to catch the tiniest sliver of the dance floor. I opt for the hero's path.

The ball comes out true, high and with just the wee draw I'd said grace for. It bounces once on the collar, kicking left onto the *poa annua* short grass for a green in reg. "Great shot!" Chris calls over from the fairway. I tell him to stick around. I've landed a sucker punch, sure, but I know it's only a matter of time before I get pummeled.

Goateed Derrick, our fearless looper, comes alive when we reach the green, where a good caddy earns his keep. Chris has a left-to-right uphiller of some 15 feet for bird; I've already missed my 20-foot bid.

"You'll want to shut the motor off right here," Derrick says, deploying a phrase he'll get excellent mileage out of the rest of the day. He points with the bottom of the flagstick to where his man should aim. "From there, gravity does the rest." Chris nearly holes the sucker. Both of us tap in for easy pars out of the box.

"Bird on the first hole at Pebble would have been too much to expect, right?" Chris grins, all slap-happy on our way down the Yellow Brick Road.

On number two awaits the typical Pebble Beach par-5 scene: three groups stacked up on a single hole—one on the green in the distance, one with hands on hips in the fairway, and one (ours) bullshitting on the tee to ward off the inevitable buzz-kill. It's hard to think about getting intimate with the hole when your ever-loving gaze takes in eight other dudes queued up in front of you. Today two crewmen wearing helmets that look like replicas of the '83 Pittsburgh Pirates have joined the sausage party, spading up a trench so deep one of them out in the fairway is in up to his ears.

Can anyone say logjam?

Chris and Rick grow impatient, pulling drivers and just about decapitating the Doozers laying pipe. Me, I give the hard-hats wide berth, pulling it safely, nay, gentlemanly, into the left rough. From the fairway, we manage nicely, Chris and Rick having a go in two while I'm forced to lay-up short of the cross bunker. Despite having to carve my approach out of some jackass's unrepaired divot short of the barranca, I manage to match Chris's par.

I'm feeling as chatty as the father of the bride as I stand on three tee, a sharp dogleg left tempting every fiber of my pilgrim's soul to cut. I walk the plank, me hearty, but the intended cap'n hook turns out to be a straight ball and plenty long enough to carry me twenty yards into the spinach. I opt for a 6-iron from a sidehill lie in the salad bar. Tugging it left off the clubface, I'm further undone by a freak carom off the steep slope left of the green, followed by a cart-path bounce that sends my Ti-tech into the landscapery at the entrance to the Beach Club.

My performance on the hole — the first real test of the first nine — degenerates from there, as I visit the first of what will be twelve bunkers in my round. There may not be as many or as famous traps on Pebble as on St. Andrews, but the links comes complete with nearly one hundred catboxes and, unlike those on The Old, they're all in play.

The fourth is, in fact, a beautiful, sandy mess, a hole that Chandler Egan redesigned in the late 1920s to include Pinehurst-like "imitation sand dunes" encircling the green like a moat. "I had never seen this type of bunkering done before, but we had faith in the idea and after a few experiments achieved a result that we hope will continue to be as good as it seemed at this writing," he wrote. Egan's faux dunes didn't last, but the present-day fourth is still awash in something resembling duneage, and it's still hell in a sand basket.

After our three-ball spends more collective time in the sand than

David Hasselhoff on *Baywatch*, we reach five bent but not broken, looking forward to the first par 3 of our desert campaign. This is Jack's hole, the only one on the course designed from the ground up by Nicklaus, as the legend goes, to restore Neville's and Grant's original intent that as many holes run along the sea as possible. With the breeze in our face, Jack's wee 3-par is a handful. After a worker drone waves us on from the green, all of us play safely away from Stillwater Cove, Chris and I, by some fluke, managing to hit our third green in reg. Once on the dance floor, I ask the uniformed worker, nametag Romero, what he's up to. Sporting a hard hat and seventies 'stache, he looks like he belongs in the Village People. He holds up for my inspection an implement six inches long.

"Jesus, it's an awl."

"Jes," he says. "I'm fixing ball marks." He sounds a bit like Cheech Marin.

"With that thing?" He smiles. "Is this what you do every day?"

"Noooo," he says, "not every day . . . maybe every other day."

"You could kill someone with that," I whistle, impressed.

"Yessss," he says, a bit too enthusiastically. "That's why I carry this . . . a *sheath*," he says, drawing the word out as if to imbue it with great meaning. "It's the only thing that keeps me from . . ." He searches for the right words.

"Stabbing yourself?"

After Romero shows us his awl, Chris and I manage routine pars on 5, which, while challenging from the gold tees, is anything but the terror confronted by the pros who play it from the 200-yard tips.

The par-5 sixth marks the beginning of the open holes on Pebble, the broad expanse of treeless, targetless golf on Arrowhead Point that comes closest to earning the Pebble Beach Golf Links its name. For the first time our trusty caddy, who's whispered his man Chris to a very respectable round thus far and many a lipped-out or made putt, leaves our side, moseying down the sixth fairway to the landing area. There he waits in the shade of the last Monterey pine on the cliff, hoping to sight our errant balls, thereby fattening his tip. I wonder what he's thinking of down there, lost in a rare private moment away from his patron. I figure he's probably trying to work out some Zen koan, something like, *If a cypress falls in the Del Monte Forest and the billionaire property owner fails to hear it, who pays for the wood chips?* Or, more apropos to the moment, *If a Top-Flite drowns in Stillwater Cove and nobody is there to see it, do you still have to count it?*

Chris cozies up to me with a confession once his caddy's out of earshot. "It's weird," he says. "There've been several putts I would have read completely differently. I've just kind of surrendered. It's sort of like riding in the backseat. Someone can ask you later how you got from point A to point B, and you don't have a clue."

I've been pretty much snowed under by my own struggle to survive the ocean holes in today's zephyr, but even I've been aware that all is not well in caddy-player relations. Like when your best buddy's marriage begins to implode, it's impossible to miss.

"Stick with it," I advise in a pathetically stereotypical bit of inane guy advice-cum marriage counseling. I recall what Tim Berg, a former PGA Tour pro who served as Pebble Beach's director of golf during the 1982 U.S. Open had told me about caddying around these links: "You always have to keep your player in focus, and at Pebble that's not easy because of all the scenery and the history . . . It's hard, but that's your job. You have to stay emotionally uninvolved . . . If they're upset, you can't get upset. You've got to stay calm and get them out of it." Writer Jim Moriarty once tackled the same delicate subject for *Pebble Beach Magazine*, where he wrote, "If the caddy-player relationship is truly like a marriage (and it is), the key to success is communication. And, as in marriage, if any dispute of substance arises, you may be certain that no matter what, you're wrong and your caddy is right."

The first five holes have suggested Chris to be a stand-up guy, at least if you subscribe to the notion that golf is a revealer of character. Alone in our three-ball, he's been unfailingly polite, has brought forth no profanities or guttural noises, and has thus far refused to avail himself of any dubious drops, mulligans, or improved lies. In fact, the closest he's come to guile was on four, where, after taking at least 3 shots to exit the oceanside trap, he'd turned to me and said, "Are you counting these?"

"I see nothing. I hear nothing," I'd said.

Unlike Rick but like Chris, I have been playing the ball as it lies, though I've succumbed to the angels of my lesser nature in taking a 2-shot penalty in lieu of a proper provisional ball on hole three. In six holes Rick, God bless, has committed all golf-course transgressions short of assault and battery, and not coincidentally, he's smiled twice as much as any of us. Chris, by contrast, is strictly by the book . . . literally. Not only is he a purchaser of, and a frequent referrer to, his glossy, full-color Pebble yardage book, he's hired a caddy because, as he put it, "he thought he should." He's also playing tour-quality equipment — top-of-the-line Nike irons and factory-fresh Titleists.

The sixth daunts and damns. Severely uphill, it plays well beyond its 484 gold-tee yardage even on a normal day. Today is a normal day, in hell. Out here on the point, the wind gusts in unfathomable knots, causing me to pull my tee-ball onto the steep sidehill of variously colored grass left of the fairway.

Upon arrival I realize to my horror that I've landed in a modestly sized, perfectly rogue patch of the bane of every golfer's existence. Worse than Shinnecock rough, worse than ryegrass pumped up with fertilizer, worse than fescue gone to pot, kikuyu is — horror of horrors — a weed. Kikuyu grass in the Golden State is, to read the biological control statements, a high-priority public enemy just behind semiautomatic weapons, agri-terrorism, and trans fats. A native of southern Africa, the bandit's got no business holding down the turf on these benighted shores. Worse yet, its broad, bedhead blades have swallowed any hope of par.

I am pissed, but then again I am amused, for I have discovered a blemish on the Mona Lisa . . . two, actually, because not more than five paces from my ball is a crusted over, totally inglorious piece of dog shit. I've golfed five holes at Pebble and, while I've found plenty of unreplaced divots in the fairways and ample sand splashed onto the greens from hapless bunker shots, I have not found anything like this . . . this noxious, agronomic party crasher.

As I set up to a sand wedge, that quiet voice of reason in the back of my head—you know the one—insists on my declaring an unplayable lie. I back off and look helplessly at my playing partners farther up the fairway, easily 75 yards beyond consultation in the howling wind. Rick has crushed his gorilla tee shot straight into Davy Jones's Locker, and he's staggering the cliff like a seaman's widow. Reunited, Chris and Derrick vigorously debate whether or not Chris should try for the upper shelf in two.

I take a Ballesteros-like lash at my hopelessly buried pearl, and watch, crestfallen, as it settles into an only slightly less marginal kikuyu nest a few feet in front of me. From here I've no choice but to wedge out onto the fairway beside Chris and Derrick, from whence I will hit my fourth shot. I've parred three of the first five holes, and now, thanks to a fluke dog shit–kikuyu lie, I'm about to suffer an "X."

Six turns out to be an unmitigated disaster for all but Chris, who marches off to seven tee with his yardage book tucked smartly in his khakis like he's leading the Waste Management Open. Rick and I hunker down out of the wind beneath the point's only cypress and swap personal data—he's from Tampa and plays every now and again in the Outback Pro-Am. We're knee-deep in bullshit when, out of the blue, a woman blindsides Rick and me. He piggybacks her briefly, laughing, and when she's done straddling him, introduces her as his girlfriend, Joanna.

I'm gobsmacked, for several reasons. First, I have no idea how Joanna got here. We're shipwrecked on the farthest reaches of Arrowhead Point—an impossible walk in this kind of breeze and miles away from The Lodge. Second, Joanna is beautiful and young, easily twenty years Rick's junior. Third, she's ecstatic—upbeat, effervescent, and clearly delighted to be underdressed, cartless, and clubless on a head of land buffeted by a three-club wind. I can do naught but conclude she has risen from the sea foam like Aphrodite to don those ass-defining, jet-black spandex hot pants. I posit further that the Gods of Golf are growing these self-sacrificial, links-loving, cheerleading she-males somewhere on golf's green earth, and that they've kept their whereabouts a secret from me.

Seven, of course, is Pebble's postage stamp, a hole that has graced more glossies than Heidi Klum. It's a legend within a legend, what the *Pine Cone* called in 1972 "the most photographed hole in all of Christendom." Most of the Bunyan-sized folk tales born here concern the kind of batten-down-the-hatches gales our humble threesome—now foursome—faces today. Tom Kite hit a 6-iron on this 97-yard pitch 'n putt en route to victory in the 1992 Open; Slammin' Sammy Snead once played a Texas wedge when the slope down to the water was little more than a miniature golf–like run of hardpan.

Bottom line: the hole's damn near impossible to club for a first-timer. Money, Chris goes first and sticks a short iron in the back bunker. Rick is next with a pull-hook left near eight tee. I dial in a short iron, figuring that if Kite hit a knockdown 6 into an even stronger breeze than this, then a wind-cheating 7 should be my number. I flush it, and the ball motates upstream. Squinting into the Mediterranean glimmer of Carmel Bay, we watch it airmail the green.

"I saw it bounce," Derrick offers.

Greenside, we find Chris's ball partially buried in the back trap and mine . . . we don't find mine. All five of us meet back of the moss to form a search party, including Joanna, who gleefully informs me that her favorite way of finding balls is to step on them. I'm pussy-footing down the cliff, despite Chris's admonitions, when Derrick strikes gold. He points to a precarious tuft on the bank below, a good dozen feet sub-putting surface.

I clamber down, tenderfooting the bank, dry-running, mock addressing, trying to determine if I can get a foothold. This must be how the dead feel in their pine boxes, I think, as I look up at the four morbidly curious faces—the bereaved—staring down at me with a mixture of concern and fascination. Beneath me, the Pacific chop swirls and sizzles. "I don't know what to do," I call up.

"You either take an unplayable," our caddy calls back, "or, if you think you can get it near the green, you take a swing."

Duh. I know what my options are. And I know, for the love of golf, Bobby Jones, and all that is holy, I'm going to play it. I also know I've no chance in hell of pulling it off. Rick and Derrick look down dubiously at the sadomasochistic exercise in progress.

"Do it," Chris says, sober as an accountant. "Go for it." If I could hug Germanic Chris from here, I would. My grateful internal monologue sounds like a tearful therapy session: *All I wanted was your permission.*

I choke down on a short iron, rehearse a few sawed off, baseball-style swings, and have a lash. The ball ducks left off the clubface, caroms off the cliff in front of me, and bounces back down onto the rocks, nestling into an itty-bitty tidal pool some ten feet below. If the ball, sitting there in that rock-walled, doggie dish puddle of salt water could make a sound it would be this: *Wa-Waah.*

Fortunately, our collectively flagging spirits coming off seven green are buoyed by the irrepressibly effervescent Joanna, who, when she thinks no one is looking, gives her man a playful swat on the ass and bounces along like a rhinestone sunglasses-clad version of a Laker Girl.

Eight can, quite literally, bring a player to tears. In the First Tee Open, in a wind not unlike this, it reduced one of California's most promising junior golfers, Brianna Mao, to a puddle of saline so deep only a hug and some paternal golf whispering from pro Mark O'Meara and caddie and former Pebble Beach director of golf Tim Berg could make right again. Berg, whose tenure at Pebble lasted through the '82 Open at Pebble, had told me months ago that he agreed with Jack Nicklaus that the second shot into the eighth green is the most spectacular in golf. The cinema-worthy carry over the chasm is in fact an occasion for man to meet his Maker, for golfer to meet his GolfSmith. In the

1965 flick *The Sandpiper*, Richard Burton actually plays an Episcopal priest promised a serious infusion of cash for his chapel if he can carry the inlet. Unworthy of Yahweh but on excellent terms with the god of water hazards, Rick and I feed our approach shots to vengeful Neptune so that Chris may live.

Nine and ten buffet us with mad surf and madder winds, a cacophony of white noise worming its way into our earholes. At 441 yards straight into a three-club wind, nine is an absolute terror, a hole Tom Watson told me he would have to play as a three-shot par 5 from the back tees in the Open, a hole Berg claims is every bit as hard, if not harder, than number eight. "Those two holes have the two most difficult approach shots I know in golf," Berg had warned me.

We have begun the stretch of holes where Johnny Miller claims the Open is won or lost, and yet nine, I discover, is longer and at the same time more forgiving of a sliced tee-ball than the viewer at home imagines, the fairway opening up right where the old double fairway from the Chandler Egan 1928 renovation used to be. "There are," Egan wrote in his 1929 course notes, "decidedly two routes of play which the player should bear in mind as he tackles this hole." I take the bonehead, cliff-walking route, and pay for it with another unspeakable number.

Hole ten, the less crooked, less downhill, not-so-long sister of nine, brings Carmel Beach into play in ways that can't be appreciated on the boob tube. It's true: when the tide is out, Carmel Beach beside and below the tenth is really just one big, gorgeous bunker-of-frolic, and the ocean quite literally plays as a lateral water hazard. On any given day you're never quite sure what you'll see from ten fairway. Today, a guy who looks like he could be either Allen Ginsberg or Moses with horned-rim glasses, picks his way through the rocks, presumably in search of golf balls. Yesterday, in an event that made front-page news in the *Carmel Pine Cone*, a 250-pound sea lion heaved itself ashore, no doubt looking for its Titleist. "After snoozing in the sun, the sea lion reluctantly began to move," the hard-hitting coverage read, "and then showed his annoyance at being shooed away, turning once or twice to aggressively strike at the boards with his head." The article continues, "such behavior indicated that the animal was healthy."

Considering how many times I've smacked my own head against the Pebble wall today, I must be the goddamn picture of health. As Joanna tends pin all awkward-erotic like a cross between Fanny Sunnesson and a Playboy bunny, I drain a 15-footer from the fringe for double bogey and bask in her applause, anticipating what I hope-fear will come next: a wedgie-inducing toe-touch. Resurgent with my unexpected stroke-saver, I'm experiencing the phenomenon I coined recently as the Hunter Mahan Effect, whereby, at the 2010 Waste Management Open, Dallas Cowboy cheerleader Kandi Harris—a "cowbelle," if you will . . . and you will—buoyed her man to victory. When Mahan discovered he had a "cracked head" on his driver, Harris ran back to the car on behalf of her man to retrieve a replacement head, eliciting the comical nbcsports.com Out of Bounds blog headline, "Hunter Mahan makes Cowboys cheerleader girlfriend fetch club; wins tournament."

However, I, unlike my man Mahan, am not in contention for my second Tour win. Instead, I'm having a Talking Heads moment as I bend over and insert tee on number eleven: this is not my beautiful girlfriend; this is not my beautiful links. Water flowing underground. Bubble burst, I dutifully note eleven and twelve point us back uphill and inland, representing the turn in the farthest loop of Pebble's figure-eight routing. In the U.S. Open year of 1982 Herbert Warren Wind once observed, "The only trouble with emphasizing the grandeur of the seaside holes at Pebble Beach is that this may promote the impression that the inland holes are ordinary. They are not."

Farthest from ordinary are the spectacular homes perched above and immediately below 17-Mile Drive—the party homes that come with priceless views of the bay. Joanna, who's promised to tell me all the hot goss she and Rick learned yesterday from Rick's caddy, points out the palatial white home behind the tenth green. "Someone made an offer on that house for sixty million," she says, wide-eyed, "and the owner *turned it down.*" Joanna also informs me that the elongated, low-slung house on Pescadero Point that overlooks Pebble's eighteenth hole once belonged to Larry Flynt, though maybe she's just yanking my chain with her saucy, double entendre talk of the Hustler's so-called "strip mall."

I have been trying not to talk much to Joanna. In part because I find her incredibly, almost fatally attractive, and mostly out of solidarity with Rick, who could no doubt write a book on the bitch and bitchin' aspects of having a very young, very hot, very uninhibited girlfriend. I'm sheepish as an Amishman around my playing partner's ingénue. I'm afraid, too, she'll either interpret my distance-keeping as rudeness, or, pushing the envelope still further, consider me a "special challenge" to draw out.

Nearly three-quarters of our way around now and tacking away from the deafening Pacific, our mixed foursome has settled into a complicated yet functional polygamy. Chris and Derrick isolate themselves from the group, taking long, languid strolls up the fairways while the rest of us hack on the margins. Rick and Joanna, meanwhile, spar with one another like teenage crushes, calling one another "Babe" ad nauseam.

"Nice shot, Babe."

"Are you getting cold, Babe?"

"Babe, do you want me to pull the cart ahead?"

And just as I've been cautious of appearing flirtatious with Joanna, in the marriage that is player and caddy, I've also been careful not to cop any of Chris's purchased intimacy. Sometimes I sense him starting to pout when Derrick gives it away too easily . . . gifting Rick with a read, say, or spotting for me on one of my many errant tee shots. I don't begrudge Chris his covetousness—he'll likely be laying down a Franklin for Derrick's experienced eyeballs, and Rick and I are the partial beneficiaries. After asking goateed Derrick whether the speed of the green on the first was typical of the rest (it was), I vowed not to caddy-mooch, despite frequent exhortations from Rick that both of us feel free to bum a read. On the putting surfaces, I'm doing quite well on my own, thanks very much, having holed out from outside fifteen feet a couple of times already, including the bomb from just off the green on number ten that set Joanna to clapping.

I'm finding Pebble's famously tricksy, steeply canted *poa annua* greens to be relatively easy reads. Because they're aggressively tilted rather than moguled or hogbacked, it's all right there in front of you, adding credence, clarity, and clearwater, to Derrick's mantra: "Let gravity do the work." The trick thus far on long putts has been to figure a net break, provided you're putting across two or three distinct planes, as often you will be.

On the upgrade, par-4 eleventh I hit yet another pull-hook and find it resting on the cart path. I take a drop at the nearest point of relief, a spot of wiry rough in the crotch where a secondary path splits off to run behind the Pebble Beach maintenance shop. It's a hairy lie, an old frizzed-out wig worn far too many times. Off the map, I don't have any idea what distance I've got left to the pin.

"Lemme get out my laser," Rick offers, watching my struggles with his arm around Joanna. He fiddles around in his cart, emerging at last with his range-finder. "One hundred and thirty-eight yards," he says.

I get an 8-iron cleanly on the ball, and it shoots straight up in the air, falls gently back down to terra firma, and stops on a dime a few paces past the hole.

"Nice shot!" Chris yells from the fairway. I give him a wave.

When I step up to the slippery putt, Derrick purrs, "Hit it with a pace of a three-footer. It's straight downhill to the ocean. Anything more than that and you'll end up down here." He points grimly farther down the green as if to say, "You don't want any part of that, partner." I do just as the golf-whisperer tells me, and damned if it doesn't drop. A legit bird!

On twelve, after I've unceremoniously bladed my sand shot over the green and been distracted by—I shit you not—the Snoopy Met Life blimp turning lazy circles overhead, the strict caddy-player union I've thus far honored begins to erode. Not counting on skulling my bunker shot, I'd already counted my chickens, so to speak, leaving my bag at the next tee and having only a wedge and a putter in hand. Ordinarily I'd play the shot with whatever stick I had in my mitts but something—the knowledge that a wedge would get the chip too much up in the air, perhaps—compels me to part with societal conventions to ask Chris if I can use one of his sticks. He's close by, stalking the back of the green to divine his line.

He looks at me as if I've asked to borrow his wife rather than his Nikes, but he relents, smiling the way you do when a stranger asks to use your bathroom. Somehow this act of horse-trading precipitates a rift in the golf-space-time continuum, which finds me missing a straight-ahead uphill 10-footer and facing a slick, three-and-a-half-foot come-backer to salvage my pride, and my 2-putt. Derrick—maybe to put me out of my misery—chooses that moment to offer an unsolicited read on a putt that, I'm convinced, has no break.

He points to a spot half a cup outside the hole and I do as directed, a regular golf whore. When I miss, putting the pill precisely where he'd pointed, I'm pissed. For the first time I begin to appreciate Chris's pseudo-marital quandary, which has thus far manifested itself in the schizoid behavior expected of the injudiciously wed. Several times today Chris has avowed to his Bagger Vance, "God, I don't know what I'd do without you," after Derrick unlocked the mystery of this or that ineffable green. At other times Chris has clearly been mystified by his own inability to resist Derrick's bulldozing.

On fourteen, the hole both Jeff Sluman and Tim Berg had described to me as the "toughest 3-shot par 5 in golf," Rick is short and left off the tee and Chris shy but down the middle. I've been trying desperately all day to get my right hand to turn over my left through impact, and for once I succeed, smoking it down the pike.

"Welcome back, partner," Rick says, holding out his fist for a post–home run, knuckle-on-knuckle bump. The gesture strikes me as goofy, and then, as the warmth of it settles in, redemptive. For the first time in a long time on a golf course I can feel a playing partner's unconditional love lifting me up, easing my pain. Rick's so full of Joanna's good lovin' he's reaching out to transfer it to me like E.T.

Something in Rick's fist bump proves magical, as I arrive to find I've outdriven Chris by a good 30 yards on the 560-yard behemoth, leaving me 275 to the pin. Fourteen is a place of odd drama, the hole where in the '92 Open Nick Faldo famously shimmied up and shook a live oak to try to dislodge his lost ball. "I remember when one time Arnie was hitting his second shot to fourteen," Berg had reminded me when I'd asked him about this particular hole earlier in the fall, "and he hit his second shot down the right side and a tree kicked the ball out of bounds. During the night lightning hit that tree and knocked it down. The stump is still there."

After seeing Rick's lay-up slice into the backyard of someone's villa, I'm not shit-for-brains enough to go for it—not quite—so I opt for a punch 5-iron up the gut to a reasonable lay-up distance. I chunk it, and, though it stays on the fairway, it leaves me 165 big ones, uphill, to a landing area about as wide as a kiddy pool guarded by a gaping maw of a bunker.

I pull a 6, aim at the right side of the green, and let fly. Wonder of wonders, the thing finishes exactly on line, catching the right side of the green and kicking left, just as designed, for what turns out to be a routine par.

Hardest 3-shot par 5 in the world my ass.

I'm feeling my oats on fifteen, where, despite a prodigious poke off the tee, I manage to bunker a toed 9-iron en route to an unforced-error bogey. Sixteen is practically a carbon copy . . . a wicked good drive through the uprights to set up a perfectly juicy 130-yard fly-in. Trouble is, with the flagstick back, I'm exactly in between clubs.

"You think it's playing its yardage?" I query Derrick, who's beside me in the fairway.

"And then some," the oracle says. "You don't want to go over. I'd say you've got room to hit your 140 club."

By now it's late in the day. The wind has calmed and the shadows have deepened, the fairway grass beneath our feet beginning to moisten. The air feels heavy, so I take my "140 club," as Derrick would call it, an 8-iron, and take a Zeus-like swipe, the ball tracking true but — *Wa-Wah* once more — long, into the back bunker.

I hem and haw over what is without a doubt the hardest sand shot of my life. Even Derrick looks over the brow of the face to tell me it's DOA. The ball's nestled up against the back of the bunker behind the green, on the downslope, semi-buried. It must be played to an uphill green with my old man's ancient 56-degree wedge to a green running away from me fast as a pickpocket.

"I literally don't know what to do," I say, scratching my head.

Which is when Joanna, bless her spandex, looks down at me from the green and chirps, chipper as can be, "Just close your eyes and hit it." I do, and to my amazement, the thing splashes out, runs into the green, and stops close enough to give me a lengthy roll at par. "Pretty incredible bogey from that position," Derrick says after I've lipped out, his eyebrows raised above the tops of his polarized shades.

The ocean breeze buffets us as we emerge from the shelter of sixteen green to the hole where Nicklaus rerouted his famous 1-iron mid-swing to hit the stick on the way to his 1972 Open victory. . . the hole where a polyester-panted Watson chipped in from the spinach and leapt into his celebrated, celebratory jog, the hole where yesterday, Rick tells me, he dropped a ball in the hay left of the hole with an eye toward recreating the miracle shot. I opt not to break it to him that the precise spot from whence Watson's shot sprung is no longer there, having been washed to sea in a storm that struck the winter after the '82 Open.

Despite its rep, nothing dramatic happens to our threesome on seventeen, beyond Rick well-nigh clocking Joanna with his tee shot ("Sorry, Babe!"), she who's pulled the cart ahead to get out of a blustery damp that's descended swiftly as the Hun. I toe-pull my tee-ball short left into the bunker, where I face the second most impossible sand shot of my earthly existence. I bail out through impact, trying to get too cute, and leave it in the cat box. Chris is predictably solid, barely missing a par putt, and Rick is too preoccupied with Joanna's gooseflesh to give a rat's ass.

At long last we've reached the big daddy, the home hole, the epic slice of ocean-hugging real estate oft dubbed the "best finishing hole in golf," the unforgettable par 5, which began its life as a forgettable, 325-yard par 4 back in 1919. We arrive to find, to our chagrin, that the grounds crew has re-sodded the back of the tee, stacking the blues on top of the golds at the wussy front.

Rick's got a mischievous glint in his eye, a glint I like. "You mind if we . . . you know?" He nods to the very back of the tee like a mafia don. "You mind if we hit one from way back?"

Derrick cracks a David Duval smile, which is to say, not much of a smile at all. "I'm not gonna stop you."

That's all Rick needs to hear. He grabs his Big Dog and swishes back to the tips in his warm-up pants, and — what the hell — I'm on his heels in my tennies. The roped off tee-under-renovation is slick with a sand topdressing, and we're goddamn going for it.

Sam Morse was originally too cheap to build the hard-on-the-ocean tee Neville and Grant had fancied, but the Duke of Del Monte came around to the idea in 1921 after British golf course architect W. Herbert Fowler agreed with Neville and Grant that the original "economy" tee, located inland, be scratched for something more befitting the epic oceanside sweep. Ever since, inspired hands have been tempted to amp up the drama here still further, with Egan once recommending, and, according to Neal Hotelling's book, *Pebble Beach Golf Links*, actually building a tee further out on the rocks, behind the present promontory. Evidence suggests that Egan's seaward tee, so far out it seems like something from one of those wacky golf calendars where greens get perched atop Pacific atolls and desert islands, was actually built in 1928 and almost immediately went the way of Atlantis.

Rick pegs his tee as crazy back-left as you can without falling into Carmel Bay, then digs in, a home run hitter stepping up to the plate.

Totally blowing off Laird Small's *Play Golf the Pebble Beach Way* antidote for getting quick off the anxiety-inducing eighteenth tee ("Make
some smooth practice swings starting from the three-quarter position"), Rick takes a Visigoth whack, his pull-snipe strafing the rocks
100 yards from our perch.

"Hold on a sec," he says, digging in his pockets for more ammo.
Ranger Rick reloads and, bam, his provisional-mullie again storms
the beachhead.

After watching Rick ship two consecutive pearls c.o.d. to Ariel and
Flounder, I'm thoroughly spooked when it's my turn to assume the
position, literally in Rick's footprints. I weigh the awesome carry over
the rocks, mulling over just how much leg of the dog to cut. There's
an old man with a walking stick poking around the beach boulders at
about 175 yards out, presumably looking for golf balls. There's a gull
or two floating in the air. There's Chris and his wife, Derrick, waiting
up ahead at the sanctioned tee markers, dubious as hell.

Of course I do what any bailer-outer would do when faced with
furlongs of salty sea to carry: I block the bejesus out of it, practically
coming out of my shoes to shove it high and right.

"It's all your fault," I jest with Rick. "I'd have never come back here
if you hadn't."

He grins and holds up his talk-to-the-hand hand.

Our good-natured back and forth comes to an abrupt halt when
Chris, By-the-Book Chris, breaks huddle with his better half, pulling
his 1-wood out of the bag like it's goddamned Excalibur. He smiles a sick
little smile and marches with Bagger back to the that little sandstone
outcropping folks at Pebble call a pro tee. I resist the urge to chant
"Chris Chris Chris" as if he were a tight-ass pre-med student doing a
Jaeger bomb at a frat party. What can I say . . . I'm proud of him.

Once "Chris Chris Chris" is safely off the tee, we hack our way up
eighteen in fine amateur fashion, spraying balls left, then right, then
left again, defacing the golf equivalent of the Wailing Wall. I lip out an
uphill thirty-footer on eighteen green and earn a coveted Rick knuckle

bump for another near miss. Rick, in a rush to get back to Joanna, who's retreated to The Lodge, is already in the hole, so to speak.

We're the last group of the day, just in under the daylight wire after a five-plus-hour tour. As we shake hands, the last rays of sun skip across the bay and eighteen green disappears in shadow. From the balcony a flash blanches the gloaming, and a woman in a red dress lowers a camera. Tourist? Femme fatale? Whoever she is, she waves the wave of a fiancée at the arrivals gate.

We walk behind The Lodge, where the sweet autumnal smell of woodsmoke lingers, past the laundry room, where a thousand bright white towels bathe under sanitary light, past the putting green, where the Rolex clock illumes in pleasing art-deco neon. Opposite the pro shop, Chris and Derrick settle up, a wad of bills exchanging hands. I overhear our looper tell Chris, "You know, you did . . . you did okay out there. You're pretty good players." It's a guarded compliment, but we'll take it.

I shake hands with Chris one more time, wishing him luck back in Cambridge. "Tell me you knew that woman on the balcony," I say. I'm thinking if he doesn't, maybe I should.

"My girlfriend," he explains, sheepishly.

Rick and Joanna ride off into the sunset with a backward wave, toward their waiting car and then on to the Inn at Spanish Bay. Chris and the lady in red will liaison for surf-and-turf. Me, I'm on my way to a hot date with an experienced car with Iowa plates, a jalopy that's spent the afternoon whispering sweet nothings into the tailpipes of Lexuses and Mercedes. Today both the driver and the driven have mingled above their caste.

"We're not trying for an overwhelming chemical attack." A few days after losing my Pebble Beach virginity, I find myself sitting across from Pebble Beach course superintendent Chris Dalhamer, trying to get his blood boiling about the kikuyu on the hillside left of six where my dream round went to die. He tells me his crew has removed fifteen acres of the junk. I don't mention the dogshit. "We're always fight-ing non-natives," he concedes, mentioning that Pebble had to methyl bromide the stuff into submission in the nineties.

The very fact that Dalhamer deploys words like "nonchemical meth-ods" and "surgical removal" in reference to his preferred means of dealing with the Hun of grasses is just one indicator that he's not your father's course superintendent, but rather the point man for a more environmentally friendly resort that has been named one of the Top 10 Eco-Friendly Courses by *Links* magazine and has been certified by Audubon International for its ecologically sound land-management. A company once celebrated for its excesses, Pebble now irrigates its turf with 100 percent recycled water, makes compost of an unimagin-ably noxious brew of grass clippings and a couple thousand pounds of AT&T Pro-Am food waste, and shuns styrofoam resort-wide.

At six-four and, I'm guessing, about 225 in steel-toed boots, Dal-hamer looks more like he should be playing linebacker at Ohio State than hugging trees. In fact, his family traces its working-class roots to Dayton, Ohio, though he grew up on the Monterey Peninsula mowing lawns. The kid who cut grass for spending cash went on to major in business and minor in plant science at Chico State. While hitting the books he got what he calls a once-in-a-lifetime opportunity to intern at Pebble. From there he accepted a gig as superintendent at the Pete Dye–designed Carmel Valley Ranch and at Robert Trent Jones's Spy-glass Hill, from whence he made the ultimate leap to Pebble in 2005.

He describes the Pebble Beach Company as "big on promoting within the company." While most superintendents have to beg their bosses for cash to make course improvements, Dalhamer calls the Pebble powers-that-be "very supportive when it comes to resources," adding, "they're always trying to be at the top."

Dalhamer's handicap hovers around an eight, which ain't half bad for a young guy with kids and a Monterey mortgage who shows up at 4:30 a.m. in the winter to preen America's most beloved links. He typically begins his day with a quick meeting with his regular staff of around twenty-seven, which includes a crew of seven or eight eager-beaver interns. Afterward, Dalhamer's army quickly disperses onto the course, where tee times begin at sunrise. "The big push here company-wise is not to interfere with the guest," he explains. "So we're trying to get as much done in those first four-and-a-half hours before the golfer. Then we come in and take our lunch break."

After vittles, Dalhamer and crew do the Pebble Beach Co. "huddle," which he describes as "a little two- or three-minute talk about what's doing on company—issues, something going on, maybe a quote of the day." That's when the boss asks his men if they've seen any issues with the course needing resolving. "Everybody's set of eyes is imperative," Dalhamer tells me. Post-dejeuner he and his crew of what he calls "wily veterans" keep a low profile, the course lousy with pilgrims who don't want their most precious memory to be a Cushman cart backfiring mid-swing.

Since Dalhamer knows the on-the-ground nuances of the fabled links better than anyone, I ask him to dish on his favorite holes. Naturally, he hedges, saying, "I've always liked number sixteen. It's a great tee shot . . . I've always liked that second shot going in, the framing downhill over a barranca bunker. It's a hole I think is overlooked. It's not long, but it can be one that can bite you . . . One of the most aesthetically pleasing holes to me is four. I just really like the bunkering and the backdrop of seven and the hillside of six as you come up. The second shot on eight is like no other shot . . . Seven is always great, but I think everyone would say that."

If individual golf holes are like children to a course superintendent, I also want to know which is the problem child. "In the winter months it's number eighteen," Dalhamer admits. "We're out there in 50 mph winds, and we're putting water on the greens because the waves are crashing over the seawall." Salt water is death on close-cropped *poa annua*. "Every hole has its own personality, its own challenges. The majority of the golf course is on the coastline, so we don't have many shade issues, but we have some here and there. Sixteen green can get a little shady. One fairway can get a little tough."

Dalhamer confirms for me what anyone who's ever played Pebble knows: the not-so-subtle macro differences between the lusher, wetter inland holes versus the seaward ones. "One, two, three, fifteen, sixteen . . . a little bit on twelve. Those four or five holes play a lot different, or maintain a lot different, than the others," Pebble's boss of the moss explains. "People don't realize how much wind takes out the uniformity of your irrigation system, what it does to the plant . . . the soils."

Being the caretaker of the most famous public course west of St. Andrews brings with it some unique challenges, including not just microclimatological vagaries but the human predation of events like August's famed Concours D' Elegance, an event aptly described as "tire meets turf" and "one of the most competitive events in the automotive world." That tagline translates to Dalhamer as twenty-five thousand people ogling three hundred head-turning autos parked on the fairway of his most difficult, colicky hole — eighteen — which already gets roughed up by the skyboxes and grandstands in February's AT&T National Pro-Am.

Combine nearly 365 days of sunup to sundown play — seventy thousand rounds in a good year, Dalhamer tells me — with a handful of big-time tournaments per annum and Carmel-by-the-Sea's fickle meteorology, and it's no wonder Pebble sometimes gets knocked for falling short of the hyper-green, not-a-blade-out-of-place Augusta standard. "The wind is the biggest thing," Dalhamer explains of the seasonal browning that happens on Abalone Corner. "That's more of a true links look. I kind of enjoy it when it gets like that. But there's a happy medium, obviously."

Since Dalhamer knows every corner of the track, and has seen it under every possible atmospheric and prismatic condition, I work my way up to asking him if he agrees with Michael Murphy that while Pebble Beach may not be haunted, it is most certainly enchanted. He's not willing to go there, quite, so he tells me about feats of nature he's seen on the links, among them hungry seagulls diving into carts on number nine to take off with golfers' hot dogs and hotel keys. "We've seen some mountain lions, which is kind of neat but sometimes a little scary. One year we did see some large squid that had washed up down by the eighteenth . . . We see dolphins going by and whales spouting out."

It's in comments like these that I begin to appreciate the delicate balance of Type A/Type B, Left-Brain/Right-Brain required of the Pebble course superintendent. "I try to get my assistants to drive around with little voice recorders and make notes," Dalhamer tells me. I drop the word *perfectionist* and my interviewee lowers his head in acknowledgment. "That's one of my biggest challenges. You're always driving, and maybe you drive too hard. Sometimes things can't be perfect . . . I'm pretty organized as an individual, and sometimes you can't organize 100 acres the same way you do your desk."

In a way, being chief groundskeeper of one of the most sacred sporting grounds in the world requires a certain amount of Zen-mind, or what my dad always termed "creative avoidance." If da Vinci's genius had been burdened every morning by the certain knowledge that he was painting the world's most enigmatic woman—that one missed brushstroke might be the difference between enduring enchantment and utter forgetability—he would, in golfer parlance, have psyched himself out. On the other hand, Dalhamer wouldn't be human if he failed to attend to the gift history has given him. "I feel very fortunate to be where I'm at," he avows. "Someone's entrusted me to take care of a golf course with the history of this place."

Dalhamer's habitual M.O. is to ask if he can do it a little bit better today than he did it yesterday, and he admits sometimes he puts too much pressure on himself and others. "That's the drive, personally. We try to instill that all the way down to our crewmembers. Just because you've been here fifteen to twenty years doesn't mean that's it," he says, adding, "we've got to be better." In Dalhamer's world, "every customer is a valued customer" and every tournament or round is "an opportunity to shine a little bit."

Given the potential for burnout, it's little wonder that superintendent jobs tend to have high turnover. As happy as Dalhamer is, and as artistically engaged, he admits that over the last ten years something has changed in the way he approaches the game. "I don't want to say golf isn't as enjoyable, but it's definitely changed from when I was playing when I was young and you were just going out and having a good time. It's hard a lot of times for me to play here because you're seeing things you want to change."

I'd opened our interview by confessing to Dalhamer that at the acne-ravaged age of fifteen I'd begun working in the maintenance shop of a university golf course in exchange for greens fees and minimum wage. I'd worked for bearded Ted the Super, nicknamed Bear, who called me, in his drowsy baritone, the "Young Turk" among his mostly college-aged, binge-prone, work-study students. Bear ran the ultimate loose ship, turning Jimmy loose on the fairway mower with a six-pack of Schlitz that would find him shit-faced and sleeping it off beneath the pines right of fourteen by noon, and leaving me to entertain myself by mowing large punctuation mark patterns in the rough (I favored the comma) or dizzying myself in the making of complex geometric patterns with the rake I pulled behind the Sand Pro.

The Young Turk in me, wrapping my interview with Dalhamer, can't resist glancing on my way out into the long, low-slung Pebble shop with its fleet of pristine Jacobsen and Toro mowers and Cushman carts. As I drive my piece-of-shit Japanese auto back down the lane to the password-protected maintenance gate from whence I came—idling momentarily while I wait to *drive my car* in front of the golfers teeing off on eleven, I decide that taking care of a masterpiece would be the most perfect kind of hell.

7

The Ballad of Bobby Clampett
and Casey Boyns

"Pat," Bobby Clampett tells the barman, winding up the way a good storyteller does when an old friend's playing straight man for him, "my last nine on the second round I hit every green and both par 5s in 2 and 1 shot over par. The final round I shot a 67 and putted horribly. I had a hole in one. I had a chip-in. My only bogey of the day was 3-putt. I'm calling it the greatest 67 in the world."

"See your mom. Give her some love. That should help you out of the yips," the barman advises, dispensing short-order wisdom on the CBS Sports golf commentator's recent putter-derailed attempt at qualifying for the Champions Tour, down in Scottsdale. The site of our current pity party, Carmel's Quail Golf Club, stars tonight as the Old Building and Loan, Bobby Clampett as Jimmy Stewart, and, as Mr. Potter, Shanghai Hotels, Ltd., the entity that a couple months back dumped the struggling Quail Lodge and cut a couple hundred jobs in a preholiday bloodletting.

Not long after arriving in Carmel I'd read about the closure of Quail Lodge, the venerable 1960s-era resort hotel built by Ed Habbard whose fairways once hosted the likes of Arnold Palmer and Gary Player. While the golf club would remain open, the closing of the resort proper struck me as an odd headline to encounter in a thriving mecca, so I'd read the front-page story in the *Carmel Pine Cone* with macabre interest.

Union leaders quoted in the write-up called the resort hotel's closure a "shattering loss." But the *Pine Cone* eulogy seemed less for the famed golf resort than for the loss in property and hotel taxes, the latter of which had added over half a million dollars annually to county coffers. Still, no one could put a number on the cultural loss of boarding up the lodge that had given so many area golf pros, including Laird Small, their start, or that had sheltered a young Jackie Clampett, recently divorced, when she arrived here with her talented ten-year-old son, Bobby, a boy who would go on to become arguably California's greatest-ever amateur.

Months before the sudden and unexpected shuttering of the resort, Clampett and his family had purchased a second home in Carmel Valley. Like his hero, pilot-golfer Arnold Palmer, Clampett had planned to fly the family into Monterey from their home in Raleigh, North Carolina, for an occasional dip into the magic he felt growing up there.

When I'd heard Clampett would be touching down for a weekend to teach at his Impact Zone Golf Academy, I jumped in the jalopy and beat it down Carmel Valley Road to meet him. I'd stopped first at the old lodge, just inside the gates of the defunct resort, where a solitary woman attendant lingered beneath a green-glass lamp, lonely as a dame in an Edward Hopper painting.

Shortly after I'd rolled to a stop, two spooked rent-a-cops had descended on my out-of-state wheels like I was parked, ticking, in the Baghdad Green Zone. After a minor confrontation followed by an explanation that I was here to meet Clampett, we'd laughed to let off the steam that had built up, our nervousness belying mutual heebie-jeebies, none of us knowing quite how to act, all three of us having come of age in a golf boom that appeared never-ending.

Before us in the Carmel gloaming stood a deserted hotel, a reminder that just as there was a "housing bubble" there may also be a "golfing bubble." If Quail Lodge—an iconic place where PGA Tour greats once stayed and played—can go down, then surely lesser courses could fall too. Its shuttering has sent shock waves through the Peninsula golfing community, exposing the first big bullet holes in a golfing economy that seemed to wear Kevlar.

You can literally feel the whole of Edgar's Restaurant—where I'm sipping my latté and talking shop with the Carmel Valley equivalent of Prince Andrew—pick up its game in Clampett's presence, behaving like patrons of a first-class resort again. If tonight's interviewee knows the shot-in-the-arm he's providing—and I have a feeling he does—he's too humble to let on.

Already the evening is steeped in paradox. I am sitting down to a candlelight coffee at a club that's operating on "reduced services," with a golfing legend that's struggling to make cuts on the Nationwide Tour and has lately been thwarted even in his attempts to qualify for the old man's circuit. Yet, out there, tomorrow, he's slated to run a full golf academy with a single female enrollee who's flying all the way out here from the East Coast and is about to get the treat of a lifetime. If this were Iowa, it'd be *Field of Dreams*.

Clampett, the wunderkind, has made a living out of the impossible. He earned his first Northern California Junior Championship within a year of starting the game, won his first National Junior Championship at fifteen, and added a couple of California State Ams for good measure. He studied French, of all esoteric subjects, at Brigham Young University, made it on the honor roll every semester, and, oh yes, he was also a three-time All-American. When he was eighteen, *Golf* and *Golf Digest*—and when do those quibbling siblings ever agree—both ranked him the top amateur in the country. That same year Clampett pulled another nifty little trick: finishing in the top twenty-four at the Masters at the tender age of eighteen, a distinction that remains his alone. And, of course, there's his impressive record at Pebble: a winner at the Spalding Invitation and a near-miss in a four-way playoff at the Crosby.

In a way, Clampett is the missing link—the most successful men's golfer of his or his parents' generation who grew up in Carmel. And if this really is the golfing capital of the United States, if not the world, and if that title amounts to more than cocktail-fueled propaganda, there ought to have been some damned good golfers bred from these sandy soils—some fortunate sons, to paraphrase CCR—though their numbers, much like those at St. Andrews, are conspicuously modest for a mecca. Beyond Clampett, and Al Espinoza—a long-ago Ryder Cupper who grew up in Monterey and finished runner-up to Leo Diegel and Bobby Jones—the ranks of truly world-class native golfers are conspicuously thin here, making Clampett's case all the more instructive.

Arguably, none of Clampett's impressive amateur achievements would have been possible had his family not come to Carmel and Carmel Valley because, while the twice-felt burden of being a golfer and a golfer from an American mecca can be inhibiting, it's also enabling. As he reaches middle age Clampett is just getting in touch with the special insight his singular upbringing has lent him. "It was a culture that was mystical in a lot of ways," he allows, "an amalgamation of so many different people."

In sum, Clampett's roots in Carmel-by-the-Sea are braided with the fated history of golf on the Peninsula. Clampett's grandfather, Fred, left San Francisco after the earthquake to settle on the corner of San Antonio and Seventh, from whence he would become one of the founding members of Carmel Point, the first pasture golf course in Carmel, that preceded Pebble by years and whose "clubhouse" would later stand on poet Robinson Jeffers's property. Bobby's birthdad, crippled in later life, lived on Torres Street and, because he couldn't go see his wunderkind play, set up a backyard practice area where he could watch his son's textbook swing take shape. Bobby's stepfather, meanwhile, made what might just be the most boneheaded or boldest choice in modern golf when he declined Arnold Palmer's invitation to become his manager. Not only did Bobby's stepdad decline, he actually introduced The King to eventual agent Mark McCormack. The rest, as they say, is history.

"Arnold would stay at Quail Lodge and hit balls right here," Clampett remembers, pointing out the window into the Carmel Valley twilight. "In '72 when the Open came here, Arnold, Gary Player, Bob Charles, David Graham, and Bruce Devlin stayed at Quail Lodge. Back in those days the pros had their own shag bag, and the caddies had catchers mitts and they'd shag the balls. Rabbit Dyer was out there with Gary Player. Creamy was out there with Arnold . . . And I'm out there with David Graham, with my little baseball glove. I've Rabbit Dyer teaching me." Clampett shakes his head at the uncanniness of it, of coming of age, of discovering the game, at exactly the right place and the right time. "As a kid growing up here it was phenomenal. I was really blessed."

Clampett's Carmel roots cross Tiger's, too. Wally Goodwin was the athletic director and golf coach at Robert Louis Stevenson School in Pebble Beach, where Bobby was the freshman class president and budding star. The same Wally Goodwin who would go on to coach Tiger at Stanford routinely played best-ball tourneys with the teenage phenom, helping young Bobby polish his game. Such synchronicities, such right-place-right-time mojo seem to define the golfing mecca. For a kind of quasi-religious experience to happen, greats must rub shoulders, must buzz with one another's energies, must jostle and vie like pilgrims in Medinah or Jerusalem or Gay Paree. The reason why the ten-year-old, ragamuffin son of Jackie Clampett could go on to become arguably the greatest boy amateur California golfer of all time has something to do with talent, something to do with "calling," and everything to do with meeting the right teachers in the right place—a community that lived and breathed golf 24-7.

"I golfed morning, noon, and night," Clampett recalls of growing up at Quail. "It was just a whole culture here. I'd go up into employee dining and help Jimmie make hamburgers. They gave me reign of the whole place. There was trust. I was a kid who had a strong desire to be a golfer . . . everybody saw that. They wanted to help and nurture it. Everybody took part."

It wasn't easy. No one at Quail Lodge was out to give Jackie Clampett's kid a free ride. He remembers a lesson in tough love received at the hands of his elders when he was eleven. "I whack my 7-iron into my bag and the shaft breaks. Lee [Martin] and Jack Fox, who was the assistant, are there in the shop watching me. I come in with this club broken in two. I'm a month away from competing in the Junior World for the first time . . . "

My interviewee stops to smile at the irony. "I come in, and I have this look of shame. Jack's in the shop . . . He's an ex-Army sergeant. It was his turn to teach little Bobby a lesson. He said, "Do you know what it takes to have to reshaft a club? We'll have to send it away, and it could be months before you get it back.""

Two and a half months later, young Bobby got his 7-iron back all right, a good month after the indignity of being the only kid at the Junior World forced to play without a full set. Couldn't someone have rushed the club repair? Couldn't some balding benefactor, some Daddy Warbucks, have taken pity on poor Bobby and gifted him with the missing blade? No one did. To paraphrase a certain former First Lady and secretary of state whose name is like Voldemort in these parts, it takes a village, and Jackie Clampett had happened upon a tightly knit one for her son. "It was a small town," Clampett remembers of the Carmel Valley of his youth. "Everyone knew one another. Members would come by and put me in a cart, and we'd go play some holes together."

There existed in Carmel at the time a critical mass of middle-class intellectuals who likewise shaped Clampett's renaissance interests. Jack Beardwood, an avid golfer who wrote the definitive history of the Los Angeles Country Club, used to call Bobby "Ninety-Nine Pounds of Dynamite" and seek him out as a playing partner. "In the afternoon

I'd go hunt golf balls and sit on the first tee, and I'd lay 'em all out and sell them to the members. I was learning business. They'd come and negotiate with me," Clampett recalls, adding that his "clients" were anything but pushovers. The competition was tough, too, as Bobby routinely golfed against older kids and locked horns with other California up-and-comers, including a feisty Corey Pavin, who he first encountered at age fifteen.

Like Laird Small and others kid golfers who grew up here, Clampett figured out early how to slip onto the famous links undetected. "First time I played Pebble, a couple of high school kids said, 'Hey, I know how to sneak on.' They kind of had the system down. Ray Parga would be in the shop and it would be like 4:00 in the afternoon. He knew the pairing sheet. It was $35 greens fees, so Pebble didn't get much play. It was private until 1969. It wasn't in that good of shape. But it was still Pebble Beach."

"Ray would say, 'Oh, go tee off on the fourth hole and don't tell anybody!' We'd go park at the Beach Club with my high school buddies, and we'd play. It was part of the culture of growing up here—loving golf and getting to play golf."

Clampett grew up playing the famed links at events as mundane as high school golf tourneys. "I remember one time I found my ball on the fourth hole in a high school match . . . Somebody must have taken it from the beach and put it there. I'd hit it off the cliff. The ball was on this far little peninsula darting way out into the beach. It was right on the top . . . on the dirt . . . right on a sheer cliff. So the ball's on this precipice that's not even there anymore. It's been long washed away into the ocean."

What did the Carmel Valley wonderboy do? "I actually knocked it up on the green from there and two-putted for par," he recalls, remembering how his opponents that day had assumed he'd cheated, and how the ensuing argument had grown so heated they nearly had to quit the match.

Clampett remembers twilight at Pebble best, remembers the

shimmering mix of colors, the ambient light off the ocean, and the surprising speed with which darkness descended on the Del Monte Forest. "We'd finish high school matches on the twelfth hole all the time. They'd get called for lack of light," he recollects. That atmosphere—the very "prismatic beauty" that Michael Murphy speaks of—burned its way into Clampett's psyche, making an indelible impression on his future golf course architecture. "It's not just the Pebble Beach golf course I love," Clampett hastens to add. "It's all of the Peninsula. But Pebble Beach is the granddaddy."

"Growing up here as a golfer and then having the opportunity to play the best courses in the best tournament conditions, you learn a lot. You see a lot. You feel a lot . . . Part of the art that's being lost in golf course architecture today is in the stripping of the land." Clampett believes in the Jack Neville–Douglas Grant school of design: pick the best, most aesthetically pleasing routing through a property's natural endowments, move as little dirt as possible, and ask the player to shape his shots. Here, too, Pebble offers an enduring template. "The old fifteen at Pebble . . . you used to have to draw it around there. Fourteen, you had to fade it around the cypress tree. Technology plays a part in this loss because people say the ball doesn't curve like it used to. Therefore we build courses that just go straight. I feel like we're losing the essence of the game. You look at the Tiger Woods and Phil Mickelsons . . . they're still great artists who shape their shots. They see the picture."

Like many golfing traditionalists on these cypress-studded shores, Clampett is of the dance-with-the-one-that-brung-ya, don't-fix-it-if-it-ain't-broke school. As a golf course architect he believes in *au naturel*, an aesthetic he likewise chalks up to being born under a Monterey star. "There's a history here of golf course building and design, incorporating some of the most beautiful land in the world . . . They couldn't move much dirt, and yet they created some of the world's best golf courses, including Cypress Point."

"I think it's the most beautiful place on earth," Clampett confesses.

"There's a uniqueness to the Monterey Peninsula that's not to be found anywhere else on the globe. Just the fact that you look out at the Monterey Bay, one of the deepest canyons in the Pacific Ocean. It's over 12,000 feet deep. And in it live creatures that only live there . . . creatures not found anywhere else in the world. It's the exploration and the wonder and the excitement . . . Carmel Mission was a very central mission in the whole Catholic Church. So much took place here. The gold miners. The Sierra Nevadas. Stillwater Cove was an old Chinese village in the 1600s."

At the height of Clampett's rhapsody, as if on cue, Pat the barman slips by with the check, gently informing Bobby that his next appointment is here. I have a feeling the next person on my interviewee's dance card is his wife or his mom, the "appointment" just a fabrication, a code between two friends who have one another's back. And why not? Part of the pleasure of a place like the Quail Lodge Golf Club, proudly wedded to a bygone era, is that dinner with the most important women in your life trumps coffee with a stranger. And if the home folks won't guard your time, shepherd your better energies, and shoo you on to your next dinner date, who will?

"There's about twenty or thirty different looks; people look the same." Casey Boyns, a California Golf Hall of Famer and veteran Pebble Beach caddy, has just handed me a cup of nuked-up chai tea in the kitchen of his home a lob wedge from 17-Mile Drive, and now he's handing me the hidden contents of his savant golfer-caddy brain. "There's twenty or thirty different body types and facial types. It's weird . . . This guys looks like that guy. You get the singles. And you get guys out there in gym shorts or blue jeans . . . Occasionally you'll get the guy who's with his buddies, and he's not happy with what he's paying or the course is not in tiptop shape. Or he goes to the snack shop and gets sticker shock at a thirteen-dollar cocktail."

The litany continues. "You get the dad's birthday, and the son wants to treat him, or vice versa. You get the husbands and wives. You get the foursome or eightsome of golf junkies, the club guys. They get out there on the blue tees and just get beat up . . . And then you've got guys out in plus-fours and perfect polyesters or the tacky khaki pants with blue tops. That's the standard golf guy."

Today's Hall of Fame interviewee has pegged me annoyingly well: khaki pants? Check. Dark cotton shirt bordering dangerously on blue? Double check.

Because a mecca says "Bring us your huddled foursomes, your golfing masses," it draws not just gods to its shores but their attendants as well. Make pilgrimage, and you'll find a plentiful supporting cast—the elephant trainers, the snake charmers, the so-called sideshows. Pebble's no different: you've got your real-estate wheelers and dealers sidling up to the action, getting rich by association with these sacred acres; your golf antiquarians and collectors sniffing around in the stacks, hoping they'll uncover a Bobby Jones first edition; your teachers with their tomes and gizmos; and, in a true golfing mecca, you've got your blessed yarn-spinning caddies, the "loopers," stacking up in the caddy barn waiting for some rich dude from the Bay Area to toss a few shekels their direction.

Pebble's tradition of quick-study tale-telling loopers reaches well beyond Boyns to Henry Puget, considered the Peninsula's first caddy. Puget, who got paid thirty-five cents an hour to shag balls for celebrated Pebble Beach pro Peter Hay, once told the *Monterey County Herald* that he'd collect a bounty of fifteen cents per gopher and fifty cents per mole delivered, in addition to occasional bag-toting. Peninsula-born caddies have rubbed shoulders with, and shouldered the bags of, golf's Who's Who, including Hope and Nicklaus and celebs like W. C. Fields and Jack Benny. In fact, Nicklaus's local caddy, Alvin "Didi" Gonzalez, was looping when S.F.B. Morse parted the waters and created Pebble Beach in 1919; he was still kickin' and carrying Fat Jack's sticks in the 1961 U.S. Amateur and just about every other time the Golden Bear set paws on the hallowed grounds. When the time came Ol' St. Nicklaus even paid Didi's funeral expenses.

In Pebble's yesteryear it was enough for a caddy to show up on time and sober. By comparison, today's caddie, like today's sig. fig., has to be superhuman — part personal assistant, part psychologist, part accountant, part soothsayer, part bouncer. It helps if your looper's a good stick in his own right — Mickelson's Jim "Bones" MacKay teed it up for his college squad — but still, it's hard to imagine Jim Furyk's Fluff Cowan wowing the faithful by spanking a 215-yard 2-iron.

The caddy is expected to know the game, sure, but not so well as to upstage his boss. All of which puts an accomplished player-caddy like Boyns in a sometimes awkward position. In 2009 he was elected to the California Golf Hall of Fame as one of "California's greatest amateur players." He's won the California State Amateur twice, in 1989 and 1993, and owns the hardware for just about every Northern California Golf Association (NCGA) tournament, regular and senior. And, lest he be pigeonholed as a Cali-only player, his credentials include qualifying for eight USGA events, including three U.S. Amateurs, two U.S. Mid-Amateurs, two Public Links, and one Team Championship, and a partridge in a pear tree.

Imagine you're Joe Blow from Omaha, Nebraska, and the bagel and coffee you swallowed whole back at the Inn at Spanish Bay aren't sitting too well. You're nervous as hell to play Pebble, and some wise guy in the pro shop says, "Your caddy is, like, God's gift to California Amateur Golf." It's enough to make you barf on your shoes before you've stunk up the course.

In a way, the caddie is the quintessential wingman and, as every guy knows, nothing pours more salt in the romantic wound than a wingman who wants a shot on goal. Golf is a romance, after all . . . the anticipation, the first encounter, the intermission in the middle, the turning toward home, the climax in the end. In all this you want a veteran at your side, a guy who's been through the wars and knows the lay of the land. Your caddy is to be your understudy, your pallbearer, and the executor of your estate. If you were the prez, he'd be your Joe Biden. If you were Miss America, he'd be your first runner-up . . . the one to assume the mantle in the event you could not carry out your duties.

"It's a whole new experience when you have someone to take you around," said former director of rooms at Pebble Lodge, Robert Boerner, who'd told me several months ago that if he were running the show at Pebble he'd have caddies be mandatory. "It makes you walk the course and experience it the way it should be done: old school. A caddie is someone who's analyzed my swing by hole three, and he's going to aim me in the right direction. I like that."

Boyns mostly stays mum about his skills, content to witness the tragi-comic phenomenon that is resort golfers tackling the most famous and, depending on the weather, the most difficult public golf course on the planet. Only sometimes, at Neville's Snack Shop where his State Amateur plaque hangs in plain view, does the beggar take off his shades and reveal that he is, in fact, Odysseus, slayer of Romans, smiter of 2-irons. "I'm kind of embarrassed by it," Boyns says of his golfing chops. "To a good golfer it's a good thing, but to a bad golfer it's a bad thing. I usually don't say anything to people, but if it comes out it comes out. Once in a while, if the mood's right and I know the guys will really like it, I'll let them know."

Boyns is that rarest of Peninsula breeds: a lifelong native. At five-foot-seven with sandy boyishly cut hair, he looks like a cross between a middle-aged Robert Redford and Champions Tour fan favorite Fred Funk. I would have guessed his age as early forties, tops, but it turns out he's been age-eligible for the Champions Tour for half a decade.

Swallowing some pipin' hot tea, the bard begins his song of Pebble days of yore. "Back then, in '55, Pebble hadn't had a U.S. Open . . . It was still pretty low-key. When I started golf, in maybe '65, I think it was $25 to play Pebble, and you could play all day. It wasn't a destination yet."

Boyns, who was born in the hospital in Carmel and was raised in Pebble Beach, describes a childhood full of vintage 1950s Peninsula scenes—the sons of career soldiers at the nearby Naval Postgraduate

School riding bikes together, playing cops and robbers, sneaking onto courses, and hunting lost golf balls. Among the squirts who caddied Pebble for their military dad was current Champions Tour pro Phil Blackmar who, when I'd spoken to him earlier in the summer, recalled how grateful he'd been for the deep memories looping Pebble had given him.

In Blackmar's and Boyns's day, duffers from all over the country arrived daily at the famous links to replenish the stock of lost pearls on the cliffs. "We'd head over to Pebble on a Saturday and look for balls," Boyns recalls. "We'd go through all the ocean holes and the thicket and the sagebrush and poison oak. We'd finally make it to Carmel Beach, and then we'd go swimming. Then we'd make our way back home. That took us all day."

When finally they'd hit the beach, at low tide, flush with hard-won pearls, they'd put two and two together like the shepherds of old. Boyns recalls, "We'd invent holes. We'd play on the beaches . . . You could actually roll the balls. We'd dig a little hole and golf."

When Carmel Beach, with its miles-long stretch of sugary sand, got too boring, Boyns and his crew grew bold, drifting like refugees back toward the base of the cliffs beneath the links. Boyns remembers, "On the eighth hole at Pebble . . . right now it's not a beach, it's rocky . . . but it used to be pure sand. We'd get down there and try to hit balls up on the green. It's 100 feet. You had to hit it solid and you had to hit it high." Overall, Boyns maintains that his childhood home was "boring," Carmel humdrum as any other far-flung place, maybe even more so, given its rep as a summer retreat for professors. "If we didn't golf, or surf, or play tennis," he tells me, "we'd ride our bikes around. Build forts. Play army."

"Golf was always there. We'd go play the par-three Peter Hay course at Pebble. I think it was two bucks to play all day. We'd play ten rounds a day. The market down there at Pebble used to be a 7-Eleven, so you could get yourself a Slurpee. Later on, when we got a little older, we started buying beer down there. The guy would sell us beer underage."

Boyns's adolescence coincided with the era of the Beach Boys, and Carmel Beach caught the occasional boss waves, though the bitchinest heavies weren't quite as gnarly or as dangerous as those up at Cowell Beach in Santa Cruz or farther upcoast at Half Moon Bay. Boyns wasn't much of a surfer, despite his blonde locks, but he hung with some hardcores. "Then Carmel was basically a retirement community. You had your dog-walkers. You had older people that loved it, and artists and poets. And then you had the surf crowd, the high school kids. You had a little bit of everything."

Carmel-by-the-Sea, as my interviewee describes it, was pretty much a haven for free spirits. Boyns's brother, a musician, used to carry a short keyboard piano around in the back of his vw Bus. "He and his buddies would carry that thing down on [Carmel] Beach," my interviewee recalls, "and stick it in the sand. And he'd be jamming, drinking, and surfing away. It was low-key . . . It was so much different."

After high school Boyns, along with many of his classmates, toyed around with the idea of going into the local sheet metal union but went the college route instead. When his collegiate playing days at Monterey Peninsula Community College and the University of Utah came to a close, he returned to his home turf, Pacific Grove, eventually marrying, starting a family, and winning a shitload of Northern California Golf Association Tournaments—enough to get him into the Hall of Fame before he had a single gray hair on his head. Meanwhile, he worked his way into being a sought-after professional caddy at Pebble, a looper for Charles Warren in the 2000 U.S. Open, a regular AT&T Pro-Am caddy for legendary San Francisco Giants owner Bob Lurie, and the most feared golfer in a Pebble caddy barn stacked with ringers.

Boyns's big-time caddy career started with a big-time disappointment. In the 1972 U.S. Open, contestants were forbidden from using their regular Tour caddies, so baggers drew names like Nicklaus, Palmer, and Trevino, unbelievably, from a hat. "I drew alternate," Boyns sighs. "A schoolteacher from Robert Louis Stevenson [High School] got Nicklaus. He didn't even know golf." That lucky son-of-a-bitch was Paul Latzke, a teacher at the neighborhood school located just up the hill from the Pebble Beach Lodge. Wally Goodwin, who would later become Bobby Clampett's high school coach and Tiger Woods's college skipper, had encouraged his fellow RLS colleagues to throw their names into the ring, and the thirty-year-old Latzke, who admitted to the press that he "didn't know much about the game," landed the biggest fish of all. Boyns, who knew golf inside and out, drew the ultimate bridesmaid role: ball-spotter.

"Ray Parga, the old pro, sent me out to number eight for three days," Boyns recalls. "The pros had to hit over me, basically. In three days there I only failed to find one guy's ball, Jimmy Powell. He was, like, in last place, and he hollered, 'Can you move over, son?'"

On the final day, Boyns worked the corner of the par-five fourteenth. And when Nicklaus blew by with Latzke on the bag, Boyns followed them in, watching Jack hit his famous 1-iron.

Since then his lot as a caddy has improved dramatically. For the 1982 Open at Pebble, Boyns made up for his bum draw ten years earlier by getting assigned Bill Burgen, a Monday qualifier from Atlanta. Boyns's rags to riches came full circle in 2010, the USGA calling him with a prospective loop instead of exiling him to the cliffs of Pebble. He explains, "There's a lot of really good caddies out here, but they're mostly resort caddies. When you have a Tour pro, it's a totally different ball game. Tour pros eat up a resort caddy. There's probably only 25 percent of the caddies that could handle a pro. That tourist thing doesn't work on a Tour guy . . . The numbers have to be exact."

For the Pebble resort golfer, the first-timer, it's all a martyr's heaven, seventy-two virgins, just as the prophet promised, one for every hole in four days of blissful golfing, a veritable Shangri-la. In love, the golfer willfully forgets the tens of thousands of golfers preceding him in first-hole flirtation. He forgets, too, that his Sancho Panza, his caddy, has witnessed countless Quixotes attempting to woo the fair links before, their overtures and seductions and mis-hit 5-irons all seeming to him pretty ho-hum. For the player, it's jukebox-stopping, wall-shaking love. For the caddy, it's a good walk spoiled.

Here's what Boyns sees from his end of the bag: "Most people are pretty nervous on the first hole. There's not much you say. 'How you doing? Where you from?'" Boyns explains the first-tee ritual. "You ask if they've played here before. They might say no. You say, 'Just relax. It's the same game, just a different place. Just hit the shots you know you can hit.' The second shot into number one is uphill and plays long. I always tell them it's such-and-such, but it plays more. If they pull it off, they realize you're on it. Second hole, the same thing happens. I'll tell them that the approach shot is longer. The third hole, you've got to lay up. So you're definitely giving them advice right off the bat."

Sometimes caddy and player connect from the get-go, and other times, well, you're calling in the shrink. "You're kind of like a psychologist," Boyns explains. "It's hard to pull the right trigger." As a looper you're getting the first-time Pebbler in a trauma situation—he's shot full of adrenaline, all his fears and dreams are close to the skin; he's in love, and he's insecure that he doesn't have what it takes. He's reduced to his child self, his core, his lizard brain. The id is out, and Boyns's job is to catch it.

"Some days you're just dialed in with a guy the whole way. It's perfect. Everything is going right. Other days, the guy just can't make a putt . . . He'll say it, and it makes you feel bad because he's paying you to give him advice." And the fun is only just getting started. On their prototypical round-in-progress, Boyns and his loop have holed out on number three and stand ready to tackle the cliff-hugging holes of the front nine, which, says Boyns, really aren't as bad as most people think.

"Basically the first seven are pretty easy. But any of them can derail you. The new five is an easy hole from the up tees . . . seven is just a chip shot."

"We always tell the guys on eight, 'This is where the course starts' or 'Tighten your belt' or 'Fasten your seatbelt.' Eight, nine, ten, eleven, and twelve are pretty much the core of the course. Eight, nine, and ten are the three really good par fours, but eleven is a sleeper. It's the fifth handicap hole. Number twelve is the seventeenth handicap hole. We always say it's the toughest seventeen there ever was. I tell my guys, 'You've played five or six holes easier than twelve already. The green doesn't hold.'"

Boyns offers me a caddy-cam perspective of the epic real estate that remains after his man walks off the twelfth green. "Thirteen is tough because it's uphill and everyone leaves it short. The green's severe. Fourteen is a legit number-one handicap par five. The drive's not so bad, but people hit their second shot right. There's some kind of at-traction. It's like number eight. Most people hit it right there on their second shot. I can say, 'Keep it left,' but then they hit it too far left. The third shot on fourteen is hard to put in a place where you can two-putt from. I tell people long right is the best place. The wind is always in your face there. There's more big numbers on fourteen than on any other hole."

"Fifteen and sixteen ease up. If the pin is up right on seventeen, it's not that hard a hole. Eighteen is really not a hard hole. It's just that it's the eighteenth at Pebble. Everyone freaks out at the ocean on the left and bunkers right. Most of them shy away from the ocean and hit it right o.b. Or they hit the house on the right . . . A lot of the guys will go for it and hit it in the ocean. They'll get a quick hook going."

What amazes Boyns is the kinds of recovery shots his loops will attempt to save their golfing hides. "These guys try shots I wouldn't try. It's like, 'You know what, just take your medicine. Just chip it out.'" I point out that a safety shot isn't as much fun, and my interviewee nods like he's heard that one before. "These guys are on vacation," he admits. "They're coming here from wherever, so they're going to try the shot no matter what. They're going to remember the glorious shot, not the eight or nine they made. That could be a little bit of a fault of mine as a caddy. I'm always Golf Management 101." Boyns parents a teenager, and his words sound to me eerily like my own dad's maxims: "Take your medicine. Don't try to be a hero."

When Pebble Beach caddies lose sleep, they lose it over what amounts to the bagger's Hippocratic Oath—at the very least, did they do no harm? Did they earn their keep? The caddy feels the pressure acutely in the make-or-break bottom line of his profession: better scores. "I hate the guys that on the first tee say, 'I gotta break 90,'" Boyns confesses, "and you know right off they don't have a chance. After the seventh or eighth hole they're at that 90."

"I once did this thing for Callaway Golf . . . It was 'How a Caddy Can Help a Hacker Break 100 [on Pebble].' The weather wasn't good. He [the hacker] was so far over par. The writer was down, and I was thinking, 'There goes your story, pal. Pay me anyway.' Those guys that have a target score. I just tell them, 'Right now your handicap is double.' Even a two- or three-handicapper will have a tough time breaking 80 out at Pebble on a nice day."

Because Pebble's greens fees are half a grand and the course gets continuous play, the looper's take home is about the best in the business. But the flipside of the gratuity math is this: the course they're touring their guy around, a guy who's come a long way and wants desperately to play well, is, even on a good day, one of the toughest in the world. That's where the Pebble Beach caddy's best-kept secret, the "butter up"—Boyns's phrase, not mine—usually comes in: the little, affirmative ego strokes the looper feeds his man beginning with the "easy" holes—fifteen, sixteen, and even seventeen if the pin is up and right.

These aren't insincere comments—a good caddy, like a good teacher, is able to spot and celebrate genuine improvement whenever it arrives—but there's a method to the butter up, all the same, and timing is of the essence. The savvy Pebble Beach caddy's usually wise enough to compliment not the golfer, an act which runs the risk of coming off as mere flattery, but the golfer's swing, which he observes has improved during the round. (And in almost every instance, once the jitters die down, it has.) Boyns's disclosure causes me to think back to my first round on the links, a round that concluded with an eleventh-hour affirmation from our looper, alias Derrick. I remember thinking then that it had arrived too late, as we were staggering off the eighteenth tee, ready to get drunk, commit hari-kari, or both. We'd had a great time but we were whipped, and the belated shoeshine came off sounding like your ex at her second wedding saying you weren't so bad after all.

Beyond the "butter up," Boyns's greatest caddy confidential is this: his mind and his eyes wander, and wander badly. "I've been doing it for so long, I lose concentration," he admits. "Sometimes I don't watch the golf balls . . . especially if you have two caddies in the same group, and they're out their talking about stuff. Then it's like," he whispers to mimic the moment, 'Where'd it go?'" As at St. Andrews, Pebble's Bagger Vances will, on holes with a long walk to the tee or a perilous hazard, simply walk down the fairway to do some ball-spotting.

On Pebble your looper is likely to part ways with you on six, on eight, on nine and ten, and on sixteen, where it's just as easy to sashay down the fairway as back to the tee. It's what the baggers call "standing the red line," meaning the unthinkably precipitous lateral water hazard that is the Pacific Ocean. Given the average five-plus-hour round at Pebble, a caddy can spend nearly an hour walking the red line, chewing the fat with the other baggers in his group. It's a recipe tailormade for distraction and brutally honest assessments the player probably wouldn't want to hear anyway. Thing is, the loopers minding the red line are competitive sons-of-bitches, and your wretched, over-the-top swing isn't lost on them. "We've got some good golfer-caddies," Boyns says of the annual Pebble Beach Caddies Tournament. "At one time we had three different State Am champs . . . Oregon, Utah, and California. We've got a couple pros . . . I've not won the caddy tournament a lot of times. The last one I played in I had a four-shot lead in the last round, and I shot 74, and he shot 68 at Cypress Point."

So, yeah, Pebble caddies can kick your ass, and they've also probably tried just about every impossible rescue shot you'll ham-hand. "I've been down off of eight a few times," Boyns admits. "I've been right up to the edge on eight fairway, with the ball kind of suspended in the sagebrush. You're trying to hit it, but you're trying not to put your weight forward because you'll go down the cliff." That quick hook that Boyns says his players fall victim to on eighteen . . . he's been there, done that, too. "You get on that sandstone," he says, smiling, "and the ball will just sit there. It's almost like a bunker shot. You can hit a 7-iron or a 5-iron. You can do a lot of stuff. Yeah, I've seen a lot. I wish I'd have written down a paragraph every day after I came home from caddying."

He has been making mental notes, though, both for himself and the dudes whose bags he totes. Not surprisingly, his favorite holes on Pebble are also the most challenging. "Eight's got to be the best hole out there, hitting over that chasm. It's a good, stout par four . . . Nine is probably the hardest hole out there. The second shot with the way the bunker is just doesn't set up right. Nine's the hardest par four for sure."

In the end, Boyns believes, even after walking the fabled Pebble fairways day in and day out—in fact so many times they are in danger of becoming yesterday's news—that the Monterey Peninsula is a golfing mecca, but not necessarily *the* golfing mecca. "Scotland is the roots of the game. To me the Scottish links golf is the real golf. But here you've got the notoriety. You got the U.S. Open golf course . . . Cypress Point is here . . . I think it's just the people who have walked these fairways. Bobby Jones, Lawson Little, Nicklaus, Tiger. All the greats. It's a great destination. It's easy to get to. It's a U.S. Open golf course accessible to the public."

As for caddying freelance at the U.S. Open when the camera's on and the dial on the pressure-cooker's entering the red zone, then how does the humble Pebble bagger respond on his home course? "You're the caddy, you're not the player," Boyns reminds me. "You're on a grand stage, but you don't even think about it. You don't look at the camera. They're not focused on you."

Easily enough said. But when you're a Hall of Fame golfer, scratch on one of the world's toughest tracks, and the Pebble Beach caddies tourney champ, you're a marked man, even if you are a prince disguised as a looper.

8

Where the Bodies Are Buried

Touching Up the Mona Lisa, the
Myth of the Fifth, and Other Chilling
Tales from Stillwater Cove

"I was conned into doing this," R. J. Harper, senior vice president of
golf at the Pebble Beach Company and general chairman for the 2010
U.S. Open, laughs as he wrangles the mike at the $25-a-plate Chamber
of Commerce U.S. Open preview breakfast held at Carmel's historic La
Playa Hotel. "I was told there'd be about twenty people in the room."
Harper's a short man, sandy blond, powerfully built, his hair blow-
dried and feathered to television anchor or college football coach. He's
an instantly likeable presence at the front of our lightly laissez-faire
brekkie, emanating down-to-earthedness and charm, both qualities
explaining his rags-to-riches rise from Pebble marshal to next-in-
command. Pep rally–style, he calls the 2010 U.S. Open "the greatest
championship in the game of golf, held at the greatest golf course in
the world in the greatest community in the world," before warming
up the crowd of a hundred or so well-fed Chamber mavericks and
mavens with a U.S. Open joke, circa 2000.

"I was the championship director at Pebble Beach," Harper recalls in the gather-ye-round tone of all good yarn-spinners. "We were surviving on Red Bull and adrenaline. The world was coming to our doorstep two weeks later. I received a call from the White House. The White House wanted to set up a call to the champion right after the last putt dropped on that Sunday in June . . . I was to have a cell phone with me right after it dropped. The sitting president at the time was Bill Clinton . . . who was to call and congratulate Tiger Woods."

Harper pauses for effect. "So Tiger kissed the trophy on the eighteenth green, and I took Tiger up to the media center. All of a sudden the President calls. We were just about to enter the media center. I asked Tiger, 'The president of the United States is calling and wants to talk to you.'"

"'Hold on a minute,' he said."

"I said, 'Tiger will be with you in just a moment,' all the while thinking, *Who on earth would put the leader of the free world on hold* . . . Finally, about a minute goes by, and he turns around and answers the phone. He talks for a couple of minutes and hangs up.

"I said, 'Tiger, you put the president on hold.'"

"And he says, 'I didn't vote for him, did you?'"

After the laughter dies down—the gentle tickle of a joke shared within rather than across party lines—Harper segues into his thesis, that the drama of past and future Opens only enhances the greatness of the historic links. The decision to bring the Open back to Pebble on what has in recent years been a ten-year rotation, Harper says, is "a recognition of the greatness of the golf course, the greatness of the surrounding facilities, and the warmth and the hospitality of the communities."

So much hyperbole, maybe, but the 2010 Open marks a record fifth time the links has hosted golf's national championship. "In the last five decades, no other golf course has been bestowed the honor of hosting the championship that many times," Harper crows. And the process, he reminds us, is competitive—something akin to applying to host the Olympics except that Pebble doesn't put in a bid per se; it has to wait to be invited to host the Big Dance by the USGA.

As the spoons, forks, and knives clink and the sound of masticating Republicans fills the banquet room, Harper says something so frank I almost gag on my sweet roll: "The reason we can charge the prices we charge with respect to rooms and golf etc. really is based on . . . Bing Crosby coming up north in the forties to host the old Crosby Clambake, and" — Harper garnishes his remarks with a pregnant pause — "the fact that the U.S. Open is played at Pebble Beach."

This is the first time I've heard anyone, let alone a senior vice president at Pebble, admit that it's not the ocean, nor the layout, nor the management that makes Pebble a mecca, but, essentially, it's the exposure, the publicity, the brand. Unlike St. Andrews, whose fame and prominence predate its position in the Open Championship rota, Pebble didn't really become the we-are-not-worthy track of today until Americans began ogling it on the boob tube.

While I'm savoring the refreshing candor of the Pebble veep's admission, he comes at us with another, this one of the dollars and sense variety: "From what I understand of the nature of the businesses in this room and beyond this room," he opines, "we're all in need of a big boost like this where the world is drawn to our community. There is nothing greater than the public relations, the media exposure you get from 120 countries witnessing a great championship . . . The shots you get of Pebble Beach . . . you cannot buy that kind of advertising. We tried to put a dollar amount to it . . . Many of you look at the Super Bowl, where they say it costs a half million dollars to buy a thirty-second spot. So you reduce that a little bit, and multiple that out by thirty-six hours of live coverage, and you're talking about half a billion dollars worth of exposure to our community." Harper has also crunched the numbers on the estimated direct economic impact on the community vis-à-vis food, drink, lodging, retail purchases, and the like. "We've conservatively estimated the impact for our community is about 135 million dollars for the week. That's a nice big boon to our community," he says.

Big boon? Where I come from, we call $130 mil a winning Powerball ticket.

The once-a-decade USGA windfall Harper hints at is sizeable enough to cause me to ask existential questions of the sliced pineapple on my plate: Why did Carmel hit the jackpot? Because God made Carmel and California? Because the Pacific Ocean laps at its shores and some Invisible Hand thought to carve some of the world's deepest oceanic canyons just offshore? Because Junipero Serra made a Catholic mission that led him to either "protect" or indenture the local Indians? Because S.F.B. Morse had a dream? Because of Bing? No wonder Peninsulans are known for their Zen mind-set, their no-worries New Ageisms. If you think too hard, Carmel's abundant blessings can make you feel abundantly resentful.

During the Q and A that follows, I stand among the property managers and innkeepers and small business owners to ask Harper if Pebble Beach hopes to profit from the Open. It's as if the jukebox has stopped. People turn around in their seats. *Do they hope to profit?* Does a harbor seal scratch its ass on Bird Rock?

The Chamber crowd may be amused, but Harper takes the question seriously. "The incremental business that we're going to generate as a company at our resort . . . is far greater than any kind of income," he explains. "Will Pebble Beach company profit? We sure hope so . . . Our hotels are going be full, our golf is going to be full beyond Pebble Beach, and the other golf courses will be full because everybody is going to want to golf. All the visitors aren't going to be here 24-7 watching golf. They'll be playing golf and enjoying what our community has to offer."

Drawing the Open crowd, Harper intimates, returning to my question after he's answered a couple of bottom-line, what's-my-cut queries from local merchants, requires some financial sacrifice on the part of the Pebble Beach Company. He fills in the ledger. "Sixty days out, we restrict to 80 percent of capacity. Thirty days out we restrict to 50 percent of capacity. That hurts us. But when you talk about profits," he says, looking back in my direction, "when you start cutting back, not only golf is cut in half but that means we don't have the ability to sell hotels rooms leveraging Pebble Beach to do it. So there's some impacts there. Two weeks out we cut to 30 percent . . . and there are some days when we don't have any players at all. We're trying to reduce the amount of divots, the amount of wear and tear on the golf course."

He's glancing at his watch now, as we've entered what today's emcee keeps describing as "the nine o'clock hour." But our featured speaker has time for one more question.

Any course changes for the Open? "Thanks for asking that question," Harper says, grinning, and grateful to be back on a talking point. "Arnold Palmer is one of our owners. Arnold Palmer is the king of golf. We've enjoyed working with Mr. Palmer on design changes, tree movement, bunker locations, etc . . . The USGA set the golf course up in 2000 literally to move the fairways off the coastline. So it took the greatest water hazard in the world, the Pacific Ocean, out of play in many regards. The gentleman's who's in charge of the course setup this year, Mike Davis, said let's go back to the way the golf course was intended to be played, which is hugging the coastline and making the water a true penalty. We didn't do anything materially different to the golf course, no rerouting of the holes, but we've had some really nice feedback from the Tour pros who have been out to play."

Augusta National's a stately Southern belle with an azalea pinned in her dark, piney locks. Pebble's a luscious, full-bodied beauty, as oceanic in her moods as the Pacific itself. Pinehurst's a dignified society lady with a classy cloche and an ageless figure. Many duffers would risk marital bliss for a swingin' one-night stand with any of them. In short, every golfer personifies his favorite tracks: he's damn near as likely to gender them, even eroticize them, as he is his own car.

Still, even the most jaw-dropping leading ladies eventually grow old. Ask Bette Davis or Gretta Garbo. Tastes change. Audiences evolve. Cary Grant transitions to Hugh Grant; Carrie Fisher to Jenna Fischer.

It's a difficult paradox, for golf especially, this evolution of tastes in an allegedly timeless game. If golf courses really are human in their lines and curves and moods—as Michael Murphy, Steve Cohen, Fred Shoemaker, and others of the Peninsula's golferati claim—they are, as a consequence, prone to aging, to ebb and flow, and, ultimately, to decline. And yet they're also reckoned to be art—or artifice—as changeless as a da Vinci or Dick Clark.

If you're running the Louvre, your job description is mercifully simple: if you keep the madding crowds from defacing the unblinking lady and stop the harsh light from damaging her famous visage, the people will come, year after year, to adore her in her agelessness. But golf is a shifting target, a cruel mistress that leaves Pebble with a Meryl Streep dilemma: how do you avoid getting upstaged by some younger sexpot, demoted from Oscar-worthy to Oil of Olay-ready?

Every year someone's building a new, upstart mecca rumored to be bigger, better, and bustier than its predecessors. News of the latest resort destination gets splashed across the centerfolds of *Golf Digest* and *Golf,* where the debutante puts on a little black dress and makes a provocative debut in the Top 50 Courses in America. One year's Bandon Dunes is another year's Whistling Straits. Old or upstart, all contestants in golf's beauty pageant must jockey for attention, often comparing and contrasting themselves in competition for the corporate dollar, as in *GolfWeek*'s description of Bandon's charms as "a cross between Pebble Beach and Carnoustie with a pinch of Pine Valley for good measure." In golf, as in celebrity—and the two are joined at the hip at Pebble Beach as in no other locale in the world—the game becomes differentiating your brand and, thereby, keeping yourself in the headlines, lest your star fade.

But running a classic golf course like Pebble isn't quite akin to running a museum, or a widget factory. It's more like operating a classic theme park, where you're pretty much compelled to introduce new thrills every few years to justify the price of admission; that rickety old rollercoaster that used to be all the rage in your parents' day now seems a little hokey. Sure, you want to preserve tradition, but you also want to acknowledge the escalation of challenge sportsmen are hardwired to want, and to need. Thus the U.S. Open, when it arrives in Carmel, along with the next-generation brawn and brain and ballistics the pros bring to lay siege, provides the perfect pretext for a few nips and tucks, for tricking the old lady out, for providing something beyond original allure.

According to a press release issued by Pebble Public Relations, titled *Acclaimed Pebble Beach Golf Links Updated for 2010 U.S. Open Championship,* "Pebble Beach Golf Links has continuously strengthened the course facets to enhance player appreciation, heighten the challenge, and exceed guest expectations." The language of the marketing blurb — using words like *enhanced, strengthened, heighten, exceed expectations* — reads unintentionally like a mail-order Viagra ad. The release next summarizes the monster renovations in toto: "Four greens and sixteen bunkers have been rebuilt, altered, or installed, eleven tees have benefited from enhancements, six holes have seen the addition or adjustment of trees (including cypresses), and the total length of the course has been extended to 7,040 yards."

A select inventory of the most significant Open changes as listed in the press release reads as follows:

Hole #1: Rebuilt #1 green to USGA specifications and enlarged by 700 sq. ft. (2007); Extended left greenside bunker to wrap the length of the green (2007); Split right greenside bunker into two bunkers (2007)

Hole #2: Added new championship tee (15 yards) (2003); Planted trees to create a narrow chute for the second shot just prior to the barranca bunker (2003); Extended last righthand side fairway bunker into landing area (2003); Rebuilt green to USGA specs (2003); Pinched front two bunkers into approach area to create a smaller opening from the fairway (2003); Installed a fairway bunker on lefthand side of fairway near landing area (2004)

Hole #3: Rebuilt green to USGA Specifications and enlarged by 200 sq. ft. (2006); Tent pad renovations—lowering and re-grading (2006); Installed cypress trees along left side of the dogleg (2006); Added new championship tee (15 yards) (2007); Installed three new fairway bunkers along right side of the fairway (2007)

Hole #4: Planned changes to fairway bunkers—flipped pot bunker toward coastline and added a bunker to the upper left of the landing area in the fairway (2009)

Hole #6: Added new fairway bunker 75 yards short of the green on the left side of the second shot landing area (2004); Removed large bunker at lower fairway landing area and installed five new bunkers along the left side (2008)

Hole #8: Added upper tee surface (2001)

Hole #9: Added new championship tee—50 yards total since 2000

Hole #10: Planned change to add a new championship tee—35 to 50 yards (2009)

Hole #11: Added a new championship tee—10 yards (2008)

Hole #13: Added new championship tee (2009)

Hole #14: Installed two bunkers along the left side of the fairway to pinch the landing area (2003); Installed one bunker along the right side of the fairway to pinch the landing area (2003); Rebuilt and lowered teeing area (2004); Planted one large cypress on right side of the fairway 100 yards out from the green, to pinch the landing area (2004)

Hole #15: Removed roadway (Live Oak Meadow Road) in front of teeing area (2003); Rebuilt green to USGA specifications (2004); Installed five new bunkers along the left side of the fairway, which includes a pot bunker placed 10 yards in the fairway, all near the landing area (2005); Planted cypress trees along righthand side of fairway (2006)

Hole #16: Rebuilt teeing grounds (2003); Planted three large cypress trees (two before the barranca bunker to create a chute toward the green and one near the bridge to create a true dogleg on the hole) (2005–2006)

Hole #18: Replaced big pine in front of the green with a large cypress tree (2002); Installed one fairway bunker along the right side of the landing area near trees in the fairway (2002); Replaced two trees in the fairway and adjusted them toward green to protect new landing area 20 yards (2003); Seawall fairway bunker expanded (2003)

At the year's first two major tournaments, the WalMart First Tee Open and the Callaway Invitational, I'd sampled pros old and young on the changes, and found the reviews mixed, even among a handpicked guest list sympathetic to the vision of the Pebble Beach Company. Some, like Jerry Pate, claimed the course was pretty much the same old lady. Tom Kite, asked if the course was still the same classic he'd won on in 1992, left me with this terse chestnut: "Same golf course. All they've done is add a few tees and lost a few tees." Callaway champ Mark Brooks, who contended with Kite for the title in '92, commented somewhat ambivalently, "It hasn't changed a lot. It's only been in the last ten years they started to do much to it in my opinion . . . The three new tees are pretty big . . . potentially . . . If they catch those holes into the wind, it'll just be flat-out ridiculous."

Phil Blackmar, the tallest pro ever to win on the PGA Tour and, long ago, a kid-caddy here when his Monterey-based military dad played Pebble Beach, fell in a similar camp to Brooks. He liked the new tees on nine and ten, assuming they would be used "with intelligence, depending on the weather," though he hastened to add, "I hope that one day the USGA understands that if someone shoots under par it won't ruin the game . . . If Tiger wins by fifteen shots, take your hat off and congratulate him."

PGA Tour pro J. J. Henry was sort of embarrassed that he hadn't thought of such far-reaching changes himself. "I saw where some of the tees are . . . obviously they build them based on what could happen," he told me, "But some of them, it's like, I wouldn't even think to put a tee back there."

Among those willing to speak at length, PGA Tour advisory board member and pro Steve Flesch sounded the most cautionary note: "The way the game's going . . . everything is longer, longer, longer," he told me as we chatted outside The Lodge. "I don't think that's the answer to how to make the courses better."

Given the pinched fairways on nine and ten, Flesch claimed tee placement is more important than ever on the so-called links. "Strategy is a bigger element than it used to be ten years ago when there was more room . . . I think it [Pebble] is harder now than it was ten years ago," he concluded, adding that 2010's mandated return to the old V-grooves will likewise increase the challenge. "Without spin on these little greens, short-siding yourself is death. If you can't spin the ball like we've been spoiled and used to, it's going to make a big difference."

Lanny Wadkins, the victor in the 1977 PGA Championship held at Pebble, sounded a similar note to Flesch's when I spoke with him at the First Tee Open, saying that the changes in Pebble, coupled with the migration from square groves back to the old V-grooves would create an exciting X factor. "I can't wait to get back to V-grooves. Tiger is the only one playing with them now. My generation's been adjusting for thirty years. It's time these kids do the same."

At our dinner date I asked Bobby Clampett, who'd played in both the 1982 and the 2000 U.S. Opens at Pebble, what he made of the changes. He, too, walked an ambivalent line: "It saddens me a bit," he confessed. "But, then again, some of it needed to be done."

"I always thought the fairway on six should be closer to the ocean. I think the bunkering is too severe over there personally. They've really made Pebble a lot harder . . . the new bunkers on fifteen down the left side where they lost trees. The character of the course has definitely changed on certain holes; fifteen is a great example of that. Pitch canker disease has hurt."

In unison, Clampett and I listed off several holes were the blight had taken its toll—enough to make the Lorax weep. Strategic trees have been lost throughout the back nine, including on the two classic par 5s, fourteen and eighteen, and the now considerably easier short par-4 fifteenth and sixteenth holes about which Champions Tour pro Andy Bean and I had chatted back in September. "There were two big trees to the left of sixteen. I mean you had to hit it through the uprights off fifteen tee," Bean had told me. "I mean, you had to hit it *through* the trees. One of my amateur partners could never get it past the road there because he could never hit it through the damn trees." Bean said he hoped the Pebble Beach Co. would restore more of the trees, as they had in transplanting a seventy-foot, 400,000-pound cypress to replace the eighty-foot pine that guarded the approach to eighteen prior to a lightning strike in 2001.

Clampett also expressed concern over the lengthening of the course, which, like the loss of so many Pebble's arboreal assets, threatened to irrevocably alter time-tested shot values. "Pebble Beach has the smallest greens of any course in the world of major championship caliber," Clampett pointed out. "It's never been length that's made it what it is. Pebble always had that perfect blend of the short hitter being just as capable of playing as the long hitter . . . I haven't gone out and seen it yet, but knowing that nine is over 500 yards and ten is so much longer and thirteen has a new tee that's now 252 yards to carry the cross bunker, I'm concerned that they haven't gone a little too far. In 2000 they played number two as a par 4; I was fine with that. I thought it was a great decision . . . So, we'll have to see. They take a lot of care with Pebble Beach. They really treat it with kid gloves."

While Pebble vies with St. Andrews for the title of world's most famous links, it departs dramatically from the St. Andrews Links Trust and the Royal and Ancient when it comes to course improvements. Consider Pebble's fifth hole, replaced in its entirety and with relish by Jack Nicklaus's design team in advance of the 2000 Open. Imagine, for comparison's sake, St. Andrews announcing that it intended to swap out the Road Hole for something a little more aesthetically pleasing, a little more in keeping with the original lay of the links before the railroad charged through.

From the beginning, the "old" fifth hole had been problematic. Pebble course architects Jack Neville and Douglas Grant wanted as many holes along the coastline as possible, an unbroken stretch from The Lodge to Carmel Beach. The only thing preventing S.F.B. Morse's own doctrine of Manifest Destiny was the piece of property owned by one W. T. Beatty—the by-now infamous Lot 3, Block 137, totaling scarcely over 5 acres. Beatty, an industrial baron from the Windy City, had plenty of ready cash and wasn't about to be moved by Morse's penny-ante offers. "I offered Mr. Beatty his choice of any property in the whole area in exchange for it," Morse later recalled, "but he couldn't be tempted with anything else. The result was, we designed the course around the property." That much—that the original course designs show a detour around the Beatty fiefdom—is verifiable in the April 1916 Map of Proposed Golf Links, which shows a sharp swerve around the old boy's property.

In its eighty-year run no one ever said much positive about the hole, as Jim Moriarty wryly notes in his article on the hole's 1999 from-scratch rebuild, "The New Fifth": "The most charitable description of the Pebble Beach's original fifth hole is that it was the shortest way for players to get from four to six. Uphill and blind, it was an anomaly. A plow horse among thoroughbreds." In his preview of the course for the *Monterey Herald*, sportswriter Lewis Leader echoed the long-standing dig at the fifth as "the world's only dogleg par 3." Robert Trent Jones wrote in 1982 that the hole was "out of place." That same year, commissioned by Pebble to offer a hole-by-hole description for that year's Open, U.S. Open Champ Hale Irwin turned to the classic cop-out, quoting a friend who had called it a "mean hole."

To give the poor, maligned fifth a fighting chance, I call up the most level-headed source on Pebble I know, former Pebble Beach director of golf Tim Berg, and ask him an open-ended question: Were there any holes he didn't like on the links he helped prep for the 1982 U.S. Open? By way of answer, he recounts a moment on the twelfth hole at Pebble when then-superintendent at the Old Course at St. Andrews,

Walter Wood, turned to Berg and asked, "Where are the bad holes out here?" Berg remembers assuring his incredulous overseas guest that there were no bad holes. But Berg pauses here in his recollection of events, his thoughts trailing off like ellipses. "The only hole I had negative feelings about was the original number five. I thought it was the only bad hole on the golf course . . . It just seemed to be a transition hole that didn't belong."

The old fifth had been tried and condemned, fair enough, but the scapegoating and shame thrust upon it speaks volumes about Pebble's drive for perfection and about the original engine—real estate—too little talked about amid recitations of the links' Cinderella story. Like a regal family history that manages to leave out the bastard children, the myth of the fifth is a peck more complicated than first blush allows. Like the bastard child, the old fifth stuck in the craw of Pebble backers for another, more fundamental reason: its awkward design had been necessitated for one reason and one reason only: the original, shotgun sale of the Beatty plot by seemingly infallible progenitor Samuel Morse himself.

In fact, the earliest designs of Pebble Beach were not for a course at all, but for residential lots with ocean views. From these blueprints a young Morse worked, when he took over as property manager for Pacific Improvement's Del Monte Properties in the waning months of 1915. He proceeded to sell off with unprecedented vigor as many Pebble Beach lots as he could, sales that included the $6,000 paid by Beatty for his plot. In short, the Beatty ground was long sold off, by Morse's own hand, by the time the so-called Duke of Del Monte commissioned Jack Neville and Douglas Grant to dream up a links with as many holes tiptoeing the edge of the Pacific as possible.

Neville and Grant had drawn up a still-born fifth, a ghost hole never to be built on account of one William Beatty—or so goes the myth that many golfers bought, if in fact they knew anything about the hole's origins at all, when Jack Nicklaus dedicated the new three-million-dollar fifth hole on November 18, 1998. They knew only that the old fifth, with its cramped quarters and confining trees, had been a pain in the ass, a blemish. What they didn't know was that the original obstacle that had thwarted an interrupted flow of seaside holes was not the scapegoat buyer, Beatty, but the hasty seller, Morse. In a seldom reported comment quoted by Moriarty, Morse says, "That [the Beatty property] was the first deed that I signed after becoming a member of the Pacific Improvement Company. I remember saying at the time, 'I will probably regret this.'"

In hiring Nicklaus to build a completely new fifth hole on the old Beatty property for the 2000 U.S. Open, Pebble literally broke new ground, defining a more aggressive doctrine that blew out of the water any don't-fix-it-if-it-ain't-broke fuddy-duddyism. The old unspoken rule had been that, in the modern era anyway, a Top 10 in the world course would only really go under the knife in the event of natural calamity—a flood, tornado, or hurricane—and even then the affected hole or holes were nearly always rebuilt to specs, as if restoring the Statue of David.

As it turns out, that mournful wail you swear you hear playing the fifth may not be early onset Turrets or your imagination playing flop shots—it may be the subterranean damns of the unquiet dead. Though few resort hacks realize it, the fifth is where the Pebble bodies are buried, both literally and figuratively. I had read that long ago, before Jack Neville and Douglas Grant wrapped a legendary golf course around the graceful bend of Stillwater Cove, the inlet had been home to everything from ancient Esselen Indians to native grizzly bears and barracuda to a Chinese fishing village that lasted into the twentieth century. So I called up Salinas anthropologist Dr. Gary Breschini, an expert on the prehistoric Indian tribes of Monterey and, along with his wife, Pebble Beach's archaeological consultant of choice, to ask what really is buried beneath Pebble's feted fairways.

Breschini told me that when the Pebble Beach Company began moving dirt on the fifth in preparation for Jack Nicklaus's new gem, they found abalone shell ornaments, mussel shell–carved fishhooks, and other treasures from a 1,000-year-old settlement of Indians that may have been "the finest basketmakers in the world." Breschini and his crew found something else, too . . . a "burial."

"Whenever you encounter human remains, you have to stop and inform the coroner," Breschini explained. "The coroner will investigate, and if it's likely Native American, then a representative is appointed by the Native American Heritage Commission in Sacramento, then that representative makes recommendations. In this case, as is nearly every case, the remains were reburied in that area with as little disturbance as possible."

Dead bodies and haunts aside, in breaking ground on a replacement par 3 in 2000, Pebble had altered sacred ground and, in the same fell swoop, had utterly rewritten the classic golf course restoration manual to read, in effect: Fix it if it ain't perfect. The doctrine was conjured once more in 2009 when Pebble announced that it would again be performing surgery on the greatest course in America. The release cited golf's chief barrister, its Matlock, Clarence Darrow, and William Rehnquist all rolled in one, the Honorable Arnold Palmer, who's quoted as follows:

> In the work we did to enhance the holes in preparation for the 2010 U.S. Open, the team reviewed countless historical photographs and documents to make sure we maintained the integrity, drama, and grit of the original design.
>
> Our goal has been to strengthen Pebble Beach for today's player, while maintaining its timeliness. I believe we have accomplished this goal with the many improvements made over these past few years.
>
> Pebble Beach is a national treasure to the game of golf. I am proud to have a hand in preparing it for the 2010 U.S. Open and for all golfers who come to Pebble Beach to enjoy its many challenges.

It's an exquisite case The King pleads in pitch-perfect rhetoric. Pebble is only trying to maintain the links' integrity, the statement suggests. Only an infidel would want to see its honor compromised by bombers like Álvaro Quirós, who make Boom-Boom Couples look like Bam-Bam. Arnie and his firm are only "preparing" the course for the USGA party, the same way you and I might prepare our bungalow for an open house — a little Endust here, a fresh coat of paint there, and voila! What could possibly be wrong with that?

Foolhardy or not, it takes Palmer-level guts to monkey with a masterpiece. And what's still more ballsy is that while Pebble Beach performed major surgery, it invited the press to witness, purposefully courting local and national media to spread the gospel. Exhibit A is an article entitled "Pebble Turns Back Clock for 2010 U.S. Open" by Kevin Merfield and published in what amounts to Pebble Beach's hometown paper, the *Monterey County Herald,* wherein Senior Vice President Harper is quoted as saying, "If you go way back through a series of decades and you look at photos from superintendent to superintendent, all these golf holes have evolved. . . . We wanted to keep the golf course and its original integrity in mind and make sure we didn't do anything that's odd or looks awkward or misplaced. Everything we did got a final stamp of approval from Arnold."

Again, the conjuration of The King's name as carte blanche, alibi, and defense; again, the notion that the wholesale changes wrought in Pebble are somehow a restoration rather than a renovation; again, the repeated leitmotif that Pebble is merely returning to some long-lost blueprint, some divine charter. A similar spin had been put on the building of a new fifth, circa which cherry-picked histories had been expediently cited and where the wisdom of the renovation had been tied from the get-go to Jack Nicklaus's unassailable credibility. As *Pebble Beach* magazine put it, "Who better to work on Pebble Beach than the greatest player who ever lived, Jack Nicklaus."

It's vexing argument to make: on the one hand Pebble is fine as she is; on the other, we had to, you know, do some things. As far back as Pebble's U.S. Open year in '72, Tour pro Frank Beard, the outspoken Gary McCord of his day, opined in his *Golf Digest* column that the public had been "brainwashed" into accepting the doctrine of Pebble superiority based solely on the track's selection as a U.S. Open site. Beard went on to write, "The USGA says it has selected a great course, but in the next breath says that there will have to be three new tees and half a dozen new bunkers. If it's a great course, you shouldn't have to do all that."

At Pebble, as at any national treasure with a rich and complicated history, fact is perennially difficult to distinguish from fiction, history from hype. Exhibit A is Pebble's very own calling card: "The Pebble Beach Golf Links," which I have on good authority is a big-time misnomer, that is, if you consider the opinion of a guy named Watson legit. In my first-ever interview with the five-time British Open champ at Pebble, I'd assigned the misappellation myself, and the legend of the links promptly disabused me of any false notions, saying, "A links course is on links land . . . sandy soil where the ball bounces. The ball doesn't bounce here. This is a seaside golf course. Spanish Bay is more of a links golf course." After recovering from the indignity of being found clueless before my golfing hero, I felt a little cheated—like learning Santa Claus doesn't exist—"Pebble Beach Seaside Golf Course" not quite having the same ring to it. Understandably, for the Pebble brass, "links" is close enough, its philosophy on the "links question" closely aligned with the sentiments expressed in Bob Weisgerber's article in *Pebble Beach*, "Lure of the Links: Pebble Beach Celebrates Golf's Beautiful Heritage." "Today there are many variations—true 'links' courses, 'links-like' courses, 'links-styled' courses, and 'links-land' layouts," he writes, crafting the golf equivalent of the Bill Clinton-ism, "it depends on what the meaning of *is* is."

The poet's license taken with the term "links" is emblematic of other, more timely Pebble Beach representations. Consider the case study offered by the conventional narrative pushed by Pebble Public Relations, namely that Arnold spied a need for changes and Arnold made those changes. Case closed. One can almost picture him next to a roaring fire, gumming a pipe, stroking his dog with one hand while he ruminates over the possibilities, an everyman genius at work. The real narrative, though, as told in Arnie's own *Kingdom Magazine*, is more prosaic. It begins with Harper approaching Arnold with some ideas for course changes, not the other way around. Harper's ideas then go to the Pebble Board, which includes Palmer, Eastwood, and L.A. Olympics icon Peter Ueberroth, among others. Afterward, the King goes back to his design team with sketches and asks for help on small matters like design, drainage, environmental compliance, specs, etc.

Later in the August 2009 *Kingdom* article, Thad Layton, the Arnold Palmer Design Corporation architect charged with putting Arnold's vision into practice, says, "We were googly-eyed about it. . . . Digging up some old photos from the early 1900s of the golf course, it looks a lot different than it does today. It got a bit rounded off over time. The old black-and-white photos are really flamboyant, really splashy. We tried to inject a little of that old character back into it, and bring it up to today's standards in terms of length."

The trouble with architects going gaga over old photos is, as anyone who knows their Pebble Beach history knows, Pebble's early looks were so protean, so totally schizo, it'd be impossible to reverse-engineer them even if it were advisable to do so. Fresh from the drawing board in 1919, Pebble topped out around 6,000 yards; the ninth was a short par 4; the tenth a dogleg par 5; the sixteenth barely topped 275 yards; and the eighteenth was a short par 4 approached from an inland tee.

Understandably eager to please the golfing public in the course's first ten years, many of Morse's early design moves were whimsically uncertain. Harold Simpson, the pro at Del Monte, mucked around with Neville's course at Morse's behest, as did Francis McComas, a landscape painter who wrote the line, "the greatest meeting of land and sea," not about Pebble, as is oft-believed, but about nearby Point Lobos. Donald Ross and Alister Mackenize were each consulted on how to improve the links before Chandler Egan was commissioned in 1928 to bring the course up to par for its first USGA major, the 1929 U.S. Amateur.

Eerily like Palmer's, Egan's design notes, entitled "What We Have

Done at Pebble Beach," begin with a careful disclaimer that read, "The committee went to work with a high admiration and real love and respect for the old course. We were desirous of making a minimum of changes." Egan goes on to annotate what were, in fact, incredibly far-reaching renovations: the rebuild and reshaping of greens on sixteen of eighteen holes, the introduction of new tees on more than half the holes, a completely new style of bunkering, and the addition of three hundred yards of length and one to two strokes of difficulty. While the course went through the expected growing pains and metamorphoses in its first ten years, it had finally, subsequent to the Egan reworking, found a sustainable route, shape, and length that was held substantially sacrosanct until the 1990s.

While the myth of Pebble's timelessness may itself be timeless, in comparison with other major championship venues Pebble has been defined not by making a sacred cow of tradition but, conversely, by its near-continuous shaping by restless hands, by trends, by impulsive motifs later abandoned, and, above all, by the constant perceived need for escalating rigor, style, and drama. For example, Egan's gimmicky, Pinehurst-styled faux sand dunes circa 1928 were subsequently abandoned as cooler architectural heads prevailed, and yet it's exactly that anomalous "splashy" era that Arnie and his team cite not just to legitimize but to lionize their own course changes. It's a bit of selective remembering, an example of wag-the-dog revisionist thinking. Still, in today's golfing cosmos, if the USGA, Pebble Beach, and Arnold Palmer say the Titleist is flat, then so it was written, and so shall it be.

In my earlier conversation with him, Pebble course superintendent Chris Dalhamer had affirmed the In Arnie We Trust creedo: "People don't realize how good he is and how down-to-earth he is, Dalhamer told me. "He's just like one of us . . . puts his shoes on the same way. I've had the opportunity to play golf with him, eat breakfast with him . . . He's obviously very knowledgeable. Any chance you get to tour around with him you take those nuggets of wisdom with him and listen. The best thing you can do is . . . absorb him."

While the controversy over Pebble's "strengthening" seems of the now, the truth is Pebble hasn't been itself for a couple of decades. In fact, golfers hell-bent on hacking out their seventy thousand rounds a year here have been playing a substantially reconstructed course without ever knowing it. Many of the famously tricksy greens that have caused Joe Q. Duffer to pull his hair out over the last few years are, in fact, laser-mapped facsimiles of the originals rebuilt and resurfaced with *poa annua* sod carefully cut from the green and kept in cold storage before the putting surface went under the knife. Since *poa annua* is considered a weed and weed farms and weed seed banks are mercifully hard to come by, only a re-laying of the original weed-grass would do. "Pebble had mainly native soil greens," Dalhamer told me. "So we've been plucking away one green a year to get those up to USGA specs and improve the drainage."

Bringing greens up to spec doesn't exactly sound invasive, but what it means in practice, Pebble's keeper of the greens explained to me, is that the existing putting surface is computer-mapped on one foot by one foot centers, laser gridded to the nth degree, and rebuilt from the ground up in the manner of your mom's seven-layer salad—four inches of gravel followed by twelve inches of sand followed by the preserved sheets of poa. It's reconstructive surgery, and while Dalhamer affirmed the process was 99 percent accurate, most of Pebble's fabled putting surfaces are reconstructions—copies of the originals. Thus when Joe Q. Duffer imagines he's reading the same frog hairs that have flummoxed Jones and Palmer, Nicklaus and Watson, Kite and Wadkins and Woods, what he's really putting is an artful reconstruction.

Put that poa in your pipe and smoke it.

The realization that the Pebble Beach I waited thirty-some years to play is, in truth, a rehab, initially throws me for a loop, the way it would if you'd kissed the wrong twin.

Attempting to console myself over the loss of innocence and to re-establish my In-Pebble-We-Trust dogma, I recall, with a smile, the climax of the Chamber of Commerce breakfast I'd earlier attended, where the emcee announced a raffle drawing for an arrangement from a Carmel-by-the-Sea floral shop called the Twiggery.

We were asked to put our business cards in a hat, and the response was lukewarm. Then Harper stood up and threw in the whole kielbasa, as they say in Green Bay Packer country: a round of golf at Pebble Beach.

The crowd of characteristically even-keeled business types literally gasped at the news, and the hat was passed again, this time with relish. There was even talk of Chicago-style ballot stuffing. And when the card of the lucky winner—a middle aged woman—was drawn, she shrieked as if she'd just won the Showcase Showdown.

A miracle is a miracle, I convince myself, a twin is a twin, a win is a win. Pebble, no matter how worked over, no matter how done-up, is always a thrill.

9

Links, Love, and Lust in
the Garden of Eastwood

A few months after arriving in Carmel-by-the-Sea it happened — love at first sight. I'd been at Pebble covering a tournament, when a steel gray Audi piloted by a distinguished silver-hair rolled by — so close I might have fingerprinted its glass — on the road that bisects sixteen and seventeen tee and eased into the Beach Club. From the passenger side emerged a vision: a raven-haired goddess with copper-toned arms swaddling virginally white beach towels. She was everything I'd hoped for: homey, sweet as honey, handsome as hell, and handy with a 9-iron, though not in the Elin Nordegren way.

And her name is Dina Eastwood.

Like everyone else on the Monterey Peninsula, I am unhealthily obsessed with Dina Eastwood. First, she is foxy. The mix of Euro, Japanese, African American, and Native American descent (her father was adopted, hence her maiden name Ruiz) makes her exotic in a

Tiger Woods sort of way. Second, she's unfailingly generous, giving her time to too many Peninsula charities to count. Third, she's both cosmetically humble and economically frugal, having once admitted to *Carmel Magazine* that she had a "real problem with [her] looks" until she was twenty. In interviews she has continued to deploy, long after marrying the stud said to be one of the richest in showbiz, such quaint, holdover aphorisms from her working-class days as, "I watch what I spend." Fourth, I have personally witnessed her, she of the perky smile and tumble-dry towels, wave to her man giddily in parting, head over heels like a schoolgirl. Fifth, and finally, she shares my father's birthday, meaning she's a brooding Cancer. I understand Cancers.

The way I figure it, Dirty Harry exists in an almost superhuman, pride-goeth-before-the-fall state of marital bliss. "Come on Dina, wake-up and smell the roses!" I want to say, playing the part of the concerned guy friend. "What does Clint have that the other guy—the golf writer—doesn't? There are more important things in life than ownership of Pebble Beach, a gazillion-dollar home at Tehama Golf Club in Carmel Valley, a closet full of Oscars, a clothing line—Tehama Clint—and a self-titled brand of beer, Pale Rider."

Here is the hard math the man in question did for *Carmel Magazine* when asked why Clint+Dina=love: "Oh, I don't know," mused Clint. "The big doe eyes. . . . It's one of those things you can't quite put your finger on because it's pheromones or something. So we got married, and we had a child. And we're still together."

Ode to pheromones aside, we are actually quite similar, Clint and I, I convince myself, meaning that if Dina's sweet on Dirty Harry, then by jiminy she'd be sweet on me. We've both been disappointed in love—the Big E. flight attendants and actresses ravished pre-Dina, me by a scant few unstable yet kind midwestern prospects; we both love Dina; and, most importantly, we both like her just the way her multiracial God made her. Clint finds her most beautiful, she reports, in "no makeup, wet hair, and just khakis and a T-shirt." Me, too. Harry gets "irritated," Dina says, when her busy schedule precludes a tee time together. Me, too!

I *feel* the Eastwoods, not just because I have glimpsed their sweet-lovin' up close, but also because I have read *Clint Eastwood: Billion Dollar Man* by one Douglas Thompson, wherein Dirty Harry does a little better fielding questions about his relationship with the missus: "Dina keeps me on my toes, let's put it that way. We both enjoy family a lot, we both enjoy pets, and we love to play golf. To me, as I said, life is like the back nine in golf. Sometimes you play better on the back nine. You may not be stronger, but hopefully you're wiser." When a man who's part-owner of one of the most difficult inward nines in the world says marriage can be more of a bitch than his back side, that's saying something.

The 1996 Dina Ruiz–Clint Eastwood storybook union pretty much sealed Carmel's claim to fame as a town so fairy-tale romantic it could make the Brothers Grimm turn Brothers Schmaltzy. She was a smart, pretty co-anchor of the evening news on KSBW-TV in Salinas, California, the one all the husbands and even some of the wives crushed on in their living rooms. He was an actor-director turned mayor-do-gooder, steely in his gaze, firm in his Republicanism. Three years after Ruiz interviewed Eastwood at KSBW — and, says Clint, they "flirted" — the tricksy cowpoke slipped her a ruby-and-diamond ring and hitched her to his wagon in Vegas while the band played "Does Eyes" and "Unforgettable."

A younger, brasher Dirty Harry was once quoted as saying, "They say all marriages are made in heaven, but so is thunder and lightning." And, according to *Clint Eastwood: Interviews*, Harry once said this while hitched to first wife Maggie, a swimsuit model he met on a blind date: "I've been married to the same chick for seventeen years. I'd better check my pulse. She's lived through all the changes in me, and she hasn't thrown me out, so I think I'll hang around."

Clint and Maggie actually honeymooned in Carmel-by-the-Sea in December 1953. Eastwood had fallen in love with the Peninsula well before then, having been stationed in Fort Ord during his soldier days, where, according to Mark Eliot's biography, *American Rebel*, he was known for his "sexual appetites," saving his trips off the military base to frolic "in the emerald expanse of Carmel," where the girls "always took to the surf wearing as little as possible to soak up the California sun." Though Maggie and her personal Pale Rider stayed legally married until 1978, the song had ended many years before. Eastwood had moved on to Academy Award–nominated Sondra Locke, an actress who played the role of a pioneer woman opposite Eastwood in *Outlaw Josey Wales* and would later perform parts in a number of Dirty Harry flicks, including a vengeful woman scorned in 1983's *Sudden Impact*—a fiction a little too close to real, as it would later turn out. Locke was Clint's flame from 1975 through the late 1980s, at which time she filed a palimony suit against him, slapping Tehama Clint with another suit in the mid nineties and writing a tell-all memoir whose title—*The Good, the Bad, and the Very Ugly*—pretty much captures the ax Locke ground.

Even while Eastwood was married to Maggie and was alleged to be messing around with Locke at his new house on San Antonio Street in Carmel, he was, according to Richard Schickel's biography, *Clint Eastwood*, "living a lie," still keeping a wider harem of hotties in a "regular rotation," including flight attendant Jacelyn Reeves, who he met at his bar-restaurant, the Hog's Breath Inn, and with whom, according to Eliot, he fathered a kid, Scott, in 1986. By the time Dina announced her pregnancy to her betrothed whilst riding shotgun in L.A. a few weeks after their honeymoon in Hawaii in 1996, Eastwood had fathered, according to biographer Eliot, his "seventh child by five different women."

And what does Dina—sweet, beautiful, intelligent, charming, saintly Dina—think of all this alleged tomfoolery? "He's a philanthropist, not a philanderer" and "the fact that I am only the second woman he has married really touches me," *Clint Eastwood: Billion Dollar Man* quoteth the fair wyfe as saying. "He's one of those people who takes bugs outside," she once told *Carmel Magazine*. "I call him Saint Francis of Assisi."

Love is, as Shakespeare said, "painted blind," and nowhere more so than in Carmel-by-the-Sea, which, much like its most famous citizen, Eastwood, patently refuses to grow stale. Renovation . . . that's the essence of romance, I'm learning, on the golf course and off. "Love is much stronger when one meets in the second half of one's life. It hits you when you least expect it. If I have a message, it is simply to say, 'Don't let anything pass,'" Schickel's *Clint Eastwood Biography* quotes the real-life Dirty Harry as saying.

What clearer man-mandate could I possibly receive in my time on the fair shores of Carmel-by-the-Sea? I'm living in, by almost all accounts, one of the most dreamy places on earth, surrounded by sand and surf, artists and alimony, dames and dachshunds. Statistically I am halfway through my wretchedly single existence. I must go forth and multiply. I must shoot for the pins. But first I must make a tee-time.

When I saddled up my mount for the sweaty, overland trek to Sex-by-the-Sea, I did consider the hopeful if not remote possibility that if "I followed my bliss," to borrow a Joseph Campbellism, I might just meet some foxy, thirty-year-old, overworked, Pebble Beach PR ingénue who, because of her devotion to the company and the long hours it entails, had miraculously not yet found her Monterey Man. I'd hoped that one day I'd be chatting with some bigwig at Pebble, only to have the salt-and-pepper exec step aside and say, "Where are my manners? I should introduce you to my assistant, [insert classically feminine name here]. Classically Feminine Name would smile demurely, and the next thing you know I'd be in bed, helping her edit press bulletins for immediate release. Another of my abiding daydreams found me marrying the comely offspring of an accidental Peninsula millionaire. I imagined Dad as an absent-minded prof. at Berkeley who'd stumbled on some gee-whiz patent but hadn't lost his humility, his daughter a dish with a goodly amount of time on her hands and a classic reserve-C finish.

Since Pebble's immaculate conception in the Year of Our Morse, 1919, such romantic notions have been kindled and fanned by a series of Pebble promotional glossies beginning with Morse's own brainchild, *Game and Gossip*, where positively titillating adverts like this one ran: "No time is spent in staring and pointing at the beauty of the place. You sense it when your ordinary attention is fixed on a golf tee or stirrup strap, and that makes it real . . . the life of the place pounds into your veins—the rush of sunlight and sea air, the sighing of the great cypresses, the tough, writhing silence of the live oaks."

Almost from infancy, Pebble served as a staging ground for courtships and intrigues between well-bred and well-heeled ladies and gents. The September 5, 1926, "These Charming People" column includes such high society drivel as "Miss Helen Crocker was hostess at her Pebble Beach home to Lady Ravensdale, who was enchanted with the Peninsula . . . . Lady Ravensdale, who was Miss Curzon, inherited the Barony of Ravensdale on the death of her father."

Like any other hot-blooded American male, I am only trying to meet my own Lady Ravensdale, merely trying to help her with the thankless upkeep of the barony whilst keeping company with my high-bred chums, chums like Viscount Waldorf Astor and his son, the Hon. William Astor, who, the same *Game and Gossip* column intimates, "stopped at Pebble Beach Lodge for a night on their way to the Bohemian Club on the Russian River. . . . 'Jolliest links we've seen,' commented the son with a wistful glance, since engagements prevented their trying their clubs." In fact, Carmel-by-the-Sea and Pebble Beach were so 24-7 sexy way back when even the charm columnist burned the candle at both ends. "There has been no lack of lords and ladies, authors and actresses, to say nothing of the usual sports men and women and the flapper set," our overstimulated reporteress opined.

If my baroness fantasy failed to phosphoresce, I hoped to get my World War II doughboy wish, the one in which I'm paired for a hot and windy day with one of the short-skirted dishes shown in the real-life Pebble wartime photos. Pictured in sepia are leggy, pin-up-worthy nymphs studying to replace shipped-out man-caddies. They wear flowers in their hair and blouses provocatively unbuttoned. They stretch out on the turf, idly listening, while some fat-ass golf pro using the grip-end of a club points to a chalkboard, on which is etched these stern commandments:

Del Monte Caddie School
No Smoking
No Cussing
No Gum Chewing
And Please Girls No Talking!

For ages Carmel has oozed eros. "Carmel-by-the-Sea is a phantasy," wrote Marcella Burke in 1928, in her column, "Our Reporter at Carmel." "It is at the same time a place of unbelievable banalities. It is a small village filled with URGES."

Eighty-plus years later the cypress canopy seen through my skylight is still noisy with URGES, as the grackles and stellar jays and woodpeckers alternately bicker and court, crooning their avian versions of Barry White get-it-on songs. Meanwhile, the Carmel-by-the-Sea streets outside my window overfloweth with classically lined Jaguars and cute-as-a-button VW bugs boasting vanity license plates reading I ♥ GOLF and I ♥ CRML.

Strolling down 6th Avenue, where I espy one of the aforementioned plates, it strikes me as fitting that the state that brought us same-sex marriage and medicinal dope would restore the rights of the marginalized, victimized heart as an alpha-numeric character. Twenty bucks says the next time I drive to San Fran I see an I ♥ DICK plate in the Tenderloin, and it won't mean Tricky.

On daily trips to Carmel Beach to do my "research," I witness countless ecstatic groomsmen and bridesmaids running pell-mell down the hill from La Playa Hotel, spilling onto the white sands in their tuxes and gowns, getting sand in their crevices, and spraying bubbly far too primo to be drunk by sea crabs. By late fall I've seen so many post-betrothal beachlandings that I know a creamy color I've dubbed "buttercup" is all the rage. Reconfirmed is my once-shaken belief that the garter shot—a snatch of bridal leg as the groom goes down on his knees—remains requisite in the wedding albums of the promising young Republicans who exchange vows and bodily fluids here. And from the number and kind of intimacies I've seen shared between dogs and humans on Carmel Beach—intimacies so steamily rabid I almost turned away—I can say with certainty that the fears of the anti–gay marriage lobby, namely, that liberalizing the laws will lead to people being betrothed to their pets, is a real possibility here in Carmel-by-the-Pedigree. For canines Carmel Beach is a hotspot if you want to give or receive a quick hump—better than South Beach, my dog friends tell me.

Indeed, Carmel-by-the-Sea was born into romance the day it drew its first, incorporated breath on Halloween 1916, which it celebrates each year as its b-day. At night here the coastal stars throb like so many of Shakespeare's "chaste queens," unmolested by streetlights, the surf crashes with its distant masculine roar, and all manner of magical strains can be heard overtopping the stockade fence of the Forest Theater up on Mountain View.

My landlady tells me that one of the first nights she and her then-husband spent in their new rental, she'd emerged into the cool Carmel air to the unmistakable sound of fairy bells. She'd naturally assumed that she'd fallen off her rocker, so stoked was she to be able to play house with her hubby in the hills in the village-by-the-sea that she'd dreamt up an angel choir. Only later did she learn that the Forest Theater had been staging Peter Pan that weekend, and that those airy vibes had in fact been Tinkerbell's.

Historically, when folks fall in love with Carmel, it's head over heels, ass over Audi. The recitations are so gushing they're almost embarrassing. Daisy Bostick counted plenty of ways to swoon over her adopted home in the early 1920s. So many, in fact, that she wrote a book called *Carmel at Work and at Play*. Bostick no doubt had a realtor's ear for hyperbole, but her descriptions are themselves practically bodice-rippers. Conjuring an "artists paradise," she describes poets and painters "caught and held by the golden sunsets, enchanted woods, gnarled cypresses, rainbow-hued waters—[who] sent for their typewriters and easels." Other saucy inventories follow suit: "The trees still whisper their secrets of love, beauty, and romance; wild things—coons, foxes, coyotes—play hide-and-seek in the moonlight." Not quite Van Morrison, but still.

Susan Porter, a theater type who first drove through the Monterey Peninsula on her way to the brighter lights of the San Francisco Exposition, avowed in a 1933 edition of the *Pine Cone* that, "Carmel won me from that day onward." Hal Bragg, another limelighter, took a pull on his pipe and said, "After living on the other side of the hill for a number of years, I decided to locate in Carmel. I met my wife-to-be here and we were married here in 1923."

Over the years artists, writers, and celebs have come here to tie the knot and start afresh. Carmel's quintessential poet-romantic, Robinson Jeffers, wooed a USC grad student, Una, away from her attorney husband, causing a scandal so great it reached the front page of the *Los Angeles Times* in 1912. Jeffers then spirited her away to these very shores, where he set about building a stone tower in her honor. Not so many years later, Ava Gardner and Mickey Rooney enjoyed marital bliss on Pebble Beach's greens, and Liz Taylor honeymooned here with the first of many beaus, Nicky (Conrad Jr.) Hilton. Joan Fontaine, whose haunty film *Rebecca* was filmed at Pebble, hitched with Brian Ahearn on the hallowed grounds in 1939, and Hollywood looker Kathryn Grayson did likewise with Jimmie Johnston a decade or so later.

The circus-barker zeal with which R. J. Harper, Arnold Palmer, Clint Eastwood, and others have pitched changes made to Pebble's layout gets me thinking. In a traditional place like Pebble Beach or Carmel-by-the-Sea, maybe change itself is a little sexy. In the late nineties, in fact, Pebble Beach routinely advertized a "Lunchtime Facelift" at its Skin Institute in the Spa at Pebble Beach.

I'm desirous of that inimitable and seemingly contradictory mix of authenticity and cosmetic plasticity—Dina Eastwood's patented swing. "What makes me feel beautiful," she once dished to *Carmel Magazine*, "is getting more comfortable in my skin as I get older, and that quarter dose of Botox right between the eyes!"

Walk down Carmel side streets any day of the week during the never-ending tourist season and you'll see hair being highlighted and dyed, mud masks being slathered, frown lines and crow's feet being microdermed away. Stay here long enough and you begin to wonder whether it's not simply change that paves the way for Eros to visit, change that makes us more desirable to our partner than we were the day before. One minute she's your Plain Jane wife of many years; the next she's the same woman you've always loved only fresh from the salon or the shopping mall or the spa and she's tarted up like Parisian call girl. And—God help you—you like it.

So if the quintessential pilgrimage to Pebble Beach is, at root, a quest for love—golf-love, self-love, buddy-love, Dina Eastwood–love—and love is all about erotic change, about swinging the wrecking ball at oneself when it needs to be swung, about personal renovations if you want to court a constituency, then I've landed not just in a capital of *recreation*, but re-creation. Hell, if Clint could literally finish his morning round on Pebble at the 1986 AT&T National Pro-Am and, minutes later, dramatically drop off the petition required for his mayoral candidacy just ahead of the filing deadline, then I ought to at least be able to petition my flagging libido.

In the civic and personal reinvention department, Dirty Harry serves as Exhibit A, for, just as Ronald Reagan and the Governator morphed into politicians, Clint went from on-screen badass and Hollywood's most ineligible bachelor to nice-guy, civic-minded patrician and part-owner of the Pebble Beach Golf Links. "He's not really a great golfer, so he accepted his talents and moved on," U.S. Open champ and former Eastwood foursome member Jerry Pate told me back in September. During the same week, Champions Tour golfer Andy Bean had spoken of his pal's legendary reclusiveness, telling me, "I felt very privileged to know him, on and off the course. You know, Clint keeps a very low profile. We'd finish a round and he'd say, 'I'll see you at Jack London's or Hog's Breath in forty minutes,' and all of a sudden you'd turn the cart in and he'd be gone . . . absolutely gone."

The actor-apparition Andy Bean calls his friend was the same ghost Carmel knew in 1986 when, after twenty-five years of living on the Peninsula, Eastwood—whose unlisted phone number quickly became a campaign hot-button—shocked his future constituency by announcing his run for mayor. "I've always been rather low-key," he admitted to the *Pine Cone* in a newsprint stump. "I don't need to bring attention to myself. I'm doing this as a resident. This is where I live; this is where I intend to live the rest of my life." In effect, The Big Man was turning over a big new leaf, as his absenteeism from his house on San Antonio had, in reality, grown so egregious, biographer McGilligan reported that, "the kitchen spices still had 1960s price tags" and "dustballs and cobwebs [were] everywhere."

Eastwood called for a "spiritual rejuvenation" and ran a change campaign against incumbent mayor Sue Townsend, an establishment candidate and a dead ringer for Eastwood pal Robin Williams's Mrs. Doubtfire. Townsend tried to point out in a public forum that a leopard can't change its spots, but was "soundly booed," the *Pine Cone* reported, when she characterized her opponent as merely "a disgruntled real-estate developer." Even reporters at Eastwood's hometown newspaper found themselves flatfooted in the face of Clint's flip-flop. "Eastwood," an incredulous McDonald wrote in the *Pine Cone*, "whose film characters are not exactly known for their talkativeness, spoken often and candidly to the press about his problems with the city."

But if Carmel-by-the-Sea residents believe in anything, it's the power of personal reinvention, and they turned out in droves to support their celebrity home makeover mayor in numbers so large the opposition cried voter registration fraud. Michael Gardner reported in the *Pine Cone* that the number of registrants in Carmel in the lead-up to the 1986 election reached an improbable 4,142 out of an estimated

4,800 residents. Gardner cited unidentified sources who claimed that pro–Pale Rider shop owners in the village's central business district were unlawfully "registering their employees who lived as far away as Marina or Seaside."

Eastwood outspent the overmatched Townsend $40,000 to $300, eventually winning the election in a landslide and causing Gardner to lead off his front-page article with mention of Eastwood's unlikely personal transformation: "In the election heard around the world," he wrote, "it is no longer Clint Eastwood the actor." In voting for their shape-shifting patron, the town born on Halloween had, symbolically at least, voted for its right to change its stripes as often as it liked. The election of Dirty Harry promised to make the image of the increasingly uptight city a little more alter-ego, a little more Mardi Gras, or at least a little more Hollywood.

At the time, Carmel-by-the-Sea had been locked in a lawsuit with the Pebble Beach Company, had threatened to shut down the Carmel Gate to Pebble at North San Antonio Street, and had repeatedly sued Monterey County. Meanwhile, the improbable was happening, as Eastwood, a man who made his living portraying a gun-slinging hardass, was quoted in the *Pine Cone* saying, "Negotiation and diplomacy is an important thing." That comment, and others like it, prompted humorist Lewis Grizzard to write a nationally syndicated column titled, "Make His Day as Mayor of Carmel," in which Grizzard put to words what the rest of a puzzled nation had been thinking: "Who's going to make Clint Eastwood's day in Carmel?" Grizzard quipped. "Some old geezer caught moving the ball in the rough? What kind of crime could there be in Carmel for Mayor Eastwood to declare war upon? People drinking red wine with fish? . . . Clint Eastwood needs to be mayor of Newark . . . Dom DeLuise should be mayor of Carmel. Or even Liberace."

Dirty Harry's is far from the only instance of celeb reinvention in the fairy-tale town of magic-wand remakes. A case in point is the good-timing Frank Sinatra, who temporarily flip-flopped into remorseful sobriety in 1964 after ending up in a Peninsula hospital bed after a late-night fight at the Pebble Beach Lodge with Richard Morse, S.F.B. Morse's son-in-law and president of Del Monte Properties. The Sinatra-instigated fisticuffs earned Old Blue Eyes an indefinite ban from Pebble under threat of arrest by the Duke of Del Monte himself.

While Pebble and Carmel-by-the-Sea have spurred Hollywood's greatest gigolos and partiers on to the highest heights of depravity, they have also played host to their uncanny reformations. A case in point is legendary night owl and Rat Packer Dean Martin, who once called the cops to his own clambake party so he'd be fit for an early tee time. Likewise, Bing Crosby's second marriage to actress Kathryn Grant and his purchase of a family home off Pebble's thirteenth fairway found him focused more on sky balls than on the high balls and dope highs alleged to have plagued his early career, when Bob Hope had called his hard-partying little friend an "economy-sized Sinatra." Pebble even mellowed hotshot astronaut and Rear Admiral Alan Shepard who, after he hit his famous 200-yard lunar chili-dip, retired to a home off the sixth fairway and once, in a very un-*Apollo* moment, confided to *Pebble Beach Magazine*, "I felt a lot more confident about my first space flight and the lunar mission than I do teeing it off in at the AT&T [Pro-Am]."

Among the fairer sex, Carmel-inspired celebrity image remakes include mid-eighties *Sports Illustrated Swimsuit Issue* sex symbol Kathy Ireland, who's repackaged herself as a businesswoman and hearts the hamlet in the forest so much she's named one of the collections in her furniture line Carmel Valley. "Carmel is a beautiful wealth of inspiration," she told Katie Perry of *Carmel Magazine*. "Just a mention of the name and you get an instant visual. It's something that people all over the country connect with. It's romantic, elegant, charming—it's got it all." And then, of course, there's Dina Eastwood, the former small-market TV anchorwoman turned co-host of *Candid Camera* turned celebrity wife and mother, not to mention—be still my beating heart—a damned fine linksteress and one-time contributing editor of *Golf Digest for Women.*

For her part Dina's totally hip to the fine line between naturalness and artifice, between restoration and wholesale renovation—no makeup, as her sig-fig likes her, but still the shot of botox "right between the eyes." About Tehama, the golf course community where she and the mister make their home, Dina said this: "Now there will be detractors who will say, 'Well you built a damn golf course.' That's true. But they replanted oaks and moved them instead of tearing them down. This is a very ungroomed course. It's xeroscaped. It's all native everything and it's not one of those fake-o places that has flowers on the fairway."

But of all these, no celebrity makeover is bigger than Pebble's which, by all accounts, was an underused, underrated, undernoticed shopgirl prior to the 1972 U.S. Open that turned, in a single generation, into an internationally known, endlessly desirable, cosmetically enhanced supermodel among golf courses.

In the face of so many fab do-overs, I find myself, not long before the holidays, responding to an ad in the *Pine Cone* for a "Golfer's Special" and "Free Body Mapping" to be conducted by Laura Austin, CMT. I pick up the phone in the spirit of journalistic inquiry, but I'm probably just craving a laying on of hands. The website for Laura's Place lists Neuromuscular Release Therapy, Swedish, Lomi-Lomi, Shiatsu, Reflexology, Reiki, Native American Healing, and Chakra Alignments to accelerate your divine and spiritual healing," among a smorgasbord of services about which I am clueless.

I show up to Austin's second-floor studio in a strip mall off Carmel Rancho Boulevard above a nail joint and a discount travel agent nervous as spit on a skillet. She puts in a New Age CD and seats me beneath a pyramidal structure to which is lashed, at its zenith, a native stone from Mexico that I gather is supposed to cleanse my dishwater aura. Austin deep-tissues golfers from Pebble, Quail Valley, and Clint Eastwood's Tehama, and makes house calls for golfers in all three locations, where, she tells me, it's not uncommon for her clients to boast their own private exercise and massage rooms. Come to find out Austin, whose father was a professional soccer player back in Mexico and an Olympian, has massaged Bobby Clampett and learned to play golf at his Academy at Quail Valley.

Austin and I talk Pebble while the music of the spheres plays. Her favorite hole is number seven ("I think I like that one a lot . . . the view, the difficulty . . . and then you get so distracted about seeing everything"), but there's no hot stones or lomi-lomi for me — my visit is diagnostic only. When I stand to go, my aching sacrum still screams like a Sam Kinison and my aura's gray as Robert Goddamned Lee.

My half hour 'neath the not-so-healing pyramid has me wondering what else my list of Pebble Beach–esque renovations might include in advance of the major championship I hope to qualify for: a date. I decide to make a short list of the key reconstructions undertaken since my move to the sea.

Month #1: Loosen mores. Trim beard to USGA specifications.

Month #2: Augment sun exposure. Increase consumption of olive oil–infused deli takeout on beach at twilight. Increase number of "hits" on online dating profile. Mitigate slice to a fade.

Month #3: Amend life story to include notion of acquiring future second home in Carmel-by-the-Sea. Expand romantic territory to Santa Cruz.

Month #4: Become regular at local coffee shop. Utilize said shop for networking. Contact sexy people for interviews. Amplify artistic persona.

Month #5: Deepen dating pool. Renovate attitudes toward relationships. Demolish personal hang-ups. Introduce new bunkering complexes.

Earlier, my Month #4 initiatives had met with ironic success. BC — Before Carmel-by-the-Sea — it had felt like death to be that achingly predictable dude, the regular, who the minute he walks in the door of some establishment the other sad regulars know exactly what he'll order, why and with whom he came, and what crossword clue he'll undertake first — *four-letter word for shepherd's game played with a stick* — once he delivers his rote lines of greeting.

Despite my resistance fate pushed me in the direction of the Carmel Coffee and Cocoa Bar. It waited for me at the bottom of a long, somewhat treacherous flight of difficult-for-a-non-morning-person stairs leading to the courtyard of the Carmel Plaza, where Mira Schumacher, the proprietor of said establishment, had, after ascertaining my habits for several weeks, slipped me a business card one day for a start-up of hers called neverendingjar.com and began calling me "professor."

When finally I got around to surfing what turned out to be a self-improvement site, I found Mira listed as the CEO, along with her statement: "I came to America 20 years ago. I am not an expert in relationships, but I am still searching for ways to develop myself and my relationship with others. From the home page I open the jars labeled "self-improvement," "intimacy," and, ominously, "single life," which titillates me in the conditional voice: "If you want to improve your dating life, if you want to make your personal life explode with some flavor right now . . ." it begins. "Knowing how to attract women means that you have to be able to flirt with women without feeling any pressure," it advises further down the page. Flirtation-retarded, I'm sufficiently spooked by Mira leaving me her calling card — at exactly the moment that I am in the throes of romantic self-doubt and hoped-for transformation — that I suspect Mira is either a) reading my mind, or b) using me as a guinea pig to test her ideas, or c) all of the above. Chickenshit that I am, I decide to temporarily suspend my play at "being a regular" experiment at the Carmel Coffee and Cocoa Bar while I keep my eyes on the bigger prize: my USGA-styled renovations.

My last action item, Month #5: social networking, pays dividends. I meet a girl, let's call her Surfing Betty, on a Big Sur–area hike sponsored by a prominent social networking website. After a sweaty climb that climaxes in a breathtaking ocean view, a handful of us do an economy lunch in Carmel, during which fair Betty shares the dregs of her pumpkin milkshake with me.

Our unsolicited mingling of straws means I return to my Carmel granny flat chock-full of newfound hormones. I decide to do what Arnie and Clint would do: take action, draw up some "plans," throw my Stetson in the ring, assume the "symbolic gavel of power" like Clint had after he whupped Townsend in the election. I will follow up with this Surfing Betty, I declare, this flagrant Sharer of Pumpkin Shakes. I will play a practice round.

I'm off the tee with a light, mildly flirty e-mail and, less than twenty-four hours later, the act-now-ask-questions-later swing technique I learned from Clint and Arnie finds me in play on the very difficult par 5 aptly named Long-shot Dating. Taking as my model the old ball masque invitations from Pebble Beach days of yore, I issue the sponsor's exemption, the special invite, thusly:

You are cordially invited
to a winetasting
romp and revel
in Carmel Valley

Let me be clear, friends, as the politicians say: I face steep odds courting my constituency. As a single man from Middle America with a yearly take-home pay somewhere south of $50,000, I am the darkest of dark horses in Carmel-by-the Sea, where love, like most other commodities, is yours by ballot. In a slate crowded with major candidates, I'm the Green Party; in a field of Boom-Booms, I'm wee Tom Kite.

It's a demanding electorate, the area's unmarried twenty- and thirty-somethings perfectly accustomed to voting you off the proverbial island. Indeed, several of Carmel's hot young things have risen to stardom via the vote of reality TV. My nearest and dearest example is Bobby Clampett's musician daughter, Katelyn, who, in front of a salivating national audience, was deemed the "full package" (I prefer "playing the full yardage") by *American Idol* judge Kara Dioguardi. Meanwhile, Carmel High's 2000 graduate Jon Jonsson was declared "America's Most Gorgeous Model" by Carmen Elektra on the BRAVO series *Manhunt*.

So intertwined, in fact, are love and hanging chads here in my fairy-tale village-by-the-absentee that splashed across the same November issue of *Pine Cone* that highlighted contentious local votes against Carmel Valley incorporation and in favor of selling off the city-owned money pit, the Flanders Mansion, I uncover a get-out-the-vote story of a different sort: contractor Robert Darley's impassioned plea to his fellow citizens of Carmel-by-the-Sea to cast their lot for his "lovely, beautiful daughter," the 2004 Carmel High grad Jamielee, who is one of ten finalists for the 2010 *Victoria's Secret Fashion Show* on CBS and whose hot bod accompanies her old man's plea. In the contest for Carmel's prettiest miss, who could forget Dina Eastwood's stepdaughter, Alison Eastwood, Dirty Harry's child, a talented, Carmel-born-and-raised model-actress who may just give her stepmama a run for her money in my Top 10 Infatuations.

"A professional at golf, an amateur at love" read the tagline for the late-eighties golf flick *Dead Solid Perfect*, and, believe me, I'll need to bring my A Game to compete with the likes of Jonsson, America's most beautiful male, who, btw, studies astrophysics and in his spare time plays piano, clarinet, guitar, and—salt to the wound—plenty of sax. Then, as if the TV survival of the fittest weren't fevered enough, there's the new bull in town who made a front-page splash on Carmel Beach earlier this week, a 250-pound male who, the *Pine Cone's* Mary Brownfield reports, boasts "clear eyes, pink mouth, good teeth, and a non-runny nose." Sure, he's a sea lion, but a bull can never be too careful with his cows, you know what I'm saying?

Thus, when Betty says yes to my cornball invitation, I celebrate a personal makeover that has transformed me from a stuck-in-the-mud, perfectly innocent Iowa farm boy into a ladies' man, just as Ronald

Reagan and the Governator morphed from actors into politicians and Clint switched from on-screen badass to nice guy patrician.

Turns out my Gal Friday is a former sportswriter, so we decide, when it turns out she's also free on Friday night, on a home and away game (home for her being Santa Cruz, home for me being Carmel-by-the-Sea). It's a weird clash of adopted cultures, by which I've come to represent by proxy the rich Republicans of Carmel and she, originally a lawyer's daughter from So Cal, has come to stand in for the dope-smoking, left-leaning hippies of Santa Cruz. Ours is a mixed twosome, to be sure, but par for the Cali course.

I played just well enough in our "away" game in Santa Cruz to earn a rubber match, game 1 having boiled down to a bottle of organic red consumed fireside in an opium den–like hipster lounge called The Red, and Betty's shiver-me-timbers admission that she wanted a baby and she wanted it pronto.

Game 2, on Sunday, finds us at a decent altitude, having hiked to a break in the live oaks and Spanish moss canopy from whose vantage we can see the whole of Carmel Valley, with its well-ordered horse pastures and bucolic vineyards, spread out below us. Betty of the formerly firelit eyes, big and liquid as tidal pools, I learn is an erstwhile surf reporter and one of the top she-boarders upcoast. She's tall and toned and might be able to kick my ass in an arm wrestling contest. In her company, my golf amours seem so lame, so fuddy-duddy, so Eisenhower era. Friday at the Red she'd told me harrowing tales of drugs, big pealing waves, and implied rolls in the hay with surf dudes and adrenaline junkies; I returned serve with banal talk of Iowa farms and saving pars.

The live oak canopy just now is a riot of birdsong and she's asking me what kind of love brought me to live in unforgivably upscale yet oh-so-beautiful Carmel. I tell her the raison d'être for my being here can be summed up in one plosive: *Pebble,* the holy of holies. She chews on that for a while, telling me that in her sport, what's more revealing than the big wave, which can be had in many places, is the mystery of what draws the particular surfer to the particular surf. Returning service, I explain to her the notion of "horses for courses" — the guys, like Phil and Tiger, who play well on the Left Coast; the guys, like Arnold, who never did. The guys, like Tom Kite and Justin Leonard and Lee Trevino, who thrive in the wind, and others, who can't play a blowy links to save their bloody lives. I explain that the lay of the land, the routing of the course sometimes "fits the golfer's eye." I mention guys like Crenshaw, whose prowess as an intuitive, course-sensitive player led him to an almost mystical appreciation of golf course architecture.

Betty responds in kind, telling me surfers sometimes attain the status of *watermen* once their knowledge of the ocean catches up with their infatuation for it. She tells me it's not uncommon for boarders to develop secondary careers in oceanography or marine biology, eventually growing so close with the life aquatic they all but grow webbed feet. Only surfers, she claims, really know wave action up close, paddling out to it and seeing a barrel backlit by the sun, glowing just so. They, more than the physicists, know how the wave will move and how and if it will hold. She recalls times where she's been on the bluffs overlooking the legendary Cowell's Beach in Santa Cruz and seen wave after perfect wave marching in from the sea. In Cruz and Half Moon Bay, perfect waves are a dime a dozen, thick as great golf courses on the Monterey Peninsula.

Betty's down on shortboards like I'm death on so-called "game-improvement" clubs. "It's just back and forth" she says, noodling her arm like a flopsy fish. The longboard, she insists, is the true art because the only way the surfer can slow himself and maintain the ride is to move to the very edge of the board, to "hang ten" right over the edge. Her fact rings true in my golf mind: the juice and splash exist in a thin band on the outermost edge — the difference between an epic ride and a tragic one just a matter of inches.

To get up on a good wave means you can't be out in front of it and you can't be behind. "The perfect ride's right up there with good sex or killer food as an endorphin," she says, fixing me in those tidal pools of hers. Though we're talking surfing, it's clear we're also talking Cali and the life lived on either side of a deepwater bay, a life to which she is native and I am émigré. We're talking about the possibility of us, a golfer and a surfer. Am I a good wave? Is she? How did we choose this mountain valley, a little swell of an afternoon of wine and hiking, over the next equally inviting one? Dumb luck? Fate? Destiny? Chaos? Who rules the seas? Are the gods of golf in heaven? Pray tell, who hurls the lightning bolts? Who strikes the 1-irons?

The surfer girl looks for the perfect tube to shoot. The golfer guy plunks down a half grand at the Pebble pro shop for a five-hour romp with a full-bodied beauty as unpredictable and drama queen as the sea.

Betty's finished with philosophy now, kaput with surfology. As we turn around on the trail she has transitioned into dating confessions — something akin to the golfer's list of his worst-ever holes. She tells me she's dated all the wrong men, namely the adrenaline junkies she covered on her beat. She sought the edge through them, she says.

But I don't want to know about her most recent flame, or any of the dudes before him — all the water under the bridge. I'm looking for the feeling I had on the first tee at Pebble, the feeling that even though it's late and dozens of other golfers have already plied the fairways, it's just me and the Aphrodite wave.

The day after our "away game," my Surfing Betty pens the impossibly complicated ghosting every guy half expects and fully fears: "I met a wonderful man yesterday but I also have a powerful, wild need that's growing increasingly urgent by the moment. Ten years ago, even five, things would be completely different. I would have had time to invest and less to possibly lose."

I am hasty in my reply, pulling the wrong club, getting quick on it, yanking down from the top, all my recent renovations and band-aid swing fixes crumbling. I write, "Totally don't get the logic here. The way to have a baby is with a wonderful man. That's step number one, or at least it used to be back when. So the man's the chicken, and the egg is, well, the egg. How could it be otherwise?"

A few paragraphs later, I'm still hacking out of the rough. "To get to that bambino, barring the miracle of modern medicine, you'll have to grasp a relationship—a good one—with just as much vigor and commitment and risk as you'd reach for that baby."

Weeks go by. I hear nothing. Then 'I have a hunch. I sort back through my inbox and reread her final email. Upon further review, as they say in the broadcast booth, it's clear in hindsight what my would-be surfer girl was intimating all along—even circa our away game at The Red—that she likely had already tried at a local sperm bank or fertility clinic or wherever, and then I came along, a naive midwestern farm kid dropping old-fogey slights like "the miracle of modern medicine."

Maybe back in the Heartland you need a Jack to have baby, but not here in Cali. My attitudes about dating are so hopelessly 1950s I might as well be some pimpled pipsqueak leaving my house on Mountain View in my Edsell to pick up my best gal to watch the picture show down at the Golden Bough on Monte Verde. I have failed Dirty Harry, I have failed Arnie. My personal renovations have, for the time being, been bulldozed, swept out to sea.

I am worse than a square. Worse than a dweeb. Worse than a golf nerd.

Clint Eastwood help me, I am me.

10

Bubba Watson Tweets Cheats; Rickie Fowler Ducks Haircut; Mark Brooks Smokes Field, Fags; and All the Other News That's Fit to Print from Pebble's Other Pro-Am

I arrive at the tenth hole on Day One of Pebble's other pro-am, the Callaway Invitational, to a blinding blue tedium. On Carmel Bay a covey of a dozen or so boarders ride the mondo waves whipped up in advance of California's first pre-winter storm. Hazardous sea warnings have been posted up and down the coast and the surfers have loaded up their woodies.

The air of this afterlife is nose-bleed, sunburn dry, the sky a cloudless shade of periwinkle. "Just another Monterey day," a blissed-out volunteer ho-hums to me, hamming it up with a mock yawn. The volunteers, dressed in Johnny Cash/Callaway black, are out in force this week, easily outnumbering the spectators five to one. One goes out of his way to brake for me in his cart in one of those "you-go-no-you-go" hyperpolite encounters. "I was told I had be nice to the spectators," he says, shooting me a wry, chamber of commerce grin.

Below me, five yards from the cliff on the tenth fairway—no more than an easy, downwind wedge from the green on the 430-yard hole—looms the lithe figure of Bubba Watson, windblown and visored, lollygagging while the four amateurs behind him hit their approaches. Bubba is silhouetted against the dappled, Mediterranean glint in another of the picture-perfect moments that routinely fall like manna here into the laps of even the most egregious point-and-shooters.

After Bubba somehow manages to three-putt for bogey, I catch up with erstwhile PGA Championship winner Mark Brooks. Pushing fifty, he looks the spittin' image of his 1980s in-contention self. Same hipsy, chase-after-it, Texas windcheater move à la Justin Leonard and Lee Trevino. Same drapey pleated pants and snug-fitting black wool sweater. Same everything except for the new fluorescent-shafted woods and a few more wrinkles around those Texas squints of his.

I'm close enough to choke on his cigarette smoke, near enough to hear him good-naturedly ribbing his playing partners—all of whom are big-stick amateurs who consistently and unapologetically outdrive him. The remarkable thing about the Callaway Invitational—"the best kept secret in golf," a tournament official will tell me—is absolute, unfettered access to top pros, free of charge.

At such close range I could peel Brooksie's banana for him, or ask him what he thinks of the spread on the Iowa versus Ohio State game. Hell, I can do anything I want but shout Holy Frijoles! during his backswing. And the weird thing is, it's not just the golf writers this week who could reach out and hold Brooks's smoldering fag. At the Callaway anyone can be as badgering, cloying, and all-around irksome as a sportswriter.

The tourney debuted in 1972, and prides itself in being what the Crosby Clambake used to be—low-key, lighthearted, and loungey. In truth there's no other event like it in golf—not only because the pros aren't sequestered behind gallery ropes but also because the pros in the pro-ams are drawn from all four professional tours to compete on a level playing field made possible by "the tournament's innovative tee-placement system . . . based on the average length of shots in each tour." It's pretty loose math, though, and the ladies and the old fogies come out aces. Monterey Peninsula native and LPGA up-and-comer Mina Harigae confesses to me that the course actually plays "easy" from her up-tees, and her eventual 6-under tally proves it.

In sum, the Callaway is a spectator's dream, elevating uncanny combinations to an art form. It's a good-timing battle royale, a free-for-all somehow still governed by USGA rules, where the final putt falls just a few days before the Thanksgiving bird gets stuffed and jolly pros dispense with the usual shackles slapped on them by their respective tours. Out come the golf carts. Out come the cigars. Out come the rangefinders and good cheer. It's a spectator's dream, but for the approximately three hundred amateurs who, by the grace of God and corporate expense accounts, descend on the hallowed grounds determined to get their money's worth swing by awful swing.

As I watch the Brooks fivesome make a mess of the fourteenth hole, I remember why some people liken watching golf to watching paint dry. At times like this it's agonizing. It's tedious. It's downright grotesque. Like reliving a disastrous high school prom ad nauseum. In short, it's a goddamned glossary of golfing errors without any of the mitigating, comedic effects of Bill Murray. Put a finesse-needy 9-iron in the hands of a manager who can otherwise flowchart and spreadsheet like Carmello Villegas can read greens, and he'll barf all over his wingtips.

On fourteen Brooksie actually plays first from the fairway, out-sticked by his playing pals. He lays it up perfectly down the right side while his partners enact a litany of fourteenth hole sins. One, fairway wood in hand, chunks it badly, holding his finish like you do when you know damn well it's dribbling to a stop right in front of you. Another sets up and slices the bejesus out of the ball in the direction of the plate-glass Mediterranean villas with their shatter-proof glass, 20 yards O.B. easy. The third, who manages a sweet lay-up, tugs his wedge approach left and long, hitting the live oak on his greenside pitch, turning chickenshit on the comeback flop shot from behind the pin, then ramming his better-safe-than-sorry chip past the cup all the way down to the lonesome lower tier of the dance floor. Meanwhile, Brooks waits patiently to attempt his birdie putt, wearing his no-drama-Obama face.

As a pro you don't get asked to the Callaway Invitational unless you have a beatific bedside manner and a love of these links. And, if you lack those pre-reqs, you'd better be Manny Villegas– or Rickie Fowler–good-looking. If you're an LPGA pro, it doesn't hurt if you're a hottie, a pixie with a pitching wedge or else a spunky tomboy who doesn't mind being one of the guys for a week. If you're an amateur, Ron, a tournament official tells me as we chew the fat beside the eighteenth green, you're issued an invite but only if the folks at Pebble are pretty certain you'll accept. Refusals are bad for business. It's allegedly $8,000 a pop for amateurs to buy in, and that doesn't include the food and the lodging. That's bargain basement, I'm told, compared to what it used to be when Pebble was flush with corporate rupees. Still, if it's your lifelong dream to tee it up on Pebble in a tourney, and you or your company can pony up some dead presidents for a Facebook-worthy moment, it's money well spent. "All amateur players will leave with once-in-a-lifetime memories to share with friends, as they watch history made in June 2010," Chief Executive Officer William Perocchi summarizes in an open letter written to the week's participants.

It may be a recession year, but the Pebble marketers count the U.S. Open on their side of the ledger. They know what you know: it's "value added" if you can boast to the folks back home in Terre Haute that you played the famed course under Open conditions. You'd be telling them a white lie, of course, but close enough, right? In fact, Senior Vice President of Golf R. J. Harper will tell us at the trophy presentation that the new, tighter fairway lines have already been marked out and, as soon as Callaway play is complete, the course will grow out its hair. By June it'll sport rough gnarly as any Rastafarian's.

For your or your company's 8K, you get up to six rounds on Pebble's courses—a value of a couple/a few grand, in and of itself. You get treated like royalty while staying at The Lodge or The Inn at Spanish Bay. You get to swing some factory-fresh Callaways on a practice range, where you'll enjoy all-you-can-hit balls until the sun goes down or your tennis elbow flares up. When you complete your first round and stop to sign your card to the right of the eighteenth green, you'll get, as a carrot, a glossy booklet with color photos of your smiling fivesome and, on the inside, a frame-by-frame shot of your swing. One dude, opening the book up beside the scorer's tent, sighs and says, "My swing looks exactly like it did last year. God, it could be last year, except I'm wearing different clothes!"

No one's complaining, though. The groups invariably finish their round with a barbershop chorus of "Tap Room!" and, saddle sore from riding the cart all day, amble up the hill toward the famed Pebble watering hole. For the pros it's a chance to try out new equipment, to get wined and dined, to get some practice rounds in before February's higher-stakes AT&T National Pro-Am, to reward long-suffering girlfriends or spouses for sticking it out during the less glamorous Tour stops—like Moline, Illinois, say.

An unofficial event, the Callaway also offers a chance for the straight-laced PGA pros to let their hair down as if they've entered a Funk-adelic time warp back to the Carmel heyday of good-timers like Roger Maltbie, Fuzzy Zoeller, Andy Bean, and Jerry Pate. They'll use their rangefinders (a definite no-no during official rounds on Tour), ride a cart (likewise forbidden), and smoke as un-self-consciously and joyfully as chimneys.

Like many of the delightful oddities at the Callaway, it takes some getting used to, to see pros driving their own golf carts—kind of like seeing Barack Obama behind the wheel of a Dodge minivan instead of the tinted, bullet-proof glass of a motorcade; like seeing your elementary school teacher at the liquor store buying a fifth of Jack. Occasionally you'll even see pros schlepping their own bags here, fixing their own divots there, calculating their own yardages. In a don't-get-your-hands-dirty game like modern golf, all this self-service strikes the unprepared viewer as almost indecent. Twice I'm nearly run over by fellow Iowan and sweet-swinging Champions Tour pro Tom Purtzer. Each time he's wearing a different shade of pastel and his soft spikes are lazily swinging over the edge like he's riding a Ferris wheel at the state fair in Des Moines.

"It's not really about the golf," a sun-mellowed Bubba Watson told me earlier in the week, fresh from a bracing, gratis round at Cypress Point and from taking the wife to the Monterey Aquarium. "It's about having fun, relaxing. And you get to play golf at Pebble . . . that's the extra."

Only a Watson—Bubba or Tom, take your pick—would wake up loving the weather forecast for the Monterey Peninsula for Day Two of the Callaway: high winds and cold, soaking rains. Bubba's stoked. In his early morning Twitter he pecks out, "Morning All! The weather channel says rainy-cold-windy (40 mph guest)!" I'm tempted to type a smart-ass reply like, *Bubba Dubya, don't you just hate them 40 mph guests! They're soooo breezy.* "That's the best conditions to play in, it's more fun!"

Later that afternoon, when everyone's good and soaked, I check back in to see if Bubba's taken off his rose-colored glasses. "I shot 74 again today! The weather was fun!! When rain comes sideways it's hard to hit a golf ball. :-)"

Sure as shootin', by afternoon a brisk wind, steady rain, and bone-chilling temps more typical of February blow in and play spoiler. Tommy Armour III cards a big fat 80 after a first round 71. PGA Tour pro Aron Price limps in with a 79. The only thing dry at the end of the day is Bubba's sense of humor in his post-round Tweet: "I played in 30 mph winds and rain! My wife was relaxing!"

On Saturday, Bubba Dubya's lately up-and-down game leaks Pennzoil, but he's still tweeting. This time he drops a bombshell that finds tournament officials thanking their lucky stars he hasn't mentioned the site of the alleged offenses, lest he sully the brand name.

Saturday begins promisingly enough, with Bubba blithely tweeting a few minutes before ten, "Morning All! 9:55 tee time at Spyglass, great golf course. Hope y'all have a great Saturday!" By 5:00 p.m., after recording a 76, the wonderchild in Bubba W. has turned indignant. "I confronted the team I played with today about cheating! It was not good for golf! Was not fun today!" Bubba supporters empathize with their hero's plight, offering youthful pronouncements of the cheating-so-uncool variety that remind me just how young Bubba and his followers are. Even his Twitter bio is all aw-shucks innocence:

Name: bubba watson
Location: Scottsdale, AZ & Bagdad, FL
Bio: Christian, Husband, Pro Golfer who enjoys giving back to help others grow in life!

By bedtime the irrepressible Bubba W. has already put a positive spin on his reaction to his amateurs' alleged foot wedges and fabricated scores: "Today by protecting the rest of the field and keeping the game pure, I learned how much I love the game of golf! Night All!"

Fortunately for corporate sponsors, the cheaters prove to be the exception to the rule, as the beauty of the Callaway Invitational lies in the understated way it quietly goes about turning back the golfing clock to less fraught, less fraudulent days. The Callaway, in fact, simulates golf's version of a one-room schoolhouse where pros ages twenty-one to sixty, including those from the LPGA and the Champions circuit, join amateurs in a multigenerational, multiethnic, multigender mishmash. And, because every pro who slips on a glove for this unofficial event is an invitee rather than a qualifier, the list of pros is as revealing as any handpicked guest list. Pebble supporters, native Californians, and Monterey-savvy pros recovering from nagging injuries or competitive droughts make the roster.

With no grandstands or ropes present, and with buddies or spouses handling the bags, the pros are unusually unguarded this week, literally and figuratively. So, before the final round action heats up, I corral a half dozen and set up a kind of "pros on Pebble" listening post.

NOTAH BEGAY III

Notah Begay, a Navajo Indian, is a former teammate and long-time friend of Tiger Woods, whom he followed to Stanford University, where together they became protégés of golf coach Wally Goodwin, former athletic director at Pebble Beach's Robert Louis Stevenson School. Begay, the most successful Native American golfer ever (with four tour wins) runs his own charitable foundation back home in New Mexico and has served as a studio analyst for the Golf Channel's coverage of the Masters. Thanks to Coach Goodwin, who repeatedly brought his team down to the Peninsula to bone up on Poppy Hills, Pebble, Spyglass, and Bayonet, Begay knows Monterey golf well. "I'm really familiar with the area and have a lot of friends here. Pebble's a beautiful layout . . . When there's no wind you can shoot some good scores. Its biggest defense is the winds and the greens . . . When the green's start getting fast you have five- and six-foot putts that break two feet. It's just a classic U.S. Open golf course."

OLIN BROWNE

Paul Azinger selected three-time Tour winner Olin Browne as his assistant captain for the winning 2008 U.S. Ryder Cup team. Browne is smart—listing politics and international affairs as his hobbies—and in-your-face when he needs to be. A veteran of over four hundred career starts on the PGA Tour, I ask him to share with me the subtleties that set Pebble apart from its ho-hum pretenders:

> It's a magnificent location, and it's a great golf course. It doesn't give you much. You have to earn every shot . . . This is a course that requires a lot of skill . . . not to mention the fact that it's probably the most beautiful place that you'd ever want to be.

It's a golf course that we all know and love, and that's why we come here . . . If the weather shows its fangs, you're hanging on for dear life . . . You can see several weather conditions in the course of eighteen holes. That's what makes it so great. It's not like playing golf in Palm Springs . . . There's a lot of variety. All of us who play like that *inconsistency*.

A golf course like this has so much variety to it. You just don't pay it conventionally. You don't just rear back and hit your shot. You have to drop down and knock one in there. You have to move your ball against the wind . . . The older guys especially like playing here because it's the way they grew up playing . . . The fact is that golf has evolved, and this course has stood the test of time. It still responds to the call . . . The players with a creative side and the players who know how to manage their games and how to play when things aren't going right are the guys who will always play well here.

JOHN COOK

A dead-ringer for John Denver sans the specs, John Cook, with his sun-kissed hair and surfer dad vibe, screams Californian. He hoisted hardware eleven times during a long-lived career on the PGA Tour, including the Crosby Pro-Am in 1981. As a member of the Champion's Tour Player Advisory Board, Cook's longevity in the game has earned him the respect of peers and Tour officials alike, plus he's informed enough company that in his earlier days Tiger picked Cook, along with Mark O'Meara, as a regular practice-round partner. I pick Cook's brain on what it feels like to have walked these links for nearly forty years.

My father brought me up here in 1972 for the U.S. Open. It was a pretty special place and special time . . . I was in awe . . . to come up and see the U.S. Open which you'd seen for so many years up here in familiar territory. Then to be able to play State Amateurs and U.S. Opens here. As a kid, you just don't forget those things . . . My first California State Amateur at Pebble Beach in 1975 I ended up winning, so it just snowballed from there. I had a lot of success on the Peninsula, especially here at Pebble.

This is the weather I grew up in Southern Cal . . . We're water people. I love the ocean—love to hear it, love to get in it, love to surf it. I love looking at the Point, looking at the Ghost Tree out here.

You just know. You know the feeling. What breaks and what doesn't. One putt doesn't look like it breaks, but it breaks four feet and it's fast . . . You come to know that. It really is a lot by memory.

STEVE FLESCH

A four-time winner on the big boy's circuit, Steve Flesch is one of the sixteen elected members of the PGA Tour's Player Advisory Council, and he's known for telling it like it is. The son of a physicist, a scholarship recipient at the University of Kentucky, and a former honor roll student, he's got it going on upstairs, too. He's got strong feelings about protecting the shot values and singular challenges of one of his favorite courses, of which he says, "People don't build golf courses like this anymore." I ask him, hole by hole, how best to handle the 1,000-pound gorilla that is Pebble Beach.

One is not an attack hole . . . You've got a 7- or an 8-iron in but the green is sloped so severely, five is in the equation . . . Holes two, three, and four are the holes you've got to attack. Five through ten you've just got to get through. Make your pars and move on. I think sometimes people are mislead by length . . . thinking they can make birdies, but the greens are the size of a Volkswagen.

Day in and day out there's a reason Pebble's top five. I don't think they need to tweak it much. If they said they were going to hold the [U.S. Open] here next week, it would hold its own.

MINA HARIGAE

Mina Harigae attended Robert Louis Stevenson, the legendary neighborhood school just a few good uphill drives from the Peter Hay

Golf Course at Pebble Beach. She took her first lesson at age six at a Salvation Army clinic underwritten by the Pebble Beach Foundation, and locals have followed her meteoric rise to Duke University and the LPGA Tour ever since. Her folks, father Yasunori and mother Mafumi, both Japanese immigrants, run a popular sushi joint just up the road in Pacific Grove called Takara. She's a bona fide phenom, having twice won the California Women's Amateur Championship as a twelve-year-old and a thirteen-year-old, back to back. After her second win, *Sports Illustrated* reported that she hustled off the course to catch *Harry Potter and the Sorcerer's Stone*. I ask her what it was like hitting the books and playing golf in a worldwide mecca.

> It was great going to school in the most beautiful part of the world. Spyglass Hill was our home course . . . We [left school] for the AT&T Pro-Am all the time during our free periods and even during teacher's council. They'd say, "Ah, let's go." And I'm like, "Okay." I got Tiger's autograph the last time he played here . . . Pebble's pretty easy for me. I've played it so much. I don't really need a yardage book. I just go.

J. J. HENRY

A former Ryder Cupper, J. J. Henry is one of the handful of philanthropic golfers at the Callaway who sport their own charitable foundations. In 2006 he founded Henry House to advocate for children in Fort Worth, Texas, and in southern New England, where he grew up. I ask him to tell me something about Pebble Beach that the average golfer doesn't know.

> I think it's a lot harder than people think. You never really feel like you can make a ton of birdies. You're playing seaside *poa annua* grass, and it's hard to make a lot of putts . . . There's some slope in these greens, so it's hard to get the ball really close to the hole.
>
> As far as favoring one type of shot, you've got to hit all the shots out here at Pebble. You've got to draw it on three. You've got to kind

of cut it on one. Six probably favors a little bit of a draw. You probably want to hit a little cut off the bunker on ten. Fourteen you probably want to hit a little bit of a cut. And eighteen favors a little bit of a draw . . . It's more about the winds and the elements and putting it in the right spots . . . You watch this as a kid on TV and you see the AT&T and the U.S. Opens. Actually, my buddy who's caddying for me this week . . . we just played seventeen where Watson chipped in and he said, "Man, that really is downhill" . . . TV doesn't do justice to how cool it is out here.

ROCCO MEDIATE

A personal friend of both Arnold Palmer and Tiger Woods, Rocco Mediate was David versus Goliath in a playoff lost to Woods at the 2008 U.S. Open at Torrey Pines, which earned him a book deal—*Are You Kidding Me* with John Feinstein—and an even larger following. Mediate lives for events like the Callaway that put him check by jowl with fans, and he's won plenty of shootouts and charity classics with partners like Jeff Sluman and Lee Janzen, as well as the Callaway itself in 1999. I ask him to recall for me his first time playing Pebble and the course strategy he's learned here over the years.

I didn't start playing until I was fifteen, so I had no idea what this place was . . . My first time here was in 1985 . . . It was crazy. It was great. I was in shock . . . It's the coolest place where land meets sea in the world, and it's one of my top two or three in the world . . . Riviera, here, a couple of others overseas.

If you shoot a low score coming out on one, two, three, four, five, and six—not that they're a walk in the park—you've got a chance. Then it tightens down on eight through eleven with the wind. You've got to get it early or it's hard . . . It's one of the best Open venues ever . . . Very difficult, but fair.

For Sunday's final round, the sun shines on a compelling horse race between the chain-smoking, black-clad forty-eight-years-young PGA

Tour veteran Brooks and the orange bedecked, suntanned, long-locked, painter-capped rookie Rickie Fowler, a *mano-a-mano* duel that brings honorary tournament chair Johnny Miller out to follow the drama on foot to the eighteenth, where Brooks closes the door on Fowler with a cool birdie to post 12-under. It's another horses-for-courses case study, the victory making Brooks the tourney's first three-time winner.

At the opera, it ain't over until the fat lady sings. At the Callaway Invitational it ain't over until annual emcee–cause celeb Johnny Miller coughs up the crystal. Sunday's matchup has Miller's broadcasting juices flowing. He's in an expansive mood as he takes the mike from tournament director Bill Sendell, who calls the Callaway, "the best spectator opportunity in golf." As everyone who watches NBC Sports golf coverage knows, Miller never met a mike he didn't like.

Miller needles Brooks about well-nigh losing to a kid in a painter's cap twenty-eight years his junior, and gets it right back when Miller asks the Callaway champ where he learned to be such a good ball-striker. "I grew up watching you guys," Brooks says. "I may be old, but, man, you're up there." Brooks segues from the dig to devotional with all the skill of a late-night comedian: "There's nothing like winning at Pebble," he tells the small crowd ringing the eighteenth green. "I feel like a fixture. I've been coming here almost thirty years."

When Johnny M.'s done with the obligatory needling, he makes a beeline for his car parked behind the eighteenth green. In his shades he looks like a cop in a Burt Reynolds movie or someone's dad sitting on the 50-yard line. He jukes one local reporter and suddenly I'm the only one standing between him and the end zone. I could tackle him at the knees—his Achilles heel, as everyone in golfdom knows—but I don't. "I'm from out of state," I say, begging mercy.

"Ya," he says. I decide that's Miller-speak for, "I admire sportswriters. Kindly proceed with your query."

I ask him, as a lover of Pebble and a longtime supporter, to tell me who, if anyone it, favors. "Pebble doesn't appeal to just anyone's game, but it sure appeals to Tiger's and Phil's," he says. "You almost go horses for courses."

"It happened to me. I didn't play for five years . . . then I won out of retirement here. I can play this course . . . It really appeals to California guys . . . The heavy air, the fog, the dew in the morning. All that stuff is California stuff that you get used to when you grow up here."

"The first time I ever saw Pebble," he continues, waxing nostalgic as the tournament organizers motion him back for pictures, "was when I was eight years old, at the World Long Drive contest on the second hole, and I got to watch Hogan and George Bayer. I was just a little kid. Somehow my dad talked me into hitting six balls."

Miller's earnest reminiscing at a moment as ceremonious as this should surprise me, but it doesn't. Pebble is one of those places that moves otherwise unsentimental folks to effusive storytelling, one generation often unwittingly passing the torch to the next. It's happening again today, no doubt: Brooks, who grew up watching Hogan hit balls in his native Forth Worth, and Fowler, who, with his fair hair, deep tan, and sherbet color palette, looks eerily like a young Johnny Miller. Maybe that's why the people who know are so fiercely protective of this place. You don't go mucking around with a mecca, be it St. Andrews or Pebble Beach, for fear the magic will pick up and move elsewhere. By dint of its very blessedness it makes you God-fearing and superstitious.

Earlier in the week I'd met up Steve Melnyk, the former CBS Sports golf announcer and 1969 U.S. Amateur champ who makes Miller look like a spring chicken. He's playing as an amateur this week after a painful hip replacement, his swing the over-the-top, physically inhibited move of many guys in their seventies. But his results are phenomenal: a well-struck fade, time after time.

Melnyk's one of many old-guarders who doesn't think longer necessarily equals better, especially at Pebble. "It's like in basketball," he tells me. "If you raise the goal to twelve feet, you only help the guys who jump the highest. If you move the tees back, you only help the guys who hit it farther . . . like Bubba [Watson]. You move the tees back, and he loves it. It's like Brer Rabbit saying, 'Please don't throw me in the briar patch.'"

And what would Bubba himself have to say about all this fusty, folkloric, old-man talk about lessons and tradition and how to properly navigate America's most famous links? I already know, because he'd told me as much when I'd shot the shit with him earlier in the week. "I don't like to listen to anybody," he told me. "We all play different games. I play a different game than you do . . . When it comes to how you're gonna play off the tee, you can't really listen to anyone."

Standing in front of Pebble's Stillwater Grill, I remember thinking that the world according to Bubba applied equally to golf as to life. In a phrase, maybe Pebble brings something different out in each of us, something we must grapple with alone. It makes some of us nostalgic, some rhapsodic, some heroic, and some sufficiently treacherous to foot-wedge their ball when no one's looking.

And what about me, two seasons into my pilgrimage to America's golfing mecca? I've driven more than 2,000 miles to learn what Pebble has to teach. Not quite halfway through the examination I find myself thinking that its ultimate lesson may well be a chestnut my father uttered more than a thousand times: golf is a paradigm for life.

Tournament wrapped, I follow the garlic trail to the hospitality room, where Pebble's caterers have arrived with an Italian concoction swimming in marinara and peppered with sausage cut in meaty parallelograms. Inside, it looks like any country club banquet room on awards night. Handwritten scores adorn the big board. Merlot flows. Contestants swap one-handed hugs and left-handed jokes on their way back to tables, plates loaded with carbs. Reporters, amateurs, and pros mingle easily. Olin Browne shows up sporting jeans, a worn gray sweater, and a five o'clock shadow, looking so Joe Blow I barely recognize him.

At the front desk, tournament directors Bill Sendell and Margo Daniels breathe a sigh of relief at another successful competition in the books, while thanking their lucky stars that Bubba's tweets didn't get more press.

Me? I'm heading back to Middle America for the first time in many moons, leaving my new warm-hearted but chichi home for some holiday tryptophan therapy at the old home course on the farm, Foxbriar G.C. For the moment I'm just about golf-satiated, the sound of irons clanking and belly laughs and tinkling wine glasses together making the universal sign of a golfer's most-wished for stocking stuffer: the off-season.

11

Mayors, Millionaires, (Life) Mulligans, and (Re)Morse East of Eastwood

The first twenty minutes of my phone conversation with Ray March—Monterey Peninsula native, author, and former Pebble Beach employee—amount to a ritual stoning. In the time it would take me to hit a small shag bag I've been told, by someone who knows, that golf writers are nothing but hacks, that none of them has the balls requisite to write critical copy, that Pebble Beach is founded on a myth created by S.F.B. Morse's propaganda machine, and that my mention of Pebble as iconic in a recent golf column only confirms my ballessness.

P.S. If I'd wanted this kind of abuse I would have called an ex-girlfriend.

P.P.S. Like the ex, there's a decent chance he's right.

It's an ironic pill to swallow, especially as the accusations that America's golf writers amount to Pebble whipping boys comes from the talented scribe (fully repentant) of a tome called *A Paradise Called Pebble Beach*, a flag-waving coffee table book copublished by Pebble Beach and *Golf Digest* in the early 1990s that shows frolicking harbor seals, gray whales a-migratin', and "a mind-boggling floor show" of California starfish . . . good stuff, but not exactly hard-hitting journalism. Marsh is peeved not just because he was relieved of his duties for what he openly calls "muckraking" reporting into the practices of the Pebble Beach Company back when he was editor of the *Carmel Pine Cone* in the mid 1990s, but also because Carmel and Pebble Beach, his homes, have changed almost beyond recognition. "I have memories of Pebble Beach being extremely underused," March tells me. "It was uncrowded. Before I really started playing golf I could go out there and hit a ball, and there wasn't anybody on the course to speak of. Even back in the mid 1960s this was true."

"The course as been a victim of the public relations effort, the drive, to make that course a money-making proposition. They've changed things around, and they always used some kind of reasoning like, 'This is what S.F.B. Morse would do.' Well, shit, what do they know? They weren't even born when S.F.B. Morse was there."

After living in Carmel-by-the-Sea off and on for most of his adult life, March and his wife up and sold their home in 2003, parlaying the equity into some serious acreage with a mountain view in Modoc, California, up in the windswept high desert where Cali, Oregon, and Nevada meet in a dry ménage à trois. There March and his wife, a former English professor, have started up a newspaper in their new whistlestop, the *Modoc Independent*, to keep the Republican ranchers on their toes. They also run a not-for-profit arts group called the Modoc Forum.

As Carmel coincidence has it, my rented flophouse turns out to be a flop shot away from where March grew up. In Carmel-by-the-Sea, which must be one of the world's space-time portals, synchronicities such as the March casa chancing to be catty corner from my granny flat are commonplace as parking tickets.

"Carmel is a village of paradoxes," Shirlie Stoddard opined in a

1950 edition of *Game & Gossip,* "chief among them the fact that the people who howl the loudest are the hardest to pry from their spot in the sun." Stoddard continues her analysis by assuming the voices of some representative Carmel types: "'I feel so cut off from the rest of the world,' mourns a woman who voluntarily cut herself off from the world. 'I hate Carmel,' says a woman who never leaves it. What people feel about Carmel, then, might be compared to the elements of an old, sordid love affair. Love is there and hate is there, but never complete indifference. And though frequent separations occur, and lovers shout, 'It's over! I'm through!' and depart, they think, forever, they always come back."

What is it, I ask March, that makes Pebble so uniquely desirable? Why do people romantically, even erotically desire it? "It's because they've been *told* it's uniquely desirable," March says, exasperated. "You had decades of public relations propaganda convincing people that it is that . . . When that company [Pebble Beach] first started, that was exactly the purpose of their public relations campaign . . . And people bought it, and they still buy it. But they don't realize that it's changed a great deal. Just how desirable is it anymore? How real is it anymore? Let's put it in perspective . . . People buy in. They buy into the hype—what's written about it, what's said about it, commentaries on television, sweeping panoramic views."

"Is it beautiful?" March poses the rhetorical question himself. "The whole Monterey Peninsula is a beautiful setting, no question about it. But somehow or another we lose sense of where that is in regard to how we value our place in this landscape."

It's the same old "It's hard to keep 'em down on the farm once they've seen gay Carmel-by-the-Sea" refrain, one that reaches well back into the halcyon days March uses for comparison. "Once upon a time there was an Alice-in-Wonderland-like village by the sea that was so wee, quaint, and lovely that everybody for miles around came to see it. And that is why Carmel-by-the-Sea today is a troubled town, wondering how it can be quaint and lovely, let alone wee." Gerald

Adams, writing for the *San Francisco Sunday Chronicle*, penned that prescient lead-in not in 2007 but in 1967, when Carmel was already enduring twenty thousand visitors a day and nearly a million a year. "Is economic success indeed bringing a kind of doom to this little enclave of white sandy beaches, artsy-craftsy shops, hand-lettered, carved signs, and quiet, cottage-bordered lanes?" Adams asked. Two years before Neil Armstrong moon-walked, San Franciscans were already fed up with Carmel kitsch and congestion, according to Adams. He quotes a pissed-off San Francisco housewife saying, "We've been so irked by the crowds for years, so we just avoid them," and a peeved Bay Area planning consultant who admits, "I never go there [Carmel] anymore."

Fast forward nearly four decades to John King who, when writing for the *San Francisco Chronicle*'s website, SFgate.com, sings verbatim the old sob song while Carmel just keeps right on ticking, hosting twice as many visitors now as it did the late sixties when Adams predicted apocalypse. King writes, "Carmel-by-the-Sea is one of those places that's so crowded, nobody goes there anymore. Most people I know head north for recreation and retreat. Their destination is the Mendocino coast, or a Sonoma town square, or a Napa weekend with mud the price of gold. Who needs whimsical cottages filled with Pebble Beach bling-bling and predictable art (look, another 'crashing waves at dusk'!)?" King's trenchant comments locate Carmel alongside places like Las Vegas and Branson, Missouri—places people like to caricature while nonetheless lining up to visit.

For the perpetuation of just this Carmel stereotype and others, March fingers the media. "Every other issue of *Sunset Magazine* tells you what a great place the Monterey Peninsula is. The whole idea of getting that golf course [Pebble Beach] on television was to promote it. They go overboard. Sometimes you have to look at it from the perspective of the people living there, eking out a living. They're working two jobs. And they're renting places somewhere outside of town. And then there's tourists who come down and say, 'You live in such a beautiful place.' How is someone supposed to appreciate it when they're working their ass off?"

Carmel makes it virtually impossible to find a reasonably priced, short-term sublet, having gone all the way to the Supreme Court to fight for and ultimately win its battle to prevent private homeowners from taking in fly-by-night renters as boarders. The *Carmel-by-the Sea A to Z Guide*, produced by the Carmel Residents' Association, is jubilant in its "R" entry for "Rental Properties," which cites the rule that no "home or subordinate unit" may be rented for less than thirty consecutive days and crows that, "This ordinance was challenged and taken all the way to the U.S. Supreme Court. The city's position prevailed." On the surface the codes insure the viability of the town's hotels, and the hotels, in return, keep the city afloat through TOT (transient occupancy tax). When Clint Eastwood was elected mayor, he called those opposed to so-called second kitchen (i.e., shorter-term) rentals a housing "gestapo" and opposed any efforts to force homeowners who took in room-and-boarders into a contract with the city that dictated who could be rented to and for how long.

To see the quiet influx of out-of-sight, out-of-town hourly labor, one need only get up early enough to see the early morning buses from Monterey disgorge their busloads of mostly Hispanic workers hired to clean up last night's mess. A second group of mostly young, attractive women arrive in the village around 9:00 a.m., well before most tourists have left their hotels. They park their cars up Mountain View and Junipero streets, their heels echoing through the Monterey pines as they hotfoot it to unlock the doors on time. These fairer-skinned shopgirls open up the retail outlets and coffee shops up and down Ocean Avenue, readying a smile for the day-trippers who'll come trickling in later in the morning. Carmel's is a high-minded, benevolent segregation. At a distance it's workable and amicable. Even the street sweeps on Ocean Avenue wear a genuine smile most days. Nobody seems to have a chip on their shoulder about it.

"It [Carmel] is one of the easiest place in the world to have a love-hate relationship with," March admits. "A lot of people don't understand what that entails . . . Frequently they'd think it's just sour grapes . . . For the most part Carmel particularly, Pebble Beach, even the golf course, have evolved and changed so much they don't come close to resembling what they were meant to be . . . Carmel has an incredibly high rate of absentee ownership. There's no residential community there anymore . . . Pebble Beach has done nothing but cash in and cash in and cash in. Granted, that was part of the purpose, but how far do you go?"

Carmel mayors past and present can't help but chuckle at the tourists who show up at council meetings still expecting the Honorable Clint Eastwood presiding. Sure, Carmel-by-the-Sea's a time warp, and a pleasant one at that, but sometimes when you're trying to govern, the Rip Van Winkle thing can be a fairy-tale pain in the ass.

The long-time mayor of the town that golf built, Sue McCloud, knows her local golf history but admits she's not a golfer, despite her dad's best efforts. As McCloud explains, "Golf was one of the first two sports, golf and baseball, played on the Carmel Point . . . We had a baseball team called the Abalone League . . . This was a summer retreat for professors from Stanford and Berkeley. And they wanted some sporting activity."

With Pebble Beach at its doorstep—a community McCloud describes as an "unincorporated area" rather than a town proper, since the vast majority of its property is privately owned—Carmel-by-the-Sea leaves the golf marketing to the Pebble Beach Company. In fact, in all things golf it's pretty laissez-faire, cooperating with Pebble on public safety and spectator paths betwixt and between, but, in general, McCloud says golf visitors here are just one part—albeit a sizable one—of the two million yearly visitors beguiled by her hamlet in the forest. "Hotel taxes used to be our number one source of revenue. It's now number two," Ms. Mayor informs me. The figures McCloud cites mark a telling shift in the golfonomics of the area, shifting the tax burden from the hotels and eateries dealing with decreasing patronage caused by the recession to well-to-do but mostly absent property owners. Property taxes now easily qualify as Carmel's number-one source of income.

In other words, Carmel-by-the-Sea is a Johnny-come-lately to the realities, fiscal and otherwise, of most municipalities. "We're a village in the forest," McCloud explains, "therefore you don't have a lot of lots, ergo we don't have streetlights . . . You do need a special permit to wear high heels in Carmel . . . What it does is it indemnifies the city. If there's a fall involved and you don't have a permit, woe is you. It's a recognition of our dark streets and uneven sidewalks and that tree roots sometimes intrude." During our conversation I make the mistake of calling the proposed public path from Carmel Beach to the lower entrance of the Pebble Beach Golf Links a sidewalk, and my faux pas gets immediately corrected. "I wouldn't say *sidewalk*," McCloud corrects me. "That conjures the idea of a cement sidewalk."

Whereas other municipalities have socked pet owners with draconian permits, doggie ghettos, and mandatory poop-scooping, Carmel has, from the beginning, rolled out the mutt welcome mat. In her locally published 1925 book, *Carmel—At Work and Play*, author, realtor, and booster Daisy Bostick observed, "Dogs are distinct and important personalities in Carmel . . . It appears to an outsider that the business section, at any hour of the day or night, contains an average of five dogs to a person." In sum, Bostick concludes, "You can scarcely be a real Carmelite without a dog." Eighty-five year later, Canine-by-the-Sea continues to market what McCloud calls a "dog-friendly atmosphere" of white sand beaches where man and master alike may frolic. In fact, the hamlet's willingness to dog-cater earns its own separate entry in *Carmel-by-the-Sea A to Z Guide*, which declares, "Many business owners are prepared to give doggy treats to our canine friends." In Carmel *Must Like Dogs* is a rule of thumb, so much so that even Dirty Harry had to answer to the pet lobby in his quest for mayordom. "I like animals, but that doesn't mean I'd go around kissing dogs," Eastwood told the *Pine Cone*

Politically, Carmel-by-the-Sea is also a freak. "Our counsel is non-partisan," McCloud explains. "We do have city politics I guess you would call that . . . But you don't run on a party position." And yet, for all Carmel's kumbaya nonpartisan rhetoric, the council is unabashedly G.O.P. "We were one of only one or two cities in the state that had a 100 percent Republican council," McCloud tells me. "Over the years that has changed as you've had more and more people who come from Silicon Valley who are senior members of their corporations, and our property values have gone up so high. I think that's brought more of a shift to the Republican side in Carmel-by-the-Sea itself."

"We don't run on a party-backed platform . . . but it so happens that those who are on the Carmel council are all Republican . . . I think it would be a big mistake if we did have party politics governing the city," McCloud tells me. "Because you don't have that much to draw as far as people who really want to be mayor these days, particularly when there's a downturn in the economy."

Translation: being mayor of Carmel-by-the-Sea is an always fraught, sometimes thankless task, as Eastwood found out when he assumed the office in a 1986 landslide vote. In very palpable ways, everyone who's followed Dirty Harry into office has done so in his shadow, a phenomenon I make sure to get McCloud's two cents on. "He [Eastwood] owns property in Carmel-by-the-Sea. And he is involved locally . . . He's very supportive of a number of things of mutual interest. When he's in town, he has a child who goes to school here. He's retained his interest in Carmel as a city," McCloud tells me.

I phone up Jean White, who ran for, and won, the mayor's race in 1988 when Eastwood's two-year term was up because, she tells me, she didn't "like the alternatives." Regarding her friend Eastwood's choice not to run for a second term, White says, "He was wise. He took his friends' advice." White claims she wasn't the least bit affected by serving in the Oscar-winner's shadow. "Clint and I were friends," she says, adding that her brother was one of his helicopter pilots. "And I love his wife, Dina."

Having grown up in Hollywood, White, the no-nonsense mayor of Carmel from '88 to '92, wasn't a candidate to wither in the Pale

Rider's shadow. "I'm not particularly impressed with the film industry . . . I used to tell Clint I didn't like any of his movies," White tells me, adding that she now likes his movie *Bird*. As for filling the Academy Award–winner's shoes as mayor, "I wasn't the least bit affected," White declares. "I don't always agree with him on things." The biggest difficulty, she recalls, came in suffering crowds that were "just like paparazzi. They would crowd into our chambers thinking Clint was still mayor . . . It's been a quarter of a century since he's been mayor. We still get older folks who ask if he's still in charge. They haven't the foggiest idea who is."

Eastwood's brief but much ballyhooed mayorship—heralded by bumper stickers that read "Go ahead, make me mayor!"—gets mixed reviews from his friend Jean White. "When Clint was mayor, he wasn't here a lot. He hired a woman to sit in the mayor's office, deciding who would and wouldn't get to see him. It created a lot of resentment in town. It wasn't the way things were supposed to work. I was much more involved than Clint would ever dream of being."

As for golf, one of Eastwood's passions and an integral public relations component of his celebrity mayorship, White is likewise nonplussed. "I know there's a hole, a green, and a tee," she confesses. At one point during our conversation she asks me what to call the people watching the tournament. "Yes, the gallery," she enthuses after I've filled in the blank. "I love the fact that the gallery is so quiet."

Politics aside, White shares a passion for Carmel with her fellow ex-mayor friend. "When I was thirteen I decided I wanted to live here," White tells me. "It's a precious place to me. I would not live anywhere else." Like every mayor of Carmel from Eastwood to McCloud, she was paid a small stipend, $200 per month, for innumerable hours of work. "It pays just enough to pay for your clothes at the cleaners," she says, agreeing with McCloud that it's getting harder and harder to find diverse candidates who aren't simply retired or independently wealthy but who are still qualified to tackle the complicated issues facing the town. "Clint and I were the only mayors in the past forty years who were still wage-earners," White reminds me.

While golf may be Carmel's calling card, the biggest issue facing Sue McCloud is Sacramento's proposed cap on water consumption on the Peninsula. A chronic shortage of agua in this semi-arid climate means Carmel residents must be encouraged to plant drought-resistant "xerophytic landscaping" — the sole "X" entry in the *A to Z Guide.*

Carmel pulls its H_2o from the 36-mile-long Carmel River which, year by year, is drying up due to the alleged overpumping of the Carmel aquifer that consequently endangers the steelhead trout, on whose behalf widely publicized "fish rescues" have become the norm. Steelhead conservation associations have filed suit and the California Water Resources Control Board has moved to curb overpumping, leaving Carmel between the devil and the deep blue sea, quite literally, or at least between a dam and a proposed desalination plant. "We try to talk reason into some of them to show what would happen if you tried to cut usage to 70 gallons per person per day," McCloud says of the proposed restrictions. "We have probably the best water conservation in the state. There's a 193-gallon average in the state, and it's around 250 in Sacramento, and yet they're ready to lower the boom on us."

Carmel faces, on a grander scale, the core issue facing all prosperous historic communities: how to open the door without inviting the flood. "One of our greatest challenges is, How do you keep Carmel Carmel," McCloud tells me. "There are fewer and fewer of us who were really raised here."

Since its inception, Carmel has always been about second homes, a word whose definition has evolved over the years as the owners of vacation homes have visited less and less frequently. "It sounds like deep dark history," March tells me, "but lots of people used to come for the summer. They'd rent a house or a bungalow and stay the whole season . . . They weren't weekenders, or one-day trippers driving down from San Jose."

Even in its immigration, the fairy-tale village has enjoyed a historically privileged position, with its hard-to-come-by lots and highly competitive real-estate markets allowing it to recruit certain immigrants and discourage others. Encouraged early on were professors and other middle-class professionals from Berkeley and Palo Alto. San Francisco, too, supplied its share of émigrés, especially in the years following the San Francisco earthquake, Carmel being exactly the kind of place you think of retreating after a disaster, whether personal, corporate, or natural.

March's family bought a piece of the dream-by-the-sea when Ray was a freshman in high school, moving from nearby Monterey to a house on Santa Fe, between Ocean Avenue and Mountain View. It was his mother's greatest wish to call a lot in the handsome village her own, and back then it could be had for a song. The March family bought its slice of heaven for $10,000 in 1949, and afforded the mortgage on mom's hourly wages as an occasional secretary at the naval postgraduate school and dad's income as clothier in town.

Like yachts and plantations, Carmel's houses are named—nothing so pedestrian as a street number for a town settled by artists and freethinkers. "To help identify locations," reads the *Carmel-by-the-Sea A to Z Guide*, "Carmel cottages often are given names such as *Tinker Bell, Doll House, This Is It*, and its next door neighbor, *This Isn't*."

The March bungalow was called *Papoose*. It was a stucco affair, Ray recalls, and a few years after their arrival the family moved just down the street to the house on the corner with the walled garden, a pitching wedge away from the famous Forest Theater. March would have been close enough to the outdoor amphitheater to go to bed listening to Hamlet deliver his agonized soliloquy each night. All around him were other kids his age and younger, a palette of age-diverse playmates that the few kids in today's Carmel-by-the-Sea would kill for. "They varied from middle class to the very wealthy," March tells me. "There were no real class distinctions. There were kids in our class whose fathers were writers . . . This was a writing and artistic community. It wasn't unusual to go to someone's house and be in a rather eccentric environment."

When March and Bobby Clampett were growing up here, they might have gone home to play with one of the grandchildren of poet Robinson Jeffers, who lived in Tor House, the wonderfully weird stone cottage he built with his own two hands and into which he embedded all manner of artistic bells and whistles—secret passageways, rare stones from around the world, miniature peepholes allowing for clandestine, spyglass views of Carmel Bay. Carmel was one big rumpus room, a place where kids roughhoused under the watchful eyes of the village that raised them. "There was always things to do," March says. "And most of it was outdoors."

To hear March and others of his generation tell it, the Carmel-by-the-Sea of the 1950s and 1960s felt more Mayberry than Monterey. High school graduating classes did well to surpass one hundred students. Today's Carmel-by-the-Sea, by contrast, has no public schools within its borders and buses kids to school and back. "The school was so small, every able-bodied boy went out for sports . . . It gave all of us a wonderful background in sportsmanship and teamwork," March remembers, recalling Coach Mosolf in particular, the man who taught most of the village how to swim. Meanwhile, Carmel's Barney Fifes were merciful with the town's juvies. "The police all knew me," March confesses. "That was a virtue because if you did a prank or borrowed someone else's car for a day without telling them, you didn't go to juvenile court. You were told to put it back." In sum, Carmel felt normal back then to Ray and his cronies, on par with the rest of America. "It was never boring. I never saw it as conservative. I was just a typical teenager not doing very well in high school."

One of the kid highlights each year was the Crosby Clambake. To hear March tell it, it was like Carnivale, a passel of celebrities with their strange fashions and stellar ways descending on a quiet, middle-class town in need of an annual shakeup. "Crosby put up $10,000, and he brought his pals, and it was a fun tournament," March says of the forerunner to the AT&T Pro-Am, which functioned as a fundraiser for the Carmel Youth Center. "The kids put up a van up there on top of the knoll where your drive should be off the eighth tee. That was the location where Coach Mosolf sold hotdogs."

The success of the Clambake, Derr Bing wrote in a 1951 open letter published in *Game and Gossip*, was "fantastic when you consider the distance from Pebble Beach to any good-sized metropolis. It adequately demonstrates what can be done by American communities when they feel wholeheartedly in the merit of any civic enterprise." Back at the WalMart First Tee Open I'd chatted with Ollie Nutt, president and C.E.O. of the 501C3 that carried on from the Crosby Youth Fund back in the 1970s, and he'd echoed Bing's sentiments: "There's a terrific spirit of volunteerism in the community going back to when I came here in 1947 . . . We have fifty volunteers with over forty years of service. It's incredible the loyalty we have here," he told me. Nutt's golf-based charitable foundation is the largest grantor in Monterey County, bar none, and provided $7 million in seed money to start the local First Tee chapter, for which Clint Eastwood serves as chair.

Ray March moved back to Carmel in 1993 with his second wife, Barbara, in time to see the last gasp of the middle-class life he'd known as a child. "The cost of living beat us up," March recalls of his return. In the wake of Eastwood's high-publicity mayorship of the fairy-tale-by-the-sea and smack dab in the middle of the dot.com boom, new money began pouring into the tiny village in a torrent so fast and furious no one quite knew what to do with it. "So they've got all this computer money, and the prices went sky high," March says, describing the deluge. "It became artificial. They're bidding on front lawns, with essentially paper money. Locals started getting priced out . . . Next thing you know it's very important what kind of car you're driving, or whether you belong to a certain club, or whether you run with certain people."

It's an old Carmel-going-to-the-dogs story, one that predates the dot.com boom by twenty five years, easy, as suggested by Adams's 1967 nostalgic assertion that the newer tourist "is no longer typified by the schoolteacher driving a Hillman Minx, but rather the very nice guy who works for Ford or IBM and comes down in his new Chevrolet to enjoy the beach and the motels." By the mid 1990s, March tells me, "the property values went so high the working stiffs couldn't afford to live in Carmel anymore. The artists couldn't afford to live there anymore, so they found somewhere else to go. What used to be a society based on wealth turned into a society based on interest in causes."

I'd seen March's perspective firsthand when, on the insistence of my landlady, I'd attended Carmel's famed annual civic celebration, a combination Halloween march and birthday bash, the town having been born on the eve of All Hallows. The kiddies in the parade of ghouls that had proceeded up San Carlos and down Ocean Ave had donned the traditional costumes—Arabian princesses, pirates, GI Joes, witches, devils, superheroes with washboard abs, and Jedi Knights—but the adults had come dressed as walking lobbyists, including two dudes covered head to toe in plastic bags representing the "Don't Trash California" gospel and wielding banners that read "Paper, plastic, or planet?" Dog advocacy clubs followed closely on their heels: the local rescue greyhound chapter, the King Charles Spaniel Club, and the Daschund Club. The wiener dogs had been slathered with faux condiments and sprinkled with lettuce on top. Next had come the corgis wearing devil horns akimbo.

Ever danced with a corgi by the pale moonlight?

I test March's homegrown housing hypotheses by visiting 17-Mile Drive open houses on sunny, autumnal weekends when the profit motive causes local realtors to throw open the gates to some of the Peninsula's most exclusive homes. My interest isn't all a put-on. I've become sufficiently drunk on my adopted, albeit temporary, hometown that I've prematurely begun scheming ways to return after my U.S. Open year is in the books. My infatuation is underscored by the fact that every time I thumb through an issue of *Pebble Beach Magazine* I flip to realtor Tom Bruce's smiling mug and full-page ad. Bruce ranks in the top 1 percent of Coldwell Banker sales associates, the literature tells me. I've walked by his office, located among the shops at the Pebble Beach Lodge, a few dozen times, and his ad has become mantric: "As you revel in the world-class golf courses, enjoy the beaches, breathe in the vibrant air, and chuckle at the antics of sea lions, seals, and otters, your mind and heart begin a dialogue. You may say to yourself, 'This is one of the most breathtaking and prestigious locations in the world. Maybe we should have a home here! But how do we make that happen?'"

By the 1930s Sam Morse's crack team of wordsmiths at the Del Monte Properties Company had found the magic words that would bring prospective home-buyers by the droves. *Game and Gossip* ads trumpeted, "A springtime climate that varies less than 10 degrees throughout the year . . . 20,000 acres of forests, hills, and streams . . . two internationally known golf courses . . . mile after mile of scenic highways . . . association with leaders in the worlds of Art, Literature, Music, Sports, and Business . . . every modern home convenience . . . health *by the sky-ful* for you and all your family."

On Friday mornings I pore over each new edition of the *Carmel Pine Cone* real-estate supplement, where the village's homely, million-dollar haciendas rub shoulders with the 10-mill-plus pleasure palaces up at Pebble. Highlighter and French roast in hand, I set up shop at a sun-dappled, hibiscus-bordered corner of Carmel Plaza, searching in vain for Carmel homes under $500,000. Meanwhile, I float a Plan B by my landlady that involves the perpetual lease of my granny flat and weekly red-eyes from Iowa or Chicago to Carmel for long week-ends—contemplating the very absenteeism that makes Ray March sick. My landlady, trying to be encouraging, tells about one of her friends, who makes the opposite commute, flying from Carmel to Chicago every week for business before returning for weekend R and R.

Mecca that she be, Carmel-by-the-Sea has a way of making you ask, "What If?" What if I say to my boss, "Go ahead, punk, make my day," slam the door behind me, and set up shop on the Monterey P., never to look back? What if I find a vacation home on the cheap and groom my game for the PGA Tour Q-School?

Today's open-house docket features an estate of nearly 5,000 square feet of polished stone. If I could just come up with the chump-change asking price of around seven mil, my shrink-wrapped *Golf Digests* would suddenly arrive at 17-Mile Drive . . . none too shabby a mailing address. The house's west-facing windows overlook the sixteenth fairway and, beyond, Stillwater Cove. In short, this is, as the propaganda sheet claims, the "real Pebble Beach."

I'm exuding shabby chic on this sun-kissed Sabbath—the only kind of chic I can afford. I'm wearing a University of Iowa t-shirt, pumpkin orange in color, and jeans. Overtop I sport my farming father's old, smoke-infused gray wool sports coat to suggest monied eccentricism. A temperate breeze blows from the backyard pool past me toward the links and out to sea.

The house I'm looking at, a second home, is empty save for appliances, window treatments, and closet organizers. It screams conspicuous consumption and soul-sucking largesse of the William Randolph Hearst kind. My footfalls echo as I round the corner into the kitchen, where the realtor gives me a wilting glance that says, "What are you really doing here, partner? You and I both know you can't afford this place."

I should have the ego strength to return serve on the withering look, but I don't. Instead, his I-see-right-through-you has me groping for my prefab explanation: I'm looking for a home on behalf of my father, who recently sold the bulk of our Iowa farm (sadly true), who would like to be closer to his son living in Carmel (somewhat true), and who is an avid golfer (erstwhile true) and wants out of the Snow Belt (too true!). I admit that this place—I motion around me to the marble and stainless steel kitchen—is "probably a bit over his budget." It's the whitest of lies, but it gets the realtor talking.

"What I like best about the kitchen," he tells me, "is there's two of everything." The dude's right . . . two sinks, two restaurant-size refrigerators, two ovens. It's the Noah's Ark of galleys.

I ask him why two. "One word for you," my host tells me. "Catering."

Having two of everything, he informs me, means the homeowner can wash a few token artichokes in one sink while the caterer wrestles a pot of steaming water in the other. Ditto for the perishables vis-à-vis the twin fridges.

The route by which this pleasure dome has come on the market—though it was built just four years ago with what the literature describes as "an incredible attention to detail and selection of materials"—is an all-too-familiar one in recessionary Pebble Beach: the owner, from the Bay Area, built the 1-acre Shangri-la in the boom years, expecting to spend weekends away from the San Fran hustle and bustle. He built according to his exact specifications—a mixture of no-maintenance mahogany walls and drywall painted the palette of salt water taffy. The casa boasts bathrooms for each of four bedrooms, plenty of closet space, Japanese tapestries depicting roly-poly Asians riding elephants and rams rumpusing through rice paddies. Then the bottom dropped out of the stock market and the rest is history. The not-so-hard-pressed seller has already shaved a cool three mil off the asking price.

I follow the only other "interested party" here for today's showing down the halls, making sure not to crowd them. The realtor tells me my "competition" hails from Texas, from whence the greatest demand for homes in Pebble originates outside of the Bay Area and the Central Valley. I duck into one of the smaller back bedrooms and the realtor follows. The windows overlook the back courtyard, where water from a small, raised hot tub cascades, waterfall-style, into the swimming pool.

"Let's play the food game with this room," he says.

Indoor food games have never turned out well for me, I tell him.

"What food does this room remind you of? The color, I mean."

He points to the sorta pink, sorta orange walls. I shrug.

"Most people say peach, and I ask them, 'You ever eaten a peach this color?'"

He's got a good point there.

"When I come into this room" — he folds his arms over his chest for dramatic effect — I think salmon pâté."

"Of course!" I say it with the eureka tone one might use when recalling a *mot juste*. In fact, I'm no closer to enlightenment than I'd been before our little guessing game commenced. I've never seen salmon pâté, let alone swallowed it.

The couple from Texas meets us in the hallway bottleneck, where the four of us jaw about the place for a few tics. The hubby claims the "ah-ha" of the place, as he puts it, is its exquisite tile work. The wife grumps that the pool looked bigger in the website pic. I'm thinking they're going to pass on this Showcase Showdown.

Real estate, just like golf, operates on a completely different planet here. Sure, what I'm dipping my feet into on this fine Monterey weekend is the same game of buyer-seller cat-and-mouse taking place at the tens of thousands of late-season open houses held this weekend in places like Wichita and Poughkeepsie, except that the big-ticket item on the selling block in each instance — the home — couldn't be more different. This hacienda's not about barbecuing with the neighbors or raising a small family. It's about keeping the madding crowds at bay — to wit, the wordsmithery in mi casa's glossy brochure: "Mahogany walls and ceiling design work enhance the sense of solitude and privacy," and "not visible from the street . . . a hot tub and pool await your undisturbed moments of self-indulgence."

The longer I linger here the more shame I feel for taking time away from the real prospective buyers from Texas, who have a legit shot at owning a deeply discounted piece of the Pebble dream. Finally, when I can stand it no longer, I break huddle, begging pardons, drifting toward the white marble front stoop, and, beyond, my blessedly thrifty car.

A couple of weeks later I repeat the experiment, telling myself not to be such a goddamn chicken, conjuring the self that delights in costumery — my inner Bill Murray. At the very least, my second round of house-shopping reflects my good taste: I'm ogling a two-story affair, just across 17-Mile Drive from Pebble so close that I could take a spirited leak off the balcony and nearly hit the thirteenth tee. Once again, I've lucked into another "motivated seller"—the very realtor who's today showing me the "built to look old" never-lived-in spec home.

The house offers the usual Pebble nouveau-riche gauche: oil paintings in crimson and gold depicting fields abloom in what looks like Provence. Showerheads the size of dinner plates, bidets in nearly every bathroom—the cumulative effect calculated to make you forget you're not living along the French Riviera.

Nearly everything I touch—no matter where I go I insist on my God-given right to squeeze the Charmin—is fake. The limestone above the fireplace is prepackaged and precut to fit. The limes in the fruit bowl, the wood in the fireplaces . . . as faux as the late Michael Jackson's nose. The realtor follows me room to room, her voice echoing under the cathedral ceilings as she lists off the amenities. I confess I'm currently living in Carmel and she nods, as if empathizing with my plight. "The only reason I go to Carmel is to one or two restaurants and the beach. It's a whole other world up here. It's so peaceful," she says, her blue eyes widening.

After Ray March "fell from journalism grace," as he puts it—by which he means swapping a shit desk job at what he describes as a "Chamber of Commerce" newspaper in Salinas for the executive suite at Pebble Beach Co. and a new title as assistant to the director of advertising and public relations—he was taken under wing by his immediate supervisor, Gwen Graham. Graham and her new assistant shared the suite with the Big Boss, the legendary Samuel B. Morse, and then-president of the Del Monte Company, Tim Michaud. "It was a fun time," March says, chuckling. "You know, some detours can be pretty. If anything, Gwen didn't know exactly what to do with me. She'd been a one-woman operation for many years . . . and was very much a part of helping create some of the original policies of the Pebble Beach Company, which at that time was the Del Monte Company." I interrupt to ask how a small-time, small-town reporter goes from the yeoman's work of news reporting in a farm town to a scribbling gig for the golf and leisure holy of holies. "I was a local boy," he explains. "I had already worked at the *Monterey Herald*. The president of Del Monte Property Company wanted to bring in people like myself who were younger and build a new image."

"You've got remember," March continues, "Morse was still alive and just in the adjacent office. Virtually everything emanated from him in terms of taste, image, and strategy." Graham had been hired in the years after World War II to help Pebble rebuild its client base after the ravages of the Depression and the depletion of the war. Twenty years later, Morse was once again looking for new blood, and new ideas, and someone to assume the aging Graham's mantle. Enter Ray March.

In assuming the new post, the young assistant was getting an education not in how to be a journalist but in how to be an elite player. "When I worked at Pebble Beach, I bought into the whole picture. It was a good, decadent life. You played tennis. You went to the beach. You went to parties. You played dominos. You ate at Club XIX." I interrupt him to ask how a middle-class kid from Carmel felt about all this high-hog living. "It was contrary to who I was," he admits. "I was basically a journalist and a writer. But you end up putting on a front that's not you to keep up appearances."

Ironically, March wasn't a serious golfer at the time, instead favoring tennis, which had helped pay his way through college when he'd worked as an assistant pro at Golden Gate Park in San Francisco. He remembers the links then being part of a larger social fabric that included the tennis club and the beach club. "It [Pebble Beach] wasn't so sacrosanct. You could walk your dog or take walks on it. In high school we used to sneak on the course."

In taking a desk alongside Graham, the young March also came into close contact with the Duke of Del Monte. "He was very gruff and brusque," March recalls of Morse. "He would come into the offices and say 'Good morning' to everybody. You didn't particularly question him." Things in the executive suite at the Del Monte Company in the late sixties pretty much worked the way they did in any dukedom: the underlings toiled away at the pleasure of their aristocratic leader, trying hard not to rock the boat or walk the plank and bracing themselves for the inevitable big blow. Working for an autocrat, however benign, meant that March found himself tasked with some rather unorthodox duties, including minding interviews with Morse, who loved to confront journalists with their own idiocy, and witnessing Morse's will, twice. "He was a very hands-on guy," March remembers. "When I say I witnessed his will . . . remember that Pebble Beach has always been a Republican enclave and his [Morse's] own son, Jack Morse, used to brag that he, Jack, was the only Democrat in Pebble Beach. Every time he [S.F.B.] would get pissed off at Jack, he would change his will."

March draws up another memory from his distant past with the Duke that illustrates not only Morse's controlling personality but the breadth and prescience of his vision: "One day he was looking for the forester, Otis . . . Morse is in the middle of the office complex, and he's really only talking to his executive secretary, but he knows he's really talking to everyone because they can hear him even though they can't see him. He said, 'When you see Otis, you tell him to quit planting those trees in straight lines. Nature doesn't put trees in straight lines!'"

Just as March was beginning to get cozy in the Dukedom, Pebble's head tennis pro up and quit, and he jumped at the chance to have a racket rather than a pen in hand. He assumed the position on an interim basis, shaping the job and its duties into what eventually became a de facto director of sports. By the end of his tenure March had pretty much seen Pebble from every angle. "I had the opportunity," he tells me, "from an insider's point of view, to witness company strategy, company philosophy."

March stayed on until Gwen Graham's death in 1969, when the company, in his words, began to "aggressively pursue a more commercial direction in their public relations." They hired an outside candidate to be the next director of advertising and marketing, and March took that as a sign to move on.

Fifteen years later, after sundry reporting gigs including a job covering the Los Angeles Olympics for an executive editor friend at the *Los Angeles Herald-Examiner*, Ray and Barbara March moved back to Carmel to do what most mid-career freelancers do—pitch pieces to glossy magazines while keeping a long list of rejections. A friend suggested that Ray and Barbara—nongolfers both—add golf writing to their repertoire, pointing out that March lived at the nexus of a travel and golf mecca. The Marchs soon found their Carmel-by-the-Sea return address alone earned them extra credibility in the eyes of golf and travel editors, but while they took advantage of their geographic clout, they were never fully comfortable with the high-dollar, highball, high-society golfing life on whose reputation they were trading. "You go through rationalizations," March admits. "First of all, as a freelance writer I was able to take and capitalize on the Monterey Peninsula by being on the Monterey Peninsula . . . Life can be very good there as long as you can live it honestly and consciously and not get caught up in the phoniness."

Though fifteen years of water has passed under the bridge since March's firing from his post as *Pine Cone* editor (for what he admits was muckraking into the practices of the Pebble Beach Company), he adheres to his belief that Pebble Beach has taken on what he calls "false airs," mythologizing and sanitizing its own origins and profit motive and hiding behind the cover of being a public golf course open to anyone. "I think that in the past Pebble might have been considered elitist, but today I don't think it's elitist," he explains. "They're the first ones who will tell you that they're the only public course that's used in the U.S. Open rotation, when in fact they price themselves out of being a public course. I don't believe that it [Pebble Beach] is available to everybody. It's been thriving off the huge wave that has crashed, called capitalism."

I interrupt March to ask what's wrong with the handsome

philanthropists I see pictured in the black tie, white zin affairs splashed across the glossy pages of *Carmel Magazine* each month and where recent, featured, full-page fêtes have included the Make-a-Wish Starry Night Dinner Auction (for children with disabilities), Pink Poker Night (for women's medical funds), Meals on Wheels Classique d'Elegance, the A.G. Davi Real Estate's White Party (for Big Brothers Big Sisters), and the Living Breath Foundation Gala (for cystic fibrosis sufferers).

He explains his objections to the fundraiser parties by analogy. "In the forties, Salvador Dali could throw a party at the Del Monte Hotel, and it's a weird party, and it's a lot of fun. They [the guests] are there for that purpose only." March is kosher with that model: the talented and beautiful—which in the Pebble Beach ball masques included the likes of Jean Harlow, Clark Gable, and Frank Capra—getting together, sans shame or apology, to party like it's 1939. What he's not okay with is the opposite: the new, more highly "evolved" Carmel that still parties hardy but hides behind a cause to do it.

"What happens . . . is this incredible level of pretense. People pretend they have more money than they have. It's a superficial kind of wealth. It's a superficial status. A superficial society . . . They may not give a rat's shit about some charity . . . It's just an excuse to go to the party and be seen." Carmel itself, according to March, has become nothing more than an inflated, hyped-up brand name that hangers-on and wannabes glom on to, the diametric opposite of the virtues of a classless utopian society writer Daisy Bostick praised as the calling cards of 1925 Carmel, where "ten cents is as good as yesterday's dollar" and "things that mattered so vitally in cities—bank accounts, conventional clothing, keeping up appearances—seem no longer of much importance." By June of 1973, however, according to the article "The Lure of Carmel," Carmel had already grown too big for its britches. "The few shops, galleries, restaurants and inns of the past era used to have the 'live-and-let-live attitude,'" the article lamented. "There was no rivalry. Everyone was sane . . . Today the story is different—the competition is keen—so keen that it's enough to drive one crazy!"

"If someone says to you, Where are you from, and you say 'I'm from Carmel,'" March reiterates, reciting an oft-faced scenario here, "what's the first impression that person is going to get? They're going to think you've got money. That's not always true. But you don't say, 'I'm from Carmel, but I don't have any money.' You say 'I'm from Carmel,' and you let them think you do. Now that's dishonest. And I accuse myself of dishonesty in that regard."

March maintains that Pebble Beach has devolved into a society based on pretence, branding, and façade. He points out that in the beginning, Pebble didn't engage in sleight of hand. It was, as March puts it, "an exclusive retreat for the wealthy and the celebrity," and it made no bones about it. "When they started the old hotel at Del Monte, that was the whole point, to bring in the wealthy, the socially accepted, the celebrity, then start promoting the real estate around it. Del Monte Properties had, since its inception, been about real estate. Golf was just one of the tools that was used . . . to develop housing tracts. That's what Pebble Beach is . . . a high-dollar housing tract."

Anger, real anger, bubbles up when March talks about the profile of the guys—and sometimes gals—who fill today's Pebble tee times. "Who are these guys?" March asks rhetorically. "They're basically high handicappers with high expense accounts. What do they know? They come away saying, 'Man, I played Pebble.'" To illustrate, March says that the new prototypical Pebble hacker is, for instance, a "guy who sells more cars than somebody else" and is rewarded by the company with a trip to golf la-la-land. That guy, he says, contrasts sharply with the visionary entrepreneur of the 1930s or 1940s who played Pebble because, say, he owned the Firestone Company rather than merely sold cars off the lot.

"The people behind it [Pebble] and the people who go to it on expense accounts have bought into the myth," he says. "It's overrated." When finally he says the words—the words that shall not be spoken—I almost gasp, and March seems suddenly tired and old, as if he's been building up to this conclusion all along and now that it's said, he's spent.

His conclusion makes me anxious, not so much because I'm unwilling to allow the notion that Pebble's worth may be inflated but because I realize my own uneasiness with his sentiments in part makes his point—that folks have become afraid to see Pebble as anything other than the best course in America, if not the world. "It's an overrated course," he says again. "They've built it into a myth. And so when a golf writer refers to Pebble Beach twice in the same story, it should be the total reverse of that."

The "golf writer" March conjures is me. He's referring to a recent article of mine in which I wrote that an Irish seaside course I reviewed compared favorably with Pebble at a fraction the price. For March, even my mention of Pebble as the standard of comparison makes me "one of them . . . a sell-out." And, as such, he sees fit to close our conversation with the same dig he began it with.

My talk with the deeply thoughtful March leaves me in a conflicted place, both about Carmel and about Pebble. I do believe that Pebble Beach is one of the greatest courses in the world, and that Carmel-by-the-Sea is a uniquely world-class destination. I do appreciate Pebble's openness to the public, even considering the exorbitant expense. I do think the company is well-run and well-intentioned, caught in the double bind likewise faced by its host city, namely, having one foot necessarily in the past and the other in its future as an environmentally friendly, community-minded organization. Yet, for all this, March's story of the Pebble Beach and Carmel-by-the-Sea of old, so closely coincident with the accounts of Jean White and Sue McCloud and many others I've talked to who love this place, makes me think theirs is no mere, and no mean, nostalgia.

12

Swinging in the New Year

High Balls, Catcalls, and Last Calls at
Ye Olde Crosby Clambake

Carmel-by-the-Sea, bless it, is like the needy ex everyone but me seems to have—it can always be returned to, consequences-free. Sure, in January it's a little mussed, a little windblown and worse-for-the wear, but it'll still throw on a blouse and meet you in a few.

A few weeks into the New Year, Carmel shakes itself out like a cat after a bath, stretches languidly, and purrs about its next 365 days of laid-back glamour. Round about Groundhog Day, Ocean Avenue begins to bustle again . . . not the bustle of summer, but a quiet bustle—a *qustle*. On balmy days, when the winter sun shines, shopkeepers open their Dutch doors again, courting the ideal recreators—folks with deep pockets and time to kill—who arrive early for the AT&T National Pro-Am.

Meanwhile, the gaggle of fair-weather Carmelites who skipped town for warmer, drier climes over the hols—"winter," as they comically call it here—have returned, rested and plucky. They're almost smug, these snowbirds, returning to their semi-deserted, full-amenity Wonderland with the same relish with which residents of college towns look forward to summer. Winter means they've got the Peninsula's largess to themselves. *Mine . . . it's all mine!* their faces seem to say.

As in any absentee resort town, sometimes we snowbirds—alas, this year, newly returned from the frozen Midwest, I have to include myself under that ironic umbrella—return to a few surprises: shingles blown off the roof, a broken window, a raccoon in the crawl space. My surprise is that I have no space. Granny has lost her flat!

With the stock market doing more flips than Cirque de Soleil, my landlady rented out my little studio during my holiday absence to a scientist guy who's studying the polar ice caps. Just hearing about the dude who's now sleeping under my borrowed quilts and egregiously stuffed pillows makes me jealous. He's young and saving penguins, and I can't even save par.

Even though I had been bracing myself for it, the news comes as a blow. I had bought so deeply into the Carmel fantasy that I had tricked myself into believing Granny of Granny Flat would live forever in her room littered with the moldering hulls of honey-roasted peanuts. I believed mine would be a permanent foothold and that, like in the movie *Groundhog Day*, each day I'd awaken to sun-kissed Monterey pines, light sea breezes, and a cup of Fog Lifter brewed special for me by Mira down the hill at Carmel Coffee and Cocoa Co.

Fortunately for me, my enterprising host has a solution: for an agreed-upon fee she'll rent me out another room for a spell—this one in the Big House proper. The desperation karma of the deal troubles me, as I find myself unable to decide whether the mistress of the house is doing me a favor out of the kindness of her heart or desperately carving up her casa piece by income-generating piece to stave off a financial crisis. The wing of the bungalow in question boasts a couch, a small gas fireplace—perfect for those damp, cold nights after coming home from Pebble—and access to the main kitchen with its plentiful supply of distilled water and Trader Joe's morsels. There are, however, a couple of catches. I'll be sharing a bathroom with my hostess—my marks for personal hygiene and overall cleanliness are among the lowest ever assigned by Swiss judges—and I'll be sharing my suite with one very nosey, mildly disabled, very territorial, exceedingly large, and, yes, occasionally sweet cat by name of Huckleberry.

To which I say, baggage in hand, *Done.* In Carmel, a bird in the bush is a roof over your head . . . or something like that. Though I'll feel the wet-nosed, sandpaper kiss of my feline companion in nights to come—nights I'll lie awake wondering if I have in fact remembered to leave the kitchen door cracked so that Huck can reach its litter box, nights I'll wonder whether a cold floor should in fact set me back the same number of shekels per night as a Super 8 back home—I'll still, stretched out on the yoga mat and foam pad, count my lucky stars I'm not instead covering up with kelp on Carmel Beach.

The locals prophesy "AT&T weather" this year, but no one's quite sure what that means. Some dispense the phrase as a pejorative signifying the preternaturally stormy, broody, downright hostile weather that once delayed the completion of the famed February Pro-Am till August and blew a full-throttle blimp backward. Others deploy the moniker like a chamber of commerce mantra intimating brochure-worthy climatological conditions. AT&T weather, whatever it means, is so open to interpretation it might as well be a statement from the federal reserve. Of Mother Nature's uncertain intentions the second week of February, Bob Hope once wrote in his golf memoir, *Confessions of a Hooker,* "The weather at the Crosby is always so chancy the family sends, with its invitations, small-craft warnings. I played in it for years with thirteen clubs and a life raft." In 1962 golf pro Jimmy Demaret awoke to snow on the ground and said, "I knew I got loaded last night, but how did I wind up at Squaw Valley?"

It's been a wet, wacky winter on the California coast—newsworthy wacky. In January snow flew in San Fran, and lent the 3,500-foot tippy top of Monterey County's Mount Toro the look of a snow-capped mountain in a beer commercial. But storms, like marital bliss and alimony, come and go around here, and with a forecast of mostly sunny skies for the run of the tournament, we are suddenly bullish about "AT&T Weather."

Once again I have managed to score a press pass to cover the fabled Crosby Clambake, calling into serious question the Bob Marleyism, "You can fool some of the people sometime, but you can't fool all the people all the time." Honestly, I feel a little performance anxiety being back in my adopted hometown during a week that's arguably more famous for men behaving badly than for cleanly-struck woods, this being the selfsame occasion when one of the heaviest of the heavy Clambake drinkers, actor-bandleader and Bing sidekick Phil Harris, one year officially declared his membership in the Jack Daniels Country Club. The pressure I feel is something akin to the impossible expectations of a first night on Bourbon Street or the Vegas Strip. In idle moments I've found myself asking if I shouldn't be upholding the standard of my gender and my profession by drinking a G&T with sportswriter pals at CBS on-course commentator David Feherty's favorite gin joint (in his drinking days), Jack London's, or sucking down ribs at the legendary watering hole Eastwood once owned, the Hog's Breath, or telling Tiger tales at the local newsies' favorite place, Brophie's.

AT&T week, like Mardi Gras, will do that to you, even if conventional wisdom holds it's not the same as it used to be. Back at the First Tee Open, U.S. Open champ and ABC Sports/ESPN golf broadcaster Andy North had grinned a big grin when I'd asked about the old days of the Clambake. He'd recalled epic storms rolling in, killer fogs, and guys falling off cliffs like chapter and verse out of some berserk Viking holy book. "Sinatra, Crosby, Hope, and those guys. It was an amazing, amazing time in our careers. I'm glad I was able to do it when stars were stars," he'd said. I'd interrupted North to ask about Bill Murray and George Lopez, and he'd replied, "Trust me, it's not the same. Those guys were just frickin' stars." Then good ol' gray-haired, Wisconsin-square Andy North had looked me right in the eye to say, "Whatever stories you've heard are true."

Even the AT&T fight stories seem lit up with rock 'em sock 'em roustabout nostalgia. Perhaps the most famous fisticuffs flew between Frank Sinatra and S.F.B. Morse's son-in-law and then-president of the Del Monte Company. That jam got Ol' Blue Eyes banned from the forest by decree of the Duke of Del Monte. An even better and lesser known golf club/fight club story happened in 1947, the first year Derr Bing moved his celebrity pro-am north from Rancho Santa Fe to Pebble Beach. The *Oakland Tribune* splashed news of the golfer-on-golfer violence across the front page of its January 13, 1947, sports pages with the headline, "Cocoran Plans Action in Carmel Row." In a nutshell, the so-called Battle of Carmel tiff went like this: PGA Tour bureau manager Freddie Corcoran had the shit beat out of him by veteran PGA Tour pro Dick Metz right in front of Sadie's Restaurant in Carmel with little more than an overcoat on his back and a portfolio in his hand. Corcoran, the golf bureaucrat, ended up on the losing end of the Kansas pro's fists, landing in Carmel Community Hospital with a mouth full of loose teeth and a bummer concussion.

When I'd asked U.S. Open champ Jerry Pate about the later, wild and wooly days of the Clambake circa Eastwood and Lemmon and Sean Connery, his response had sounded so conspiratorial it bordered on Congressional testimony: "I knew them well," he'd said, changing the subject. Andy Bean, who won the 1979 Pro-Am with his partner, Bill Bunting, was one of the lucky son of bitches allowed to run with the law firm of Eastwood, Lemmon, and Connery. "I can't tell you how many pairs of shoes I've had melted to my fireplace here," Bean had told me, issuing the single most enigmatic golf quote I've ever heard. "Playing with Clint and Sean Connery was something else . . . Connery prided himself on playing well, and once I said something about 'I think you better knock the hell out of a 3-wood,' and he says"—here Bean does an impression of Connery as spot-on as Darrell Hammond's on SNL—"'Son, I'm gonna show you a golf shot.' He hit a 4-wood, drew it in, and bounced it on the green."

After his round, Bean would meet the boys at Jack London's or the

Hog's Breath for a chaser and a recap of the round's most ridiculous or inspired shots. "I think I played . . . not up to what I could have played," the good-natured Bean drawled. "You know when you're playing with Clint and Connery . . . for a while there every hundred yards the girls would say . . . " Bean had then told me what the girls used to say, following it with a grin and a "but we won't print that."

Hearing the game's legends talk about the sixties and seventies Crosby Clambake is a bit like hearing your pop reliving his college exploits: part of you's dying to know how much better the good old days really were while the other part wants to cover your ears for fear you won't be able to live up to the old man's standard in depravity and devolution.

With so many stellar memories, nostalgia runs rampant where the AT&T is concerned. Shuttling down from San Jose to the Peninsula I'd overheard a gray-hair telling her seatmate she'd be watching the tourney again this year on TV as a protest. Ever since the days when picnics became verboten on the links, she couldn't be bothered to attend. Ray March had sounded the same nostalgic chord during our phone conversation. "It [the AT&T Pro-Am] literally got out of hand as conservative pressures were put on to tell everyone where to stand, when to applaud, when to talk, and when not to," he'd told me. "The Crosby days were wonderful days when you were a kid, and the movie stars were out there, and they were all accessible, and there was barely a gallery rope separating you. There wasn't a strict, conservative, politically correct PGA telling you what you can and can't do. What's happened," March had explained, "is that . . . Pebble Beach . . . lost its sense of humor. There's no sense of the absurd anymore . . . Granted, Bill Murray has tried, God bless his soul."

While at today's Pro-Am a kid's likely to be patted down if he so much as tries to pack a Canon, March was allowed to pull out his little Kodak on loan from his mother whenever he liked. "I would just go up and ask Randolph Scott, 'Can I take your picture Mr. Scott?' And he'd stand right there for me, right on the tee . . . There was a lot of give and take between the player and the audience right up through when Katherine Crosby took her name off of it [the Pro-Am]. It was still a clambake, and after that it never was again."

Much as I may share March's nostalgia gene, this week I won't indulge any Debbie Downers, won't allow myself to give a damn what the old guard says. Carmel's still Carmel, by Clint! There's still good golf to be watched, celebrities to be hounded, booze to be overconsumed. I'll wager it's still possible to party like it's 1969.

As in most tourist towns, it's not always easy to tell when something's afoot in fair Carmel-by-the-Sea. The same steady stream of Viagra-styled, silver-haired lovers and wasp-waisted, raven-haired Euros pad up and down Ocean Avenue. It takes a double-check of my cell phone to confirm it: It's 9 a.m. on Day 1 of the AT&T National Pro-am, Year of Our Lord Samuel Morse, and yet the only sign that the classiest, starriest regular PGA Tour stop is happening at all is the cars parked up Mountain View, reaching to the very doorstep of my rent-a-bungalow.

After a shower that leaves an embarrassing windfall of man-hair in the basin of my fair landlady's pristine tub, I follow the crowd of well-off Boomers and slow-moving geriatrics down the hill to the Carmel Chamber of Commerce shuttles lined up to take us out to Pebble for $15 a pop. Ours are luxury coaches, and yet the price for the uphill buggy ride into the Del Monte Forest less than a mile distant seems wicked steep. All our Jeeves has to do, after all, is drive a dozen or so amicable, well-educated, utterly white golf fans up the traffic-free slope in his clean-burning, nonpolluting sleigh.

One by one we dutifully pay our fare, getting branded with the impossible-to-break plastic bracelets used in college bars. We clamber aboard the bus and make polite conversation until the driver wishes us a great day of golf viewing, taking care to remind us that the last shuttle leaves at 5:30 unless we want to hitchhike home. A rumble of dissent—the last shuttles going to Monterey don't leave until 7:00—but our protestations are quickly squelched, the very unfamiliarity of bus transport having stupefied the upscale, private transportation–accustomed crowd.

I arrive at The Lodge to find that the little pressroom we scribblers used for the First Tee Open and the Callaway has, for the AT&T, given way to several annexed conference rooms. It's a little dizzying, this big-time golf event nerve center with its endless, skirted tables, all pointed frontwise as at weddings. By default all reporters face a huge plywood scoreboard painted a dark Augusta green featuring built-in steps and oversized, hole-by-hole, player-by-player tallies. Flanking the massive wall-to-wall leaderboard where Pebble Beach pro Chuck Dunbar will keep score are several flat-screen TVs showing the Golf Channel. Identifying each wireless-ready workstation is a little table tent naming the media entity that's reserved the spot. All the biggies are here this week—*Golf Digest, Sports Illustrated,* ESPN.

"Here" in a manner of speaking. If you're one of the cool kids you arrive fashionably late, fly into Monterey on Thursday or Friday, and pay only a courtesy visit to the course before you sneak out with some reporter pals for a tee time either up-Peninsula at Bayonet or Blackhorse or at the poor man's Pebble Beach, Pacific Grove Muni. I'm not one of the cool kids. For the next four days I will come early and stay late, often with pocket-sized wholesome snacks, an ethos that gives me borderline traumatic flashbacks to high school. For the first two days I'll be one of a handful of people in the cavernous pressroom actually using their work station—again, like high school minus the chicken-fried steak. I will not be seated next to the Golf Channel's Jim Gray, with his oversized Marvin the Martian head and sales manager chumminess. I will not drink complementary Cokes nor eat complementary Kettle Chips next to *Sports Illustrated*'s gift to golf writing, Alan Shipnuck, who, with his long legs, broad smirk, and unprecedented reach, can pick and choose from among the savory Tour tidbits falling around him like crumbs while the rest of us shake the trees for leads.

Instead, the powers-that-be have seen fit to position me strategically between a mute, fastidious reporter from *Tokyo Sports Press*, who I'll hereafter refer to as Pat Moriarty for his uncanny resemblance to the Bonsai-loving, peace-mongering sensei in that cinematic classic from my childhood, *Karate Kid,* and the bespectacled, uber-nice James Raia of GolfTribune.com. I'm caught between East and West and, pardon the pun, *yen* and yang. But I'm in play, and grateful for it.

I'm pleased to be next to Raia and within shouting distance of Jerry Stewart of the *Monterey County Herald.* We plebes in the "local press,"—as we'll be called hereafter, to differentiate us from the Jim Grays of the golf world—have to stick together. We may be sitting verboten at the nerd table in the proverbial cafeteria but, damn it, we're somebody. Technically I'm not local media, but since I live in Carmel and since these guys are the only ones in the press corps I'm ever seen "hanging with," I've been assigned my clique by association. A plebe is as a plebe does.

One of the convoy of Thursday afternoon media shuttles—white domestic sedans and minivans reeking of new-car smell—drops me off in front of a deserted trailer on the windswept dunesland off 17-Mile Drive just shy of Point Joe. It's a little unsettling, this far-flung, ocean-buffeted drop-off point—the kind of place a mafia don deposits his victim before helping him on with his cement shoes.

Two journalists emerge from the trailer, yelling at one another to be heard over the ocean's roar. I ask them the best route by which to hoof it to the Monterey Peninsula Country Club (MPCC for short), the new course in the Pro-Am rota and, in this Tiger-less tourney, a headliner all by itself, replacing the perennially soggy track the pros dubbed "Sloppy Hills" (Poppy Hills). I follow the finger of my media brethren across the famed 17-Mile Drive, down a winding trail in the dunes, to a throng of Japanese. Wise money back at the pressroom said today would be a good day to stay clear of the Shore Course, since Ryo Ishikawa, resplendent in a Gumby Green, zip-up-the-front jumpsuit, was sure to put the Japanese press in a feeding frenzy. Ahead,

I see them, moving in what, paradox be damned, can only be described as an orderly ameba. They move with the demure shuffling steps characteristic of their people, discernable even at a distance from the every-man-for-himself, long-limbed, he-who-shouts-the-loudest-wins cowboy lope of the American press corps member. Actually, I could care less about Ishikawa, nickname "Bashful Prince," with his self-styled head covers replicating his oversized head, wraparound shades and trademark mop of hair.

I'm a red-blooded American male from the Heartland and, as God is my witness, I'm hunting celebs and Phil Mickelson. It's been a good nine months since I last covered Lefty in the flesh at the Masters, and since Phil is the closest thing the Tour has to Elvis—the rubberbanding waistline, the schizophrenic fashion sense, the ever-fluctuating hairstyle—I need some pre-springtime Phil-time.

I catch up with Lefty as he cleans up a 3-foot par on MPCC's par-3, 176-yard eleventh, a comely postage stamp played from atop a miniature golf-styled rock outcropping to a "redan" green canted to the player's right. Mickelson's plastered head to toe in corporate internationalia, per usual: KPMG, Barclay's, and other logos so numerous and miniscule it would be indiscrete in this most heterosexual of games to permit the gaze to linger. In Tiger's absence, the de facto number one player in the world has taken his fashion sense to a whole new level, opting today for pin-striped slacks. He looks trim, like a guy who finds himself suddenly back on the market after a break-up. He's wearing an Under Armour–type top of exactly the sort his man-breasts once thwarted. "Chew on this, Tiger," the form-fitting getup and newly defined pecs seem to say. Bones is bones, unchanging as oatmeal, with his well-tanned woman thighs and Huckleberry Hound slouch as he shoulders the bag.

Mickelson does some toe reaches on the par-4 twelfth, gives his legs that just-peed shake, and lets one rip. "He's got a good swing," the gal beside me opines, master of the obvious, to which her companion says, "And I love *that hair.*" Insert postmenopausal shiver here. Lefty's long locks cascade down the back of his neck, curling into a soft fade. In sum, he is Paul McCartney–esque – circa the Wings period – in ways that transcend his pseudo-hippie 'do. Like McCartney, Mickelson is money – corporate-embraced more energetically than ever after Tiger's stunning fall from grace. Lefty's all about family values, philanthropy, and, of course, success. Like Paul, Phil's always had the counterweight of his darker doppelganger, Tiger – John Lennon by analogy – as a foil for his own ostensible wholesomeness. This year, though, Lefty seems to sense the moment is ripe for psychic as well as professional breakthrough, and he's wearing black to cultivate his inner Johnny Cash. Hence the hair, hence the McCartney post-Beatles break-up ethos, hence the designer pantaloons, hence the middle-age lady shiver.

Whatever his *je ne sais quoi*, it's working. He's playing well enough to keep it a respectable few under par, but he's leaving shots on the course, as Phil will, missing the ten-foot-and-unders that, when he's on, are as good as automatic, and when he's not, are like watching a shade-tree mechanic trying to replace his own fuel pump. Clearly, Lefty's on autopilot. He's here, he's punching the clock, he's squeezing the flesh, humoring and honoring the sponsors but, as he's wont to do, the inner Phil, the Spirit Phil, has gone elsewhere . . . the 50-yard-line at a Chargers game, maybe, or at home with Amy and the kids . . . who knows.

"Good shot, Bob," Mickelson calls over his shoulder periodically in that rote, automatic way Tour players do when compelled to play with mere mortals. He's playing with Robert Edward "Bob" Diamond Jr., president of his sponsor, Barclays, which means Phil might as well be saying, *"Nice shot, boss."* A former all-state linebacker and 10-handicapper, Diamond's muscular if not erratic game is giving Phil's vocal chords a workout. Mickelson is one of the game's most effusive complimenters, and one of its most genuine.

Overhead, the MetLife blimp blimps about in the air, Snoopy doing whatever Snoopy does up there before the real action begins. An onshore breeze blows in from Bird Rock, carrying the unmistakable scent of seals basking—one part fecund saltwater funk and two parts ammonia-infused guano. It's a heady perfume.

For my money—which I'll admit makes for empty rhetoric since I didn't pay gate—Thursday is the best day of the Pro-Am. The day after Hump Day brings the real golf fans out, the longtime locals and the Corn Belt émigrés too retiring to fight the Saturday and Sunday crowds when they could be home with the golden goose, the golden retriever, and a glass of chardonnay. They're the folks who love golf but at a civilized remove, which is to say not enough to endure the weekend's Blood Mary–swilling autograph hounds. They come with their best good friends, as Forest Gump would say, and their well-preserved spouses, and, though the days of greenside picnics died with Katherine Crosby's removal of Bing's name from the tournament in 1984, their conversation is casual and eclectic, the kind you might hear in the sixth inning of a minor league baseball game at All-Star break. In short, the Thursday crowd at one of the AT&T satellite courses is what marketers might call a highly targeted demographic: the Roth IRA slash Chuck Schwab mutual fund cohort. As your embed, I jot down, for anthropological posterity, items overheard in the gallery whilst tracking Lefty up the thirteenth and fourteenth holes at the Shore Course.

"She just does it for the tennis. She's just gadding around."

"Q: How can you write that off?" "A: One of the investors pulled back."

Though I know golf and business are rumored to be joined at the hip, for the first time in my checkered career as a golf scribbler I actually hear the words "best practices" bandied about on the links. To our left, the deer graze the dunesland. Cypress Point and Spyglass Hill come clearly into view as Mickelson putts out on the thirteenth. It's as if all of us are living in some kind of belle époque, golfers and businessmen and socialites mingling easily while Rome burns.

I leave Phil temporarily to watch quarterback Tom Brady rip the ball off the twelfth tee alongside Tour bomber Vijay Singh, the muscular, lithe Fijian looking like a toothpick next to the Patriots' future Hall-of-Famer. Promiscuously, I next check out the Huey Lewis, Don Cheadle, Jason Gore, Chris DiMarco foursome as they wend their way up the par-4 fifteenth; I'm strangely delighted to discover that Huey has some news for DiMarco, who he's outdriven by a good 20 yards.

Huey's sneaky long, and just plain sneaky—if I hadn't done my homework I'd have no way of knowing that the windbreakered everyman playing his mid-iron to the green is in fact Hugh Anthony Cregg III, purveyor of such pop standards as "I Want a New Drug," "Power of Love," and "Hip to Be Square." Wikipedia tell me Lewis's grandpa invented that unsettling, gelatinous red wrap that goes around fancy cheeses, doubling, for me, Huey's status as a cultural icon. But fame is a fickle mistress, and so is golf, and if you put the two together it partially explains the palpable weirdness surrounding the field of B-list celebs appearing at the AT&T of late, about which there is the perennial bitching about it "not being what it used to be." Meanwhile, erstwhile megastars like Huey scratch and claw anonymously for hard-earned pars while everybody and their mama join the swelling galleries of the pretty boy QBS. No wonder pop has-beens commit suicide. But I digress.

The pretty boy I'm following up the eighteenth just now, and angling for a postround interview with, is Phil McCartney-Mickelson. Only our doe-eyed press-minder, Kim, stands between me and the little Hurricane Katrina scorer's trailer where Dr. Phil is signing his prescription. The *Pocket Guide for Playing Out Front of Phil* consists of just one directive: Get your ass out of the scorer's tent staging area PDQ or get swept away by the tide. To that end, Tour veteran Jeff Maggert's trying like hell to clear the runway, zipping up his bag with the abandon of a business traveler waking up from an airport snooze to news of a gate change while simultaneously trying to talk to a couple of reporters ballsy enough to pose questions before the Mickelson tsunami strikes.

We ask him about the Phil controversy du jour: the workaround Lefty found within the square-groove policy recently implemented by the Tour for the 2010 season. Phil began the year playing old square-groove Ping wedges that predated the ruling, inciting an uproar. The whole thing came to a head a couple of weeks back with Scott McCarron all but calling Lefty a cheater, and Phil pretty much threatening to sue his ass for slander. The WWF-styled name-calling and baiting was enough to make you long for the milder spats of Fat Jack and Arnie. And now here's poor Maggert forced to field The Question with no more than 3 feet and an uninsulated trailer wall between him and the alleged Square-Groove Outlaw.

"I don't know if it's an advantage or not. It's hard to say," Maggert says. "I do know that those old Ping wedges were great around the green, regardless of the grooves. Maybe that's some of it, too. It's just a good wedge. And you put it in a good player's hands, and all of a sudden he's putting it close to the hole and people are like, 'What's going on here?'" At the sound of jostling behind him in the scorer's tent, Maggert skedaddles, and we newsies wait for Phil like teenyboppers waiting for the Beatles—quieter for sure, but no less giddy. That smile, those eyes, *that hair* . . .

"Guys, how's it going?" the Golden Boy banters as he emerges from the scorer's tent, beaming. While most of the other pros have to be flagged down by a "facilitator," Lefty walks right up to our little press corps like he wants to fill out an app to join our team. Grateful, we start with a softball, asking ask him if this week's reduced field size—along with the Shore Course itself, another of the new rollouts of this year's tourney—have cut into the legendary six-hour rounds for which the AT&T has become infamous.

"We're used to having two to three groups waiting at the turn," Phil says. "And we didn't have to wait at all. We hardly waited on anyone in front of us. And the group behind us we didn't see. It was a real difference."

"I enjoy playing with the amateurs," he continues, enunciating all three syllables in *amateur* like a prep schooler from Andover. "I enjoy learning a lot this week. Bob Diamond with Barclay's and Joe Kernen with CNBC have a lot of interesting insights into what's going on in the world today, and I enjoy listening."

And that's the extent of it. The Paul McCartney of golf breaks huddle to a veritable chorus of autograph hounds and well-wishers shouting "Phil!" It's a weirdly atonal barbershop chorus, these collective pleas, the kind professional golfers dread during their prime and come to miss in their retirement. The tenors are the cloying kids with their programs thrust in the air for signing. Next come the baritone huzzahs of the teenage boys who'd fancied themselves a bit too cool to shout crazily for another dude's attention until they'd found their pie holes involuntarily opening. Rounding out the three-part disharmony are the voices of the adult males of middle-age mandom with their moose calls.

I leave Lefty to the madding crowd for now, angling for a brief duet with Huey. The Gen-Xer in me is a little starstruck, I'll admit, when finally I look into the deeply furrowed, ruggedly handsome face of the guy who, along with Michael Landon and Harrison Ford and John Travolta, was one of the Big Four mom-crushes back in the eighties when I darkened the door of Henry Wadsworth Longfellow Elementary. Huey hasn't aged in the gentile, artistic Eastwood way, say, or in the preternatural, kidnapped-by-aliens-and-pumped-full-of-formaldehyde Dick Clark way, but he's still sexy. Huey used to live here on the Peninsula but has since moved out to Hamilton, Montana, he tells me, and the West seems to have imprinted itself on the pop rocker's character-lined face. He looks well, and not well, all at once—like the Marlboro Man.

"I *love golf,*" he enthuses, talking to me at a New York City, in-your-face rather than Hamilton, Montana, arm's range. "What's not to like? This is the Masters for an amateur. The best thing about it is the format—the two-man better ball . . . at the [Bob] Hope [Classic] you hit a lot of shots that don't matter. Here you matter."

I ask him what he did differently, if anything, preparing for the

Shore Course this year in lieu of Sloppy Hills. "I don't prepare," he says. "There's no preparing."

About now, the voice in my head is screaming, *Dude, it's Huey Lewis. What's with the yawner questions?* I try harder. Does he swing to any particular rhythm? Like a waltz maybe? Or a rumba? His map of Montana—all the coulees, and arroyos, and riverbeds, and rocky streams—folds into a grin.

"It's like golf when you want to hit a high note . . . Someone said when you look at music, the note is up, but if you think of it as up, you're in trouble. You think of it as straight ahead. Then you just go out and get the note. It's the same thing in golf. Eighty percent goes further than a hundred and ten."

So does he walk around the course with irksome songs—earworms, they call them—stuck in his head, golf and major scales mixing in his SAT-genius noggin. He's known to have aced the math section, the no-good curve-breaker. It's sort of the other way around, he tells me, with golf infecting him backstage. "In a show, we'd do, like, eighteen to twenty songs, and there's eighteen holes. We'd always come back and say we bogeyed "Heart and Soul" or birdied "Heart of Rock and Roll." Some of the songs are hard par 5s, some of 'em are easy, some of 'em are little 1-shot holes. Actually the analogies work pretty good. I say to my band, 'What is Heart and Soul?' And they say, 'It's just a par three.'"

"I got my gopher, Bill. Can you sign my gopher?" I'm just the other side of the ropes from the Bill Murray circus and, as usual, I can't believe how positively stupid people can be in the presence of stars. Something about cozying up to a bona fide celebrity invariably lowers IQs by several touchdowns, turning women into girls and men into dumbasses. Exhibit A: "Can you sign my gopher?"

The last time I shot the shit with Billy, as his buds and wanna-be-buds like me call him, he'd been getting some good, deep-tissue lovin' at Pebble to keep his back from balking. This time around it's his knee that's gone south. Like Huey, he looks a little worse for the wear this winter, his face white like he's been hibernating in Chi-town. As usual, Murray's handling the gopher-signings with near Christ-like forbearance, which is why the crowds here adore him.

"Wanna have a drink?" Billy asks his postmenopausal sidekick-tour-guide-roadie-one-woman-hospitality-crew du jour. "Can we can go in the clubhouse here or no? I'll meet you over there . . . Wanna go work out?" Per always, Murray is multitasking, carrying on a relatively complex negotiation for booze and companionship while accommodating the fans jockeying for his John Hancock.

"You're my only autograph. And I'm so excited!" exclaims one twenty-something, turning her back on the comedy giant and pointing to a spot between her shoulder blades.

"Quick on the shoulder, Bill. Just a quickie on the coat right there."

Murray raises an eyebrow as if to say, *You sure you want me to do this?* but he obliges, dragging the black sharpie across her distressed leather jacket in a signature that might, if you use your imagination, read "Bill Murray." Meantime, Murray's geriatric sidekick responds to his earlier booze-query. "You can either go into the grill, or there's another bar that looks out over the *loggia* that looks out over the golf course."

"*Loggia,*" Murray says, repeating the term with working-class Chicago disdain. "Loggia?" He moves toward the waiting celebrity shuttle and the DMZ behind the ropes near the scorer's trailer. "I got a bum knee," he says, hoping for sympathy while parting the sea of fans.

"Okay, we're backin' up," someone in the crowd says. We should be hearing the beep-beep-beep of a heavy truck in reverse but there's no room to take anything other than baby steps backward in the impotent way golf galleries do when they're asked to clear a path. Murray stops, marooned, a head taller than the sea of autograph-seekers, an American in Tokyo. When finally he looks down it's into the eyes of a Down's syndrome girl who, unseen at the flabby equator of all these grown adults, has been patiently awaiting his autograph.

The beauty of Bill Murray—the absolute beauty of him—is he's at his best with people whom life has knocked around a little bit, folks who have drawn the proverbial short stick. Elevating his game, he looks down at the wee lass. "The thing to do is just work on your short game," he says, as if in answer to an unspoken question. "Oh, I know it's old advice . . . But if you can't make a putt, get out of my life." He works himself into a pissed-off, football-coach tizzy for the girl's benefit, roaring, "You either make a putt, or get out of my life, you understand?"

"I just got a glove from George Lopez," the Down's girl says.

"You need a tee, don't you?" Murray asks sweetly. "It could keep your mouth open while you sleep so you don't snore."

"Just like my dad." The girl grins.

"Does he snore? You tell him to lay off the hard stuff then."

"Bill," some joker calls out, "I'll trade you the Pebble Beach hat for your hat. Deal?"

"No deal!" Murray says, channeling Regis while wading, zombie-like, through the crowd again.

"Bill . . . Bill . . . Billy" solicitations dog the funnyman all the way under the press ropes, where a smaller but equally needy interest group—the sportswriters—ready themselves to pounce.

"Bill, you got a minute?" one of the bolder journalistic sucker fish asks.

"Who's asking?" Murray gives him the brush-off, not breaking stride until he reaches a small group of friends huddled around the celebrity car shuttles, where he begins making dinner plans.

"Instead of going to the club, we're gonna go to an actual restaurant," Murray mumbles to his homies. "San Tropez. Ya ya ya. We're gonna go there right after we finish."

"It's on Dolores right downtown," somebody in the inner circle ventures.

The Comcast SportsNet guy tries again, introducing himself and his affiliation. "Can I have a moment of your time?" the dude asks, all Eddie Haskell–like.

"Much better," Murray says. He lowers his head to entertain the questions he's doubtless heard year after year. For an hors d'oeuvre we newsies pose the Cadillac of clichéd queries: Why does he keep coming back?

"*When* it's fun," Murray replies, emphasizing the conditional, "it's really the most fun you have during the year. It's exhilarating to be this close to the ocean and play these great golf courses. And the crowd is silly. They're in a great mood . . . everyone's in a positive state, because they're in a natural state of bliss."

Today wasn't so blissful, though, for our man. Despite draining a putt on the eighteenth hole to collect on a dollar side bet, Murray's wheels—his knee, specifically—are pretty much shot. When word got out that Billy was ailing, the over-under in the pressroom figured it'd be a day of unprecedented liquor and high jinks, enough to make even Carl Spackler scream "Uncle."

"Alcohol wasn't going to get it done for me today. I needed a pain-killer . . . and not the ordinary kind," Murray quips. This year he's partnering with a new pro, Tim Herron, better known on Tour as Lumpy. I ask him if there's any partner-envy going on between him and his old running mates, who've now graduated to the Champions Tour—the old man's circuit.

"Jeff Sluman and Scott Simpson . . . we had the most fun anyone ever had in this tournament," Murray recalls, sounding, as many do about the AT&T, a nostalgic note. "I'm sure they wish they were here, especially with the weather getting like this . . . But Tim's great. He's one of the nicest guys. He's from Minnesota, so he's got that going for him."

Then, abruptly even for him, our interviewee hits the self-eject button. "I got to go see a man about the knee," Murray tells us, playing his favorite get-out-of-jail card.

Given his history of on-course drama and bad backs and bum knees and joyous booze, pulling for Murray at the AT&T is kind of like rooting for a hobbled Kirk Gibson to hit that walk-off home run in the 1988 World Series. You just can't help yourself.

Pro-Am days start late and end late PSVT — Pebble Standard Vacation Time — and thus they seem never to end. There's always another gag up ahead, another iron to hit, another log to feed to the fire, another shot at the bar. It's bliss. Your tokens never run out.

Earlier in the day I'd felt like a total dweeb, shooting the shit with John Daly, who'd Facebooked his fans a couple of weeks back at the Farmers Insurance Open to say he'd run out of cash, lost his game, and couldn't continue on Tour. Favre-like, he's come out of "retirement" on a sponsor's exemption for this year's Clambake. J. D. had been telling me how he considers Pebble and the Monterey Peninsula a "great wonder of the world," adding, "'cause really when you think about it there's not a whole hell of a lot else to do except play golf."

"That, and eating and drinking," I'd said.

"That's right," J. D.'d drawled before I'd realized I ought not be talking sauce with one of the circuit's most notorious and most sincerely repentant alcoholics. Open mouth, insert foot.

The Thursday nightcap is often, and oddly, the best. Since Thursday officially kicks off the tourney, it's the night where old friends meet up to regale one another with mostly untrue yarns from the year thus far. It's like the first night of a buddies vacation . . . no one's yet chronically hungover, no one's yet on someone's nerves, no one's prematurely thinking about what's waiting back home. Thursday night in Carmel-by-the-Sea is the last day of school before summer vacation; it's full-on, crazy-grinning Sinatra: the best is yet to come.

So I call up my friend Natalie and she agrees to meet me for drinks and dinner down at Clint's place, the Mission Ranch, on Dolores near where the Carmel River meanders its swampy way to the sea. Eastwood, resident do-gooder, bought the historic dump back in the eighties to save it from proposed development, thereby preserving its campy, country krafty ways for at least a generation to come.

I dial Nat hoping to partake, in some small, platonic way, in the Thursday night lovefest. She's a nurse at one of the many little outpatienty surgery-type places on the Peninsula where the rich and upper-middle-class Peninsulans go to get their elective nips and tucks and bunions done while drinking in a whole lot of TLC from winsome nurses like my dinnermate. Nat comes by her bedside manner naturally: she's pretty, with her long, dark, curly hair falling just below the shoulder and she's possessed of the straight-ahead, look-you-in-the-eye, don't-bullshit-me ethos that's surprisingly common among Peninsulans. As it turns out, Cali's so lousy with displaced middle Americans like me—we Iowans and Michiganders and Minnesotans—that we've pretty much infused the gene pool with honesty.

By 7:30 Clint's joint is jumpin', but it's early enough yet in late-supping Carmel that Nat and I are able to get a table, sans reservation, in one of the "additional" dining rooms that basically amount to a deck overstretched with an all-weather plastic tent—the upscale, temporary kind you see pitched next to artificial lakes at resort weddings. We fall into our seats gratefully, both of us having been on our feet all day, and order a couple of pales ales, ready to wang chung for the night.

Truth, I met Natalie smack dab in the middle of what she would later confess was her "yes" period. It's my feeling that when you meet someone in the throes of any "period"—their "whips and chains period" or, for the golfer, their "stack and tilt" phase—extra caution is advised. An anthropologist might define the "yes" period as a "viral social phenomenon" affecting a wide cross section of female bipedal hominids in the beginning of the second millennium, but here's the Cliff's Notes version: Nat and many of her she-peers decided they were going to give every guy a fair shake, even the swarthy, vaguely Middle Eastern, double-digit handicappers like me. Perhaps my fair dinnermate said yes because she wanted me as the designated Shakespeare and eighties TV jingle ringer on her squad for the bawdy trivia night at Monterey's Brittania Arms. In any case, the "yes" movement seemed a boon to dudes, except that when girls say yes in the platonic sense to guys they're predisposed not to want to date, they basically beget a whole lot of unlikely, ambiguous, intergender _____ships that would never ordinarily have breathed life.

While my "date" tonight isn't the young Pebble Beach golf widower or heiress I'd blueprinted prior to dropping anchor in Monterey Bay, she's pretty damn close. She went to Robert Louis Stevenson—former stompin' grounds of Mina Harigae, Bobby Clampett, Casey Boyns, and Wally Goodwin, Tiger's coach, to name a few—and used to ditch school to watch the celebs at the Clambake. She grew up on an area golf course, whiling away the hours searching for golf balls with her kid sister while, half a continent away, I did the same with my dad in the Iowa cornfields bordering our homemade pasture course. When I prattle on about hunting those prized pearls in the cornfields of my seventies and eighties youth—Flying Ladies, and Green Goblins, and those funky, two-toned, ABA-styled Ping Eye II balls—she's one of the few Gen-x femmes who understands my pathology. Her ma and pa still live on a golf course down the road and her eyes still rove instinctively for lost balls whenever she walks the pooch.

You'll understand, then, why I'm a wee sweet on her, in addition to our shared maniacal penchant for sugary carbs that somehow fail to impact our respective waistlines. The last time I saw her, we—at an impasse as to what flick we should see preholidays—had compromised on *Couples Retreat*. The movie that I'd hoped would be romantically comedic enough to grease the wheels of our nascent golfing romance turned out to be a gigantic, insultingly childish flop, not unlike my would-be courtship. However, sly devil that I am, I'd insisted on a side wager as the credits rolled and the question of the ageless Jason Bateman's age came up. Carbon dating him back to *Family Ties*, I'd argued Bateman most be well north of forty while Nat, shrewdly underbidding me in a way that would make Bob Barker proud, guessed late thirties. The bet was one giant gooey slice of yellow cake at Rosine's in Monterey and a dinner to be named later.

So here we are, the only couple under Clint's tarp under the age of forty and sans children, having a cautiously romantic Thursday Pro-Am dinner among the Mission's well-fed, guffawing, balding clientele, trying to talk above the show tunes just now cranking up at the piano bar. After the compulsory catch-up on our families and our work, Nat delivers the news that she met a guy; she delivers the fact with all due tact, the way girls will when they don't want to lose a friend. Across the two-top I'm nodding my fool head off, picking up what she's putting down, as an old friend of mine used to say. Turns out she met Greg or Gary—I forget the dude's name as soon as I hear it—during the late "yes" period, and said yes to dating an older divorced naval officer with a couple of kids in tow. Things progressed quickly, she says. In fact, tomorrow she's supposed to babysit the kiddos while what's-his-face catches up on all things nautical.

We linger a little longer over her duck and my pasta, Nat and I do, catching up like the de facto friends we've become, encouraging one another in our respective harebrained schemes for the future with reciprocal relish. I call to our waitress—a tall, statuesque mom-blonde with a dancer's body—and ask her for some goss about Clint as a boss. Does he ever crack the whip? Does he throw plates, and I don't mean for Greek weddings.

He's wonderful, she tells us, smiling demurely. In fact, the whole family is great, especially Dina Eastwood, who elicits the term "lovely" as she always seems to anywhere on the Peninsula where her fairy-tale name is summoned. Just once I want to hear one of the natives drag the Prince's or Princess's name through the mud, but tonight, no dice.

After a couple of rousing renditions of "Happy Birthday to You"—the Mission Ranch is the single singingest place you've ever been—crooned by the staff to the gray-hairs at tables adjacent, Nat and I are ready to call it a night—not for a roll in the hay in the Ranch's $285 (off-season) honeymoon suite, alas, or its slightly more affordable but no less romantic beds in the old 1860s farmhouse, but to our respective boudoirs—hers with Greg-Gary and mine a hardwood floor and yoga mat with Huckleberry the lame house cat.

There's no route back into the crisp, star-studded sea air but past the bar, past the cringe-worthy rendition of "Crazy" being belted out by a middle-aged chanteuse draped unbecomingly across the piano, no Chutes and Ladders shortcut to deposit me on the front patio with what I suspect is bougainvillea overtopping, and wisteria and jasmine intermingling with other species so sweetly floral they would positively un-man me to mention.

After my erstwhile date and I have walked the gauntlet to emerge into the night air and piney starshine, I realize I've forgotten my jacket, of course, and it's rinse and repeat—back past the punch-drunk croon of tonight's Liza Minnelli—"Crazy for feelin' so lonely"—back to the table where our Eastwood-loving, straight-as-a-string waitress waits with my windbreaker—back to an encore walk past the diva at the door singing her fool heart out—"Crazy for feeling so blue"—to Nat, who waits for me under a throbbing cosmos to walk her to her Blazer—"and I'm crazy for loving you."

13

All Shook Up at the
AT&T National Pro-Am

Son of Iowa Meets Tiger's "Big Brother" Meets Asian
King of Rock-and-Roll Meets Hungry Godzillas

Friday morning at the Pro-Am finds me walking a gauntlet of security guards—who, with their standard-issue, superhero square jaws,
dimpled chins, and wraparound shades all look uncannily like PGA
pro and fellow Iowan Zack Johnson—to make my way into the news-
hive and get the overnight scoop from my fellow drones, a detour for
which I am rewarded with several "if it bleeds it leads" items. To wit:

Apparently, a couple of guys last night at the Pebble Lodge had a
few too many, came to blows over a girl, allegedly got themselves
tazered, and were hauled off in a paddy wagon with a couple of
serious gangbangers from Salinas.
Overnight, Huey W-Ded from the tourney, complaining of short-
ness of breath, or heart pains, or some combination thereof. This
news makes me sad.
The Japanese press corps has been busted, one reporter tells me

with barely contained glee, for seriously depleting the gratis food and drink supply in the pressroom mess hall, their Asian work ethic and native thrift apparently conspiring to bring about their Godzilla-like downfall.

I enter the mess hall and verify that, yes indeed, a sign has been posted saying "Do not take food" in both English and Japanese. I nod to the seriously buff security guard–food bouncer with the earpiece, a Chicano Cerberus who guards the door, and who, over the next four days, will not smile once. On my way out I hold my cup of iced tea aloft to make sure he knows it's beverage only—no foodstuffs, see—and make a beeline for the links. Have complementary beverage; have pocket-sized Penway Composition Book with blanks for Name _____, School _____, Grade _____; have press pass, will report.

On Friday a.m. of the National Pro-Am, Pebble looks like it does on most any day of its resort life, except for the marshals who this year are more than conspicuous in their Macy's Elf–like getups—red AT&T windbreakers, starched white plus-fours, and black tennis shoes of the sort your high school shop teacher wore. The whole idea behind the jester garb is to stand out from the crowd, as marshals must, but on the front nine on a slow tourney morn, the series of Lilliputian bearded men in uniform look comically *Wizard of Oz.*

Decorum does not yet rule the way it will when the CBS cameras power up tomorrow afternoon, and Jim Nantz and Nick Faldo begin trading witticisms in library voices. Today, leaf-blowers and weed-whippers whir in the yards of the rich and famous, whose backyards back up onto America's most famous public golf course. The light is positively Asian, filtered obliquely through cypress. The day smells of soggy woodchips, damp earth, and, dimly, of fish.

Pebble draws you, the spectator, inexorably and unerringly toward the sea. From The Lodge follow Palmero Way, traipse down Whitman Drive, and before you can say "S.F.B. Morse" you're on what many consider the finest stretch of seaside golf in the world, "Abalone Corner," played atop the nearly treeless meadow, Arrowhead Point,

where sheep once grazed the steep slope down to the one-time fishing village, Stillwater Cove. Before you lies Exhibit A for the kind of
terrain Robert Louis Stevenson once called a "felicitous meeting of
land and sea." Most gawkers and rubberneckers end up on the glorious
ocean-facing holes where I am now, where the sun turns you red as a
lobster, where the hearty winds huff and puff enough most days that
it's difficult to hear words uttered at your elbow, and where invariably
you slip into your own silent communion with your Maker, or at least
with your golfing super-ego.

Bloody Marys appear in unsteady hands here at 11:00—a full hour
before the rest of the civilized world. The surf-driven sea spray off
Carmel Point is positively Aphrodite-like. The crowd moves slowly,
easing into the p.m. and away from last night's Scotch. A faux-blonde
crouches in front of the side mirror of a minivan shuttle parked alongside ten tee, putting her face on. The sun, the salt, the surf, the baking
flesh, and the uncertain sea legs—the scene gives off a Jimmy Buffet
meets Chuck Schwab vibe.

I find Ricky Barnes of Stockton, California, playing his third shot
into nine green after catching it chunky out of the fairway bunker. The
sight of him, he of the Beach Boys blonde locks, silhouetted against
the ocean, no matter how many times I've seen its pictorial variants
in glossy mags and overpriced coffee table books, takes my breath
away. Barnes holds his finish and behind him nothing—save a few
little archipelagos and some cargo ships plying the Pacific in the name
of commerce—comes between you, him, and Okinawa.

Catty-corner behind me and up the hill past Neville's Snack Shop,
one of the day's marquee groups—Padraig Harrington and Retief
Goosen—play their way up fourteen fairway, testing the new fairway
bunkers Arnie and his design army put into play to pinch the landing
area pre Open. As usual, the Harrington group is a good hole and a
half behind, though none of the usually stopwatch-happy PGA Tour
officials have put them on the clock. Even in a group as big-name as
this, the marshals and the policemen and the volunteers practically

outnumber the spectators, some of whom are still under cover of corporate awning.

As Paddy and Goose hole out on fifteen, the privileged few behind the tinted glass of the climate-controlled confines of a giant corporate hospitality tent dubbed the "The Champions Club" stare at the Golf Channel broadcast on the big screen, unaware that immediately behind them exist two of the world's biggest golfing draws in the flesh.

As I cross Whitman Drive in front of the Erik Estrada-on-*CHIPS* motorcycle cops astraddle their retro Kawasakis, I spy a familiar face walking toward me: Doug Acton, my PGA personal pro. He's tanned, smiling, and clearly happy to be out on the golf course he loves. He's following one of the amateurs he gives lessons to while checking out the "action," as he calls it—the move through impact—of various pros. Acton's got a photographic memory for both the swing and the swinger, and wonders how "my action" is coming along. My action, I confess, is MIA, having not been back out on the course since our last lesson together. But I have, I tell him (deploying some of the lingo I picked up from Tiger) been doing "rehearsals" of the new move through impact over the holidays, and I'm hopeful the graft will take. Everything else is foreplay anyway.

Meeting your golf pro after a months-long absence is sort of like running into your middle school teacher at the liquor store; it's all kinds of awkward. Acton confesses he's sold the business and will be managing the store in Carmel for an outfit from Phoenix—Hotstix, he says, pointing to his windbreaker, the breast of which is stamped with a corporate logo featuring two crossed clubs but as yet no crossbones.

I'm happy for him, I tell him, but it pains me to see my personal pro in what amounts to a uniform, another walking billboard in a sea of walking billboards . . . another corporate man. This isn't the Doug Acton I know—the guy of wild visionary entrepreneurial notions—a fold-up putting green to take on the road, golfing retreats with swing analysis built in, couples winetasting mixed with spousal golf instruction. As the next group arrives at sixteen tee—causing the marshals on either side of Whitman Drive to agitate with Acton and me standing there in the DMZ—I offer my hand to him in the good-luck-to-you-friend gesture of graduations and funerals.

The encounter reminds me of Carmel-by-the-Sea's flipside: the entrepreneurs and dreamers and schemers who, upon finding here a previously unknown *joie de vivre*, open their hearts and minds to all kinds of crackpot notions. This town, she'll coo to you, whisper sweet nothings in your ear, intimate your greatness. When you rise to the heights she's asked—as you, flush with romance, inevitably will—she'll ask more of you: more hours, more money, more risk, until finally you find yourself in the classic catch-22 of loving the impossible-to-reach, of romancing beyond your means. You're stuck, ship to shore, somewhere between sublime pleasure and unmitigated pain, between the devil and the deep blue sea.

I think of my landlady, the one whose yoga mat I'm sleeping on these days by the seldom-lit fire. She fell in love with the place at first blush and claims she's never leaving. Yet the finite supply of discretionary income she's living on gets used up quickly here, and there's only so much square footage in her little bungalow to sublet. This morning, while showing me the wobbling charts of a bipolar NYSE in her home office, she was nearly in tears at the negative trendline. Already, with three of us in the house and as many cats, her little ecosystem nears carrying capacity.

Once Harrington finishes his round, he's immediately corralled by the TV ruffians and backed up against the sea behind the eighteenth green. Retief, meanwhile, does a few quick interviews and makes like a tree. The golf media is a fickle bunch and they have their darlings. Today we want Paddy and could give a damn about the South African. Tomorrow it might be just the opposite: one man's Boer is another man's Irishman.

For-print interviews can happen with any backdrop—ugly side of the scoreboard, back of the bleachers, shade of the scorer's shack—but for TV there's only one place to set up shop: Pebble's home hole, a place so self-evident to a cameraman that there may as well be a little white circle Kryloned atop the fescue. The interviewee must be pushed to cliff's edge so that the only thing showing in the squinting camera's iris is a face backdropped by the deep blue of the ocean and lesser blue of the sky. On cue, as Harrington begins, a sailboat heads out to sea. "This is a great place to play," he says, as I suck up to the boob tube crew. "It's as good as any course in the world. When you're between shots you get to look around. You're not brooding or analyzing."

Harrington's an unusually sentient golfer, an amalgam of Ben Crenshaw's plucky sensitivities with an Irish monk's soulful proclivities. But against this transcendent backdrop even Paddy's enlightened brogue sounds like so much blah blah blah. The surf lolls in and out. The TV folks bag the interview, fold up their portable media shop, and scurry back to the truck to edit the footage for tonight's news.

I follow the school of media suckers to the next alpha male, Mark O'Meara, who's normally at Dubai this time of year along with the other world-class big shots teeing it up for sheikh and autocracy in the Emirates. O'Meara fields questions with his arm around his sunglasses-wearing second wife, Meredith, whose head rests contentedly on his shoulder. She smiles enigmatically as her man fields questions, not about the upcoming U.S. Open, not about the condition of his game, nor about his own happy betrothal redux, but about two of the most treacherous subjects a professional golfer could ever be asked to discourse on: Tiger Woods and infidelity, not necessarily in that order.

"I got calls from *US* magazine, *People* magazine, *Star, Entertainment Tonight . . . Larry King,*" O'Meara says, literally scratching his head. "A *New York Post* guy kept calling me. I finally texted him back and said, 'Listen, please leave me alone . . . I don't have any answer.'"

Golf writers know O'Meara to be one of the most genuine interviews in the game, he of the nice-guy blue eyes and baby-pink complexion that make him an unlikely star. Having himself suffered through a very public divorce from his first wife, Alicia — a divorce he didn't choose—he's been on the hook a lot lately. In an interview with *Golf Week*'s Jeff Rude following the departure of his partner of twenty-nine years, O'Meara admitted, "I did a lot of crying. A tremendous amount of crying. The last fifteen months have had more impact than anything that has ever happened to me—more than winning the Masters and the British Open." He went on to confess the breakup would have been easier had he not taken to so much crippling self-analysis. "If I was a playboy," he said, "or a guy who wasn't a committed person, it would have been easy. It would have been like, 'Okay, there's my hall pass.'" And now, irony of ironies, here's O'Meara, playing at the AT&T for the first time in years and partnered with the chairman of Augusta National, Billy Payne, having to field questions about exactly that kind of playboy, and one who just happens to have been, in the words of Forrest Gump, his best good buddy, Tiger Woods.

"Like I said to Jim Gray yesterday, I love Tiger. He's my very dear friend. I'm certainly disappointed. But time will, you know, heal, and hopefully he can get his act back together and get himself straightened out . . . I understand he's been criticized, rightfully so. But, in saying that, he has done a lot of good for the game."

"I was shocked, to be honest with you," O'Meara responds when one of us asks him about his reaction to Woods's public admission. "But I haven't been around Tiger for the last three years because I've been playing the Champions Tour, and I haven't been living in Orlando. We just have different schedules . . . But, yeah, I was like a big brother and he was like my younger brother. He helped me a lot, and even when I was going through some tough times these last few years, we had dinner and talked."

Listening to the Tour veteran labor to put his "little brother's" struggles into words, it's easy to see why the Woods-O'Meara chemistry happened in the first place. O'Meara reeks of paternal acceptance, of an avuncular benevolence very different from the ethos of Tiger's own father, Earle. As O'Meara reflects on Tiger's plight, I can almost hear the voice of my own father, were he shoved in front of the cameras and asked to comment on the peccadilloes of his prodigal son.

"I had no idea a lot of this stuff was happening," big brother avows. "I just haven't been able to be around him enough . . . I feel for my friend. I wish him well. I pray for him. I just hope he can get his act together. He's not the first human being to make a mistake."

Given the right interviewee—and O'Meara, with his good-natured willingness to gab, is definitely the right interview—golf writers will ask questions until they're literally blue in the face. It's comical to watch, actually, this *pas de deux* between a guy who makes his living in silence—the pro golfer—and the dude who could talk the fur off a dog's back. I've seen behind-the-eighteenth gab sessions that have literally lasted until the sun went down, until the only questions remaining to be asked were, "So, do you prefer chamois or terrycloth?" But O'Meara is probably the oldest professional out here this week, and he's a salty sea dog to boot, so when he says, "Thanks, fellas," we quote-fattened pigeons dutifully scatter.

When I return to The Lodge after the O'Meara sessions, it's well-nigh happy hour and the pressroom has nearly cleared out, the local scribblers carpooling home to wives and kids and roast beast while members of the national news media debate where—not if—to get dinner and drinks. Positioning myself once more at the keyboard, "Pebble Beach Wifi" pops up on my list of preferred networks as I construct my evening of theater in lieu of looking up what second-round leader Dustin Johnson majored in at Coastal Carolina. It feels damn good, patriotic even, to be doing a little personal research on the clock, especially when "the clock" is a Pebble Beach Rolex. My pressroom tablemate from GolfTribune.com, James Raia, leans over and busts me as I platoon what are essentially the same shows: *Bye-Bye Birdie* at Robert Louis Stevenson and *All Shook Up* down at the Golden Bough.

It's the pot calling the money green, though, because he's been ogling pictures of the collateral damage done yesterday from the fifty-foot rogue waves up at the Mavericks Surf Contest at Half Moon Bay alternated with scintillating pics of Indy car driver Danica Patrick. Raia, who grew up on the Peninsula, tells me he courted his future wife at the Golden Bough back when the denizens of fair Carmel-by-the-Sea indulged in quaint bits of economical Americana like hug-your-honey movie-going. My tablemate tells me he has fond memories of the old theater, memories I'm guessing involve stealing kisses in the back row if not some heavy petting, and I'm coaxed by his good vibes recounting into an evening of saccharine retro.

There's an egalitarian beauty to the Carmel Chamber of Commerce coach I've just clambered aboard for the frighteningly hairpinned downhill run to the fairy-tale village. Bucking the trend that these days finds golf writers—as spoiled as the pros they cover by media shuttles, gratis lunches, and security officials—I'm looking forward to the people-mover ride with Joe and Jane Gallery. My up-with-people sentiments are merely academic until a pair of breathless married couples sit down behind me, one of which is evidently in the midst of one of those ultra–passive aggressive snark-fights that keep our blessed unions interesting.

"Barely made it, honey," the wife says sarcastically. "Just fifteen minutes to spare." Chastened, the husband goes mum. I've been this guy—this solid, responsible, American citizen whose worst flaw is that he likes to arrive fifteen minutes early to the last shuttle of the day, only to be ridiculed by his sig. fig. A minutes-long marital cold war ensues. Then, out of the blue, as we roll past the Smokey the Bear sign at the entrance to Del Monte Forest, the wife begins gabbing about affairs which, judging from this afternoon's Tiger Woods talk and my yesterday's return ride on this very bus, are something of a trend among upwardly mobile Californians. "I'm just saying he"—gesture in the direction of brooding hubby—"has more opportunity than I do. He's out in the road and I'm home with the kids. Do you think that the stereotype about traveling salesmen is true?" she asks the other wife. Then: "What do you think, Chris?"

We three men—the two hapless husbands and me, unwilling eavesdropper—fall silent. *Danger!* our collective man-monitors wail.

Shut-down. The other wife obliges her conversational partner by talking about all the opportunities she'd had for elicit hanky-panky whilst business traveling.

"I don't want to talk about it," Chris, our brooding husband, mumbles.

Wife No. 1 and Wife No. 2 bandy the topic about for a few more minutes, alternating sex talk with a decently informed discussion of Spanish architecture, until we're safely returned to Hansel and Gretel town. By the time our coach finally brakes to a halt, my back-of-the-bus mates have moved on in the traditional Carmel-by-the-Sea tourist hierarchy of needs, from quasi-architectural ruminations to the seemingly limitless palette of food and drink options before them. The existential debate just now is whether to snag a power nap back at the hotel or to just go ahead and get their wine on. There's some jokey talk about going back to the inn to see Josh Duhamel and Fergie, a celeb couple who is likewise knee-deep in rumors of extramarital peccadilloes involving a stripper named Nicole (never good). In fact, Josh and Fergie may well be having the self-same "who has more opportunities to cheat" discussion my backseat neighbors just wrapped, only after a romp of excellent make-up sex rather than in the back of an inglorious people-mover.

At this point, Wife No. 1 asks, pseudo-innocently, "You've been quiet honey . . . What's wrong?"

Hubby mumbles reply. "He says," she says, translating to the rest of the party as they disembark, "he's uncomfortable with the conversation."

Imagine that.

To paraphrase the right reverend Ray Charles, twilight-time in Carmel is the right time to be with the one you love. Silver-haired diners negotiate the difficult hills in the dying light en route to roasted duck at some secluded bistro. The little inns and B and Bs like the Lamp Lighter and the Green Lantern blaze convivially in the gloaming, with sounds of merry guests tickling your conch as you pass.

It's instinct to point your nose toward the Pacific as the breeze freshens and the smell of the sea gets all Manifest Destiny. My habit is to head down Eighth Avenue with some Nielsen's deli food in hand, a route sure to intersect with both ends of the Carmel divide alive at this crepuscular hour: the elegant epicureans, the obnoxious Hard Rock and Hooters day-trippers, and the workaday locals who emerge under dubious cover of semi-darkness. They're folks like the woman I see this eve, grunting with the effort required to lift her surf-soaked golden retriever into the back of a beat-up Toyota Tacoma.

On misty nights like this one, Carmel-by-the-Sea seems as mysterious as Victorian London, ripe for tomfoolery if not skullduggery. It's no wonder that mysteries galore have been written or filmed about this place, including the comedic *Death at Pebble Beach* by erstwhile local eccentric Russell Coille. Carmel is home to that macabrest of macabre mystery writers, author of *L.A. Confidential* and former Hillcrest Country Club caddy James Ellroy. Halloweentown's foggy oddity appeals to crime writing's bad boy, who once described himself to *Carmel Magazine* as "a naturally ruthless guy who tries to be decent." Further back, S.F.B. Morse's mouthpiece, *Game and Gossip*, helped institute the haunt in alliteration-endowed articles like "Night Is Ruled by Cypress Witches on the Bay of Monterey," which opened, "Along the wooded drives of the Monterey Peninsula, the cypress, of a moonlight night, take on strange shapes. Hooded heads beckon, horny hands gesture—witches, wigwag with every whiffle of wind."

So when I round a twisted bend on Scenic Avenue—killing time until *All Shook Up* begins—I'm primed for mayhem when sirens split the air. Ahead of me, a fire engine trains a high-wattage searchlight on the beach below while an ambulance and several squad cars stop traffic. Leaning over the seawall, I ask one of the onlookers what happened. He tells me a surfer had been separated from his board as the sun went down and his fellow surfers had gotten anxious and called for help. I follow the guy's eyes down to the sand, where a longboard has washed up absent its rider. Below us, in the searchlight, a uniformed

Carmel cop clambers down the steep cliff to the spot where another surf dude is hauling in the victim's board. The scene looks bleak but my fellow bystander assures me everything is okay; the kid's already loaded up in the ambulance—he's just a little cold and scared. On the sands below the blond officer and the greasy-haired, flannel-wearing surf bum who's hauling in his hapless buddy's board actually exchange fist-bumps and smile over a job well done.

Carmel Beach is not at all as I remember it, the beach tonight officially closed due to "Dangerous Conditions." Gone are the 100 yards of white-sugar sand between ocean's edge and seawall. Gone are the newlyweds and dogwalkers and beachcombers and clambakers. Instead, the village's notorious rogue waves have left a hardened soufflé of eroded dirt, sand, and kelp in their wake. The difference between the beach I'm beholding now, midway through another stormy winter, and the same benign stretch during the rest of the year is the difference between a pristine sandcastle and one ravaged by wind and water and left for ruin. It's the intersection of these two forces as they meet in Carmel-by-the-Sea: the unruly, uncouth Pacific Ocean and the civilized row of Frank Lloyd Wright–style, Brady Bunch–era homes lit up like fishbowls with their objects d'art hung by the chimney with care that earns Scenic Drive its name and makes the village so ungodly appealing. Beauty and beast shack up together here.

Even allowing time to rubberneck the surf rescue made by Carmel's finest, I make it to the Golden Bough Playhouse a good forty-five minutes before curtain, making me one of the first milling about the 1950s lobby with its early NASA light fixtures that look like chromed-up crowns of thorns, its elementary school drop ceiling, and the helpful staff of postmenopausal do-gooders practically tripping over themselves to assist. Somehow I'm doubting Josh and Fergie beat me to will call.

While the matrons hook me up with a primo seat, I survey the little concessions stand—store-bought trans fats, mostly, and a few unopened bottles of cheap chardonnay. Three ladies wo-man the concessions counter tonight and, just my luck, the one charged with hooking me up to the vino I.V. is struggling with Operation Corkscrew. "My husband normally does this for me," she blushes. It turns into a production, this ritual uncorking, a regular barn raising forcing all three Fates behind the counter to put their broad shoulders to the task. I offer my services but they assure me they have it under control: one holds the bottle firm as a larded-up pig while the other ratchets the corkscrew until at last the thing comes loose with a blush-worthy pop. "I'm pouring you extra for your trouble," my wine goddess informs me, overfilling my clear plastic cup.

By showtime I'm completely, unintentionally crunked, enough to fuel an ill-considered text to a friend back home to ask if she'll read an in-progress novel of mine. It's the solipsistic scribbler's equivalent of a drunk dial, but the wine has me feeling fine, my happy Fates behind the snack counter now a three-headed blur.

By the end of the two-hour-long musical marathon featuring two dozen Elvis songs sung by an Asian American college kid playing the King of Rock-and-Roll, I'm both morose and enchanted as I file out of the Golden Bough onto Monte Verde, behind the moms and dads who've come to cheer their kin. The scene's so Middle American it feels positively Norman Rockwell—proud grandparents leaving arm in arm in blissful heterosexual monogamy, timeless as if they'd just returned from the nickelodeon.

We move as one into the cool, pine-scented air, the gray-hairs to their parked sedans, whose wheels have been turned toward the curb in textbook fashion and whose parking breaks have likewise been dutifully engaged. The local oldsters who've been walking Carmel's notorious hills for eons know to hold their betrothed lightly at the elbow, while the uninitiated husband and wives struggle solo up the steep grade of Eighth Avenue. "I'm going to change my shoes," one of the wives calls out in the darkness, meaning merely to walk the half block from the theater to the car. Shortly thereafter the husband goes down in the dark, making the ominous thud of a grown man crumpling to pavement.

He's fine. We're all fine. The seasoned Carmelites shine flashlights in front of them, making the scene seem like summer camp, the rest of us benefiting from the stray beams to navigate by.

'Neath an encore Carmel zodiac of achingly bright stars, I follow a pair of couples from the Golden Bough all the way past the Sunset Center, past Knapp Hardware on the corner of Mission, up the hill to where Eighth narrows to no more than a sidewalk's width and the tree roots begin to buckle and bulge the asphalt.

Whoever be these revelers, they're staying in the lower-rent district, as it were, away from all the action. "It smells like money," one of the guy says in the pitch black, leading his merry band down an unlit side street. "Money I don't have."

14

We Are the Major
Champions, My Friends

Pebble and Spyglass Hill on AT&T Moving Day

Two days into the AT&T National Pro-Am and two consecutive hang-overs means I'm par for the proverbial course. Thoroughly chardon-nayed and baked as any clam, today I've eschewed the motor coach with its tiresomely smiling chamber of commerce faces and inglori-ous yellow wristbands in favor of a fragile-as-glass walk through the Carmel gate to the Pebble Beach maintenance shop entrance—for the weekend, graciously opened to the herd.

Earlier in the a.m. I'd darkened the door of the Carmel Coffee and Cocoa Co. to find Mira's daughter—at least I think it was Mira's daugh-ter—waiting for me at the till, my Fog Lifter in her hand. Either she's clairvoyant or else her mom prepped her on my physical particulars: smallish, hairy, vaguely Semitic . . . usually comes in around 8:30. When I ask her if she knows where in town I can buy earphones to replace the lost Mac buds I need for transcribing interviews, she suggests Carmel Drug, but says it's a long shot. Then—strike me down—she offers to *pick me up some* at cvs on her way home to Carmel Valley, and bring them to me tomorrow, Sunday no less. If I've already found a pair by then, she says, no big deal, she'll just return the set.

I'd said, "That'd be great," when what I'd meant to say was, "Are you for real?!" Duly spooked by such egregious generosity, I'd preceded to turn the Carmel central business district upside down in a preemptive, do-for-myself search. I'd come up empty, of course, shopkeepers wagging their heads side to side when I'd made the universal sign for Steve Jobs. The cashier at Bruno's Market, my last stop, had been especially sympathetic. "You'd think . . . " he'd begun his conciliation speech, but alas and alack, no buds. It's a retail irony the Bruno's cashier and I both know too well: you can get any kind of gourmet coffee bean or brie or cut of roast beast in the fairy-tale village-by-the-sea. You can, at Carmel Plaza alone, oh-la-la at Louis Vuitton, get your Henley on at J-Crew-by-the-Sea or pick up that funky-yet-old-timey summer dress at Anthropologie, and then you can Twitter about your "deals and steals" via a hip widget on the plaza's website. But you've got to go big-box slumming across Highway 1 if you want a nonconsumable, totally utilitarian, utterly gauche set of—heavens to Betsy—ear phones.

When I arrive, pooped, at the pressroom I learn I'm not the only one that was deep in his cups last night. A fellow scribbler tells me he spotted Nick Faldo at 6 a.m. "totally hung," though I'm more inclined to believe Sir Nick was simply out giving Pebble a rigorous predawn examination. The Hog's Breath was packed last night, too, my buddy tells me, in a tone that suggests he ought to preface his sentence with "Dude." It'd been a young crowd, twenty-somethings mostly, he reports, sighing the sigh of the aged.

A quick, food-paranoid check in our journalistic mess tent shows the Japanese have been duly chastened by yesterday's laminate warning. Plenty of beverage remains. I hook myself to an iced-tea I.V., wait patiently while it slowly displaces last night's vino and bile, and ready myself to catch the media shuttle to Spyglass Hill. Most of the celebs have been scheduled for Pebble, this being Saturday—a day of epic, Kelly Slater–worthy surf which CBS hopes to parlay into a ratings bonanza. Having already mixed and mingled with Hollywood's midlist, I opt for good golf over good teeth and choose Spy—the course where Pebble Beach Academy's Laird Small works his magic, the course Michael Murphy swears over and over has him by the balls, the course where tournament leader Dustin Johnson is putting up some crazy-good numbers.

I arrive to find a crowd of one hundred enthusiasts, tops, following Johnson and his playing partner, D. J. Trahan, as they weave their way down Spy's tree-lined fairways. It's so somnambulatory here that, prior to the arrival of the Johnson entourage, amateurs James Crane and Kevin Quinn had *both* holed out from the difficult greenside bunkers on sixteen—two in a row—but had merited only a few amicable, ho-hum claps from the catatonic crowd. Pimento sandwiches falling on the ground at the Masters have caused a bigger ruckus. After a morning at bumpin' Pebble, the quiet among the Spy pines proves almost unsettling. Canvassing the back nine, I pass a scoreboard operator who's abandoned his post to talk on his cell, and a PGA rules official's cart parked, unmanned and abandoned, in the pine straw, as if its pilot had been the victim of an alien abduction. Aside from the occasional amphitheatered crack of titanium on Titleist, it's damn near postapocalyptic.

Beside me at the sun-bathed sixteenth green, a woman sighs, "We don't know any of these guys." To which her companion, a bleach-blonde wearing jewel-studded sunglasses, says, "I only know Phil Mickelson. Where is he?" How wonderfully deflationary is life these days on the Monterey Peninsula? Fifty is the new forty, forty is the new thirty, and Phil is the new Tiger.

Still, the winsome afternoon is not without excitement. As Luke Donald plays up the eighteenth, a *mano-a-mano* duel ensues not between Cool Hand Luke and playing partner Mark Wilson, both playing forgettable rounds, but between the two amateurs, John Watson and Steven John, probably the two best ams in the field at scratch and 1-handicap, respectively. John, who plays his golf at Clint's home club Tehama and routinely gives Casey Boyns a run for his money as top amateur dog on the Peninsula, arrives to find his drive buried in the spinach. He scratches his head, pulls a short iron, and takes a mighty swipe, actually driving his ball *into* the ground. It's the single most freakish shot I've seen played by a scratch golfer in a competitive round since T. C. "Two-Chip" Chen's U.S. Open double hit, and it gives me the golfing willies.

As John recovers from the mud ball, a kerfuffle breaks out further up the fairway, where a handful of cops and tournament security officials have rounded up a bunch of ne'er-do-wells. The half dozen offenders are sitting down on the turf, arms folded over their knees, facing away from the action. They're wearing Blues Brothers suits, which makes the group look like a cross between a stag prom gone wrong and a Jehovah's Witness group arrest. "This is so embarrassing, This is so embarrassing," one of the formerly merry pranksters mumbles to himself over and over.

The rowdies are allegedly fraternity brothers from Santa Clara University, whose parents are teeing it up in the tourney, a couple of marshals tell me. As it turns out, the frat boys had overdone the sauce, "forgot" to buy their tickets, and then lacked the good sense to keep quiet about it. In the end, my informants tell me, they'd been cited by the cops, charged full admission, and rounded up here to stew in very public shame until the parental units arrived.

"I told them this isn't Phoenix," the marshal tells me in a classic to-catch-a-thief gloat. Conjuring the Tour stop in Phoenix—where the chaos-loving galleries behave more like they do in an NBA playoff game—constitutes tough medicine indeed. He sniffs, "This isn't a college crowd." Actually, today it's more like a crowd of centurions, or a convention of morticians.

The controversy proves fleeting, having been quickly and adeptly handled with the Monterey equivalent of "overwhelming force." The transgression won't get reported in tomorrow's paper; unbecoming news at any of the Pebble Beach Company courses seldom does. Yesterday one of the local reporters back at the Pebble newsroom recalled that some thirty years ago his first story assignment was to a local high school golf match taking place on the storied links, way back in the Jurassic period when, unthinkably, Pebble was actually the home course for Robert Louis Stevenson High. The golf match between rival schools had turned into a brawl with actual fisticuffs, and when the cub reporter penned his story with an "if it bleeds it leads" headline, the article was pulled. Where Pebble is concerned, censorship—which never officially rises to such since the copy never makes it past the local editor—is a fact of life on the Peninsula. It's viewed by most not as a manifestation of press suppression but, as in many local newspapers around the country, as collective intervention preserving decorum.

Though it's a seaside track and, like its more smokin' sister, Pebble, a mix of "links" and inland golf, Spyglass pays homage to Augusta in many small ways, the first of which is the members' clubhouse—not the little snacky cafeteria bungalow down by the parking lot or the pro shop across the road, but the gentile, Butler Cabin–like edifice atop the hill beside the eighteenth green. Add to the Augusta cover album some of Spy's towering pines, curvilinear white sand bunkers, and verdant, rolling doglegs, and you've got yourself a dogwood-less doppelganger.

Though Morse opened Pebble in 1919 and Bobby Jones and Company didn't get around to founding their Georgia Peach until 1933, Pebble often seems to defer to its junior club and competitor for the title of most iconic American golf course. The various ways in which the two, first-name-basis layouts bookend American golf are legion: they occupy opposite ends of the coast; they've both been consecrated by the laying on of hands of the great Scottish architect Alister MacKenzie; they were both founded by benign autocrats, Morse and Clifford

Roberts, respectively; and they're both routinely rated among the top five courses in the United States.

As I mill around the scorer's trailer waiting for the first of the day's interviews, I leaf through the simple black-and-white photocopy I picked up back at the pressroom titled *2010 AT&T Pebble Beach National Pro-Am, Amateurs' Home Town and Club*. On its face it's a ho-hummer. The approximately 155 names—a de facto listing of some of the wealthiest and most talented men (and one woman) in America—are presented as plainly as a mega-church roster printed on some parishioner's home laser. On closer inspection, however, I count two representatives from Augusta National, chairman Billy Payne, Mark O'Meara's partner for the week; and Lee Styslinger III, president and chief executive of Altec Inc., a member of George W. Bush's Export Council and a trustee for the gold medal–winning ski and snowboard team at the 2010 Winter Olympics in Vancouver.

While the average ticket holder may not recognize America's corporate barons, the pros know exactly who they're better-balling with. Many Tour golfers studied marketing or business in college when they weren't studying supination and pronation, so whenever they lace up the spikes for a pro-am as big as this one, they're acutely aware of the dividends that might accrue them in return for two to four cheerful rounds of corporate escort.

"You meet some great people," Luke Donald tells me after his round. "You form some great relationships that help you down the road in terms of sponsorship . . . It's nice to see a lot of big businesses are still interested in golf. That's great for the economy and good for golf." After his round at Spy is in the books, Mike Weir intimates a similar sentiment, telling me that he comes back because he loves the area and the golf courses. And, he adds, "I have a good friend . . . George Roberts."

When Weir first dropped the name I'd simply nodded, and assumed George Roberts was some local wine aficionado, arts patron, or all-around do-gooder whom the likeable, utterly sincere Weir had happened to be befriend. Later, on a hunch, I Googled "George Roberts" and "San Francisco Country Club"—the two breadcrumbs dropped by his *Amateurs' Home Town and Club* listing—and found a total of four hits, one of which links Roberts to Charles Schwab, a fellow member of the prestigious Bay Area Country Club, and names Roberts as erstwhile director of the board of a little grocery store called Safeway and two other mom-and-pop shops you may have heard of: Duracell and Bruno's Supermarkets. One web bio describes Roberts in language so cryptic it sounds like Tom Clancy: "Texas-born private equity investor and billionaire financier." In the late eighties Roberts and his partner, Henry Cravis, pulled off one of the most famous leveraged buyouts in history, bagging RJR Nabisco. Turns out, in 2006, according to the site, eleven of Roberts's funds produced over $50 billion in profits. His influence in the markets dates all the way back to the global investment giant and ultimately ill-fated concern Bear Stearns. While some articles dub Roberts a "corporate raider," most agree that, like his buddy Chuck Schwab, Roberts is a gee-whiz venture philanthropist. And he's also a 4-handicap.

Weirsy, where can I get me friends like these?

Roberts's partner in corporate philanthropy, Charles Schwab of Schwab Investments, is likewise teeing it up this week. And while Schwab owns a home off the eighteenth at Pebble, he's still way under the radar out on the links, partnered with Aussie pro Rod Pampling. According to *Forbes* magazine, Schwab enters the list of the richest folks in the country in the top fifty at just under $5 billion in net wealth—on par with the entire annual budget for Middle American states like mine. As with most of the corporate invitees on this year's guest list, Schwab's also decidedly Republican, in the past ranking in the top one hundred in donations to the GOP, according to *Mother Jones* magazine. Also "in the house" and on the links this week, quietly tucked in with pro Joe Ogilvie, is the man at the helm of the week's corporate sponsor, AT&T big boss Randall Stephenson, and his predecessor as CEO of the telecommunications giant, Mike Armstrong.

In sum, if a terrorist ever wanted to strike a death blow to American capitalism, God forbid, he could bypass the president's inaugural ball and head straight for the AT&T Pro-Am, where there's more political, social, and monetary power per capita than any other sporting event in America.

Our first big interview of the day is with tourney leader Dustin Johnson, one of the PGA Tour's most talented rising stars and also one of its more troubled. Talented because the kid can dunk a basketball in bare feet and will average over 300 yards per drive this week; troubled because he's already pled guilty to second-degree burglary—a youthful indiscretion for which he was ultimately pardoned by his home state of South Carolina—and been arrested for DUI as recently as 2009. Johnson reminds of a minor league pitcher: a lean, long-limbed loose cannon capable of bringing some serious heat. He's got a vulture's wingspan and a slow, Low Country Carolina drawl that makes him sound like he should be driving NASCAR.

Johnson's been too busy chasing Titleists to develop an affectation. He describes his round simply—"rolled the ball good," "hit the ball good," "happy with the way I'm playin'"—stopping briefly to comment on the gnarly rough. He's accommodating enough, but you get the sense he'd just as soon whup a journalist as talk to one. He hacks a couple of goobers at the feet of us newsies while we interview him about an incendiary round where he shot 30 on the front side.

Two-time U.S. Open champion Lee Janzen, a fellow midwesterner from the Lutheran climes of Minnesota, is next on our press hit list. Janzen's second Open win in 1998 at the Olympic Club in San Francisco proved he was legit—up there with the other repeat major champs of recent vintage, the Phil Mickelsons and Padraig Harrington's of the golfing world. Like Tom Kite he's known as a potentially prickly interview. Safe to say, none of us scribblers relish the impending tête-à-tête, especially since Janzen's had a rough go of it in the first couple months of the season. His best finish was a T24 at the Waste Management

Open, which pretty much says it all. Add to that the indignity of having his U.S. Open game of short, controlled drives pretty much gobbled up and handed to him by young guns like Dustin Johnson, who on average is outdriving him 25 yards a pop, and you have a potentially unhappy camper.

"Lee, a few of us would like to ask you a couple of questions," I venture, waiting for the shoe to fall. He looks up from his golf bag, where he's zipping zippers faster than Tiger Woods. "Start askin'," he says wearily. I'm first off the diving board into the deep end, asking what keeps him coming back to this tournament. "It's Pebble," he replies, as in *duh*. "I mean, if this tournament was . . . well, I'd say if the tournament was in a cornfield, you might not get people to come."

"That means something coming from a Minnesota boy." My comment is intended not as a jab but as an admittedly awkward attempt to connect, to show my interviewee that I've done my homework. Still, he bristles. "Well, I've been living in Florida since I was twelve," he says, turning away.

Inside, I'm thwacking myself on the head. *Stupid, stupid, stupid.* Spend years covering peripatetic professionals and you learn not to ask them about their hometowns. It's a sore subject. In golf, as in Hollywood, most of the guys have had to completely remake themselves, and their swings, to get to the top. That meant, at the very least, talking their folks into moving to somewhere below the Mason-Dixon Line. Janzen's just given me the Heisman straight-arm that world-class athletes often give when asked about a hometown—Austin, Minnesota, say—that doesn't fit their carefully cultivated sporting image or sound quite so nice as *Windemere, Florida*, when called out on the first tee.

I'm still smarting from the Janzen slapdown but I tune back in when he offers a wacked-out, meteorological quack theory for what makes Pebble such a bitch: "The ball doesn't travel very well near the Pacific. It travels much better near the Atlantic. Water's colder, so that must have something to do with it . . . There's more resistance in the air here, so it's gotta be a little bit better shot."

Ocean temperature, air resistance, curve of the ball? It's invigorating to hear such an odd, pseudoscientific parsing of a course that usually merits nothing but superlative clichés: beautiful, fantastic, scenic, amazing. Janzen's sufficiently warmed up now to sing Pebble's praises. "We don't play anything like it the rest of the year," he tell us. "The variety of holes at Pebble Beach—eight, nine, and ten—could be the best stretch of three par-4s anywhere, as far as beauty and strategy . . . Six is probably my favorite hole, because the land made that hole. You couldn't go with a bulldozer and make that hole the way it is."

I'm so enthralled by the trans-Newtonian smack Janzen has been talking and his new, more expansive self that I'm emboldened to ask another question, namely, "Who's best positioned to win at Pebble?"

"Someone who hits it straight, long, hits it the distance they want to hit it, thinks really good, and makes their putts," he says, sticking the knife in and twisting it. "How's that?"

Lucky for me, the next guy out of the scorer's shack is one of the Tour's more media-friendly good-timers, Rich Beem. Beem's best known for fending off Tiger to win the PGA at Hazeltine in 2002 and, in endless highlight reels, diving onto the hood of an Altima coupe after scoring an ace at the 2007 Nissan Open. He reminds me of my best high school buddy, and that—coupled with the fact that he once quit golf to sell cell phones—endears the Beemer to me. As one of the last remaining "regular guys" on a Tour that is increasingly filled with pretty boys and prima donnas, Beem has a cross to bear, and today that cross weighs more than Brian Urlacher. Like Janzen, Beem's best finish of the new year came at the tragi-comically named Waste Management Open and, like Janzen, he's managed to miss the cut at the AT&T. As he packs up shop, I ask the Beemer if he's got time for question.

"About what?" (Golf Writer Tip Number 383: Don't ask if you can pose a pro a question anymore than you'd ask your teenage kid if they'd like to scrub the toilet. The Nike slogan applies here.) Permission granted, I ask him about the AT&T's rep for letting free spirits be free spirits. "I'll be brutally honest with you. It's more valuable for the amateurs than it is for the pros. Because . . . no offense, but some of the pros have a hard time getting out of their shell . . . I actually shied away from this event for a long time and, now, coming back . . . the golf courses are difficult and the conditions aren't always the best, but . . . it's great camaraderie, a great week."

I politely inquire after whether Beem, who early in his career took a backseat to no one but Daly in the Bacchus Department, has indulged in a little bit of the "Monterey Merlot" this week. Beemer grins his high-school hellion grin. "You're doing a disservice to yourself if you don't. I mean, hell yeah, you got to go out and have fun with it . . . I don't get involved as much as other guys. I . . . you know . . . dip my . . . foot in the water a little bit." For an anxious sec., I'm unsure what Beem is going to say he dipped in what. "I'm not scared," he adds, "that's for damn sure. You've got to have fun with it to show the amateurs a good time, and that's what I did."

And Carmel . . . does he dig it? "No, it's terrible. The views are awful. It's absolutely brutal. It sucks. Put me in the middle of the Sahara any day."

Once the ironic Beemer's out of earshot, a fellow scribbler sidles up to me and says, under his breath, "I'm surprised Beem didn't have a fifth of booze with him."

"Really?" I ask. I'm always the last to know about these things.

The guy nods solemnly at the character assassination he's just perpetuated. Sometimes sportswriters can be so high school.

While I wait for the Big Sticks to come out of the press tent before heading back to Sam Morseland, I gather my notes on what the pros have told me about Pebble so far this week. Inevitably, feelings about the granddaddy of the Monterey Peninsula courses bubbled to the surface, even if, as was the case today, they'd just been spanked by Spyglass Hill, a course many of the pros consider more difficult than Pebble and with a course rating to prove it.

Whether Pebble's a dream date or a nightmare, she's the kind that has you talking long after the stolen kiss at the door. To date, here's some dish:

RICKY BARNES

"Pebble was everything. If we won a tournament when I was young, we got to come over here and play the day after Christmas. It was kind of the reward . . . First time I played here I don't even know what I shot. I was trying to slap myself in the face, realizing I was playing Pebble Beach . . . This course is not going to get bumped out of the top five or top ten in the world at any time . . . Maybe the best piece of land I've ever played on."

AARON BADDELEY

"I'd say it's in the top twenty. I wouldn't say it's top three. I do think the more you play it, the better it gets. I remember the first time I played it, I was like, 'It's a nice course. The holes on the water are nice.' Then you play it again and you're like, 'This is good,' then you play it again and you're like, 'This place is awesome!' I love the small greens. I like the variety . . . I like the seventh hole, the short par 3 . . . You got some longer par 3s, like twelve . . . or the fourth, up the hill, the short par 4 you can hit iron off the tee or driver."

JOHN DALY

"It's a wonderful part of the country we don't get to see a lot, and Pebble, being a public golf course hosting the U.S. Opens . . . these courses are absolutely beautiful . . . It is the great wonder of the world."

LUKE DONALD

"I suppose you could classify Pebble as a links but it doesn't have that firm fast feel that St. Andrews does. Pebble is one of the most scenic courses in the world . . . I think it's a good course. It's probably not one of my favorites of all the courses I've ever played, but in terms of vistas and views, it's up there . . . I just think a few of the holes architecturally are a little bit weak. You hit good drives and you're on big side slopes . . . There are a lot of good holes . . . Definitely a course I enjoy playing. The more I play it, the more I enjoy it."

COREY PAVIN

"I've always loved Pebble. [My appreciation] can't grow any more than when I first played it. I think it's a really cool course . . . It's pretty, and if you catch it on a good day and you play well, you can shoot a good score. It can be extremely challenging when the wind blows . . . Just a fantastic place to go out and play. Great holes. Wonderful views. A shotmaker's course."

A few hours ago I'd arrived to sunshine so blindingly abundant it had caused me to shed my sweater. Now, having long since re-donned the cashmere, I'm shivering. It's ass-cold out here, as the marine layer—that creepy meteorological stalker that shadows the coast—has settled in on the couch with the remote and means to stay. The glib reporters who've come and gone this afternoon have given us off-puttingly chipper dispatches from the other side: "You still need your sunblock down at Pebble."

Maybe architect Robert Trent Jones Sr. and Company buried fog machines in the moguls to add to Spyglass Hill's *Treasure Island* ambience, or else Spy's just microclimate-doomed to miasma. In any case, the weird, wooly weather falls short of wish-you-were-here. It's more Thanksgiving at Lambeau Field than Hellos from Sunny California. Even the gallery girls have wrapped themselves in University of California throws and slipped on the mittens. I'm maintaining the cold-weather vigil for Mike Weir and Jim Furyk, who are signing their cards and making their way toward me in the roped-off press area.

It's a beautiful Canuck response Weirsy gives me when I ask him for a comment or two: "Ah, you don't want to talk to me. I'm in last place." Not the New Yorkian *Whaddya want?* Not the Nuyorican *Que Passa?* Not even the French Canadian *Qu'est-ce qui se passé?* "*Ah, you don't want to talk to me"* is Ontarian for *"I don't want to talk to you,"* but, praise the Lord and pass the Maple Leaf, Weirsy is too nice to refuse. In fact, if you can be caricatured for your underdog niceness, you're either the Chicago Cubs or the Pride of Ontario.

The first time Weirsy saw Pebble was during his rookie year on the Tour in 1998. He's come back ever since, in part because Weir is a family guy and Carmel is a family destination for those who need it to be . Part of the charm of Carmel-by-the-Sea, like any fantasy incarnate, is that it can be whatever you want it to be. To his credit, Weirsy's fun is more Tim Tebow than Lindsay Lohan. "I love wine," he tells me. "My whole family loves coming out here . . . my parents, my kids. My dog makes the trip to run around on the beach down in Carmel. He's had a heyday."

"Every hole has its own little challenge," Weirsy tells me when I ask him why he admires Pebble. "That's why I think it's such a great golf course. You use every club in the bag. You hit a lot of long irons, but you hit a short iron into seven. I can't narrow it down to one hole; they're just all so good . . . It sets up well for a lefty . . . It looks good to my eye."

Behind us Jim Furyk waits in the wings, caddie Fluff, a.k.a. Mike Cowan, busily scrubbing everything he can find to scrub while silently watching over his man like an overweening mother. Fluff's every bit as much of a legend as Furyk himself is, one of the most recognizable caddies on the Tour and progenitor of the comical headline, "Tiger Fires Fluff," when Woods gave Cowan the axe.

With Weirsy gone dog-chasing and Fluff occupied with fetching an autographed ball for a tyke, Furyk tells me he comes here mostly for the golf courses and especially for Pebble, with whom he has some history. "Early on I liked it because it was so beautiful," he tells me. "I've gotten more comfortable over the years on Pebble . . . Everyone's played Pebble a bunch of times. If you've never played it before, it's going to be a difficult place to come in and have a good event . . . For me, especially, I had a hard time with the greens and breaks and the second shot at eight, second shot at nine. It's got some difficult shots and elevation changes. Over time it's a place you can really learn a lot about the golf course and its subtleties."

Furyk puts the AT&T Pro-Am on his schedule each year for plenty of other reasons, too. "It's a beautiful area. I like the golf courses. It gets a knock out here for the weather . . . But we could be in Baltimore." Note to golf fans: Don't let anyone ever tell you the world's third best golfer doesn't have a sense of humor. It's just a dry one. Furyk continues, "My wife and I love Carmel . . . It's just cute. It's very quaint. It's got a bunch of great little restaurants and pubs. It's a very relaxing place. It's slow-moving and a good place to spend the day and not do anything."

On television, when Jim Gray or Roger Maltbie corral him after a round, Furyk usually looks pissy—like an overworked accountant during tax season. But off-camera he's one of the sweetest top-notch athletes you'll ever meet, a guy who can use the word "cute" without flinching, a guy who's actually able to *discourse* on his sport, which means improvising coherent sentences above and beyond Sport Clichés 101. With Furyk you get the sense that the words, like the shots, come hard-won. You hang on them.

Furyk's eyes, too, are a revelation. They're blue-gray as the Civil War, coldly discerning and warmly intelligent. They're golfer's eyes . . . like Arnie's, like Jack's, like Norman's and Watson's—the eyes of pilots and sea captains and corporate executives. Eyes that have seen a ton of weather, real and metaphoric, eyes that have gazed in as much as out. They're commanding, these champion golfers' soul-windows.

15

D. J. Does Valentine's Day

Clint, Climax, and Eye Candy
Sunday at the Clambake

After four or five straight days of hard-core partying and celebrity ogling, Sunday at the AT&T National Pro-Am risks anticlimax. Like the last day at an all-inclusive resort, you've had so many Bloody Marys you're practically oozing Citron and V-8. You've partied till you're pooped.

I, however, am right with the world this Sabbath morn, fresh as a flower, resilient as ice plant, having nursed a single glass of gratis merlot with Johnny Miller at a reception at Pebble's Gallery Café the night before—well, not so much *with* him as at his feet—and, afterward, having teetotaled my way through a teeth-gnashing one-man-band playing Van Morrison and Beatles covers in the courtyard of the Carmel Plaza. When the Clapton wannabe crooned a ditty he called "Syphilis" to the tune of the Beatles' "Yesterday" ("Syphilis, How the hell did I ever get this? Oh the pain whenever I take a piss, Oh I believe in syphilis") an early roll on the yoga mat with Huckleberry the lame housecat seemed suddenly ducky.

I'd begun my Sunday at the Carmel Coffee and Cocoa Co., where Mira had handed me a heart-shaped ceramic plate—color lingerie red—atop which sat a bar of chocolate. Not just chocolate, mind you, but dark chocolate, the kind packing a cacao percentage that beats the chance of rain in Monterey on Groundhog Day, the kind that trumps Tiger's percentage of putts made from inside 10 feet. She'd claimed she'd intended to give her heart to a handful of regulars, this being Valentine's morn, but it'd been no mere Hershey's she'd slipped me. To a Middle American like me, it might as well have been the Dom Perignon of cacao, the Gurkha Black Dragon cigar of chocolate, the goddamned Wonka Bar complete with Charlie Bucket's golden ticket.

Being the kid who blushed scarlet when his relatives so much as sang Happy Birthday to him, I'd thanked Mira profusely, grabbed my cheap-ass cup and gratis chocolate, and hustled out to the courtyard to sit under the hibiscus and ponder this unexpected act of radical hospitality. Is she sweet on me, this Mira? Did she hatch this plan last night with her girlfriends, dressed in a nightie, giddy as a schoolgirl?

Regardless, I strut into the pressroom feeling a little more like a man, a dark, sweet secret literally burning a hole in my pocket. Dustin Johnson is your overnight co-leader. None of my cronies really expect him to barf on his shoes unless J. B. Holmes catches fire and pushes him from behind or the wind kicks up, neither of which is forecasted. The day shapes up to be a two-man race between Johnson and two-time career Tour winner Paul Goydos, whose dark-horse status has sent us scribblers to shameless overnight Googling. To cover today's Clambake climax close as shit on stink, as we say back on the farm, I ask the PGA Tour's Dave Kellner to burn for me a DVD of CBS's final round broadcast in-progress, freeing me up to do some old-fashioned beat-the-streets—or, in this case, the greens—reporting, while checking in periodically with Jim Nantz, Nick Faldo, and the gang in TVland.

At noon one of Pebble's avowed fans, Nantz, opens the broadcast by invoking yesterday's record waves. "All-time highs," he intones. In the minutes that follow, Jimmy describes a "links world renowned for its majesty," a "Pacific paradise," where "sixty thousand flock to its shores to challenge Mother Nature's best." It's the kind of embarrassing, totally undisguised salivating that makes you want to say "enough already!" when your buddies shamelessly ogle a hottie, but it's been happening ever since cameras first trained their irises on Pebble.

I know this because, I'm almost ashamed to admit, I have amassed what I term a Pebble Beach "video library" – a.k.a. a collection of golf course porn. Shelved beside too many Chevy Chase movies and that other well-loved classic of the vhs era, *vhs Headcleaner, Wet* is the very punny *Kite Soars Over Pebble Beach*, a recap of the 1992 U.S. Open presented as a "Special Video Offer from Titleist" that allows me to rewind until I'm fully sated with host Jim McKay's opening ode to Pebble: "The Monterey Peninsula is a popular place any time of year, but for golfers in the third week in June, Pebble Beach was the only place to be," McKay claims, adding, "Pebble Beach . . . the name is magic for golfers who come to visit this national treasure." Elsewhere it's the tape's bathos that slays me, the coverage so pun-rich it's impossible to resist, complete with groaners like, "Tom Kite lifted his game to new heights in capturing his first major championship," and "Kite overcame blustery breezes," etc., etc.

My most-watched vid, though, is the recently re-released *Snead Versus Nicklaus Revisited*, from the *Shell's Wonderful World of Golf* specials from the 1960s. The show opens with the Nantz-like George Rogers, who takes it from the top, in Technicolor. "The Pebble Beach Golf Links in Pebble Beach, California, a seaside golf course unexcelled in beauty, design, and unpredictable weather on the Monterey Peninsula," Rogers baritones, as behind him a full orchestra bows their strings and a fly-over shot unveils the picturesque seventh hole bathed in sunshine and licked by light surf. The course's familiar outline takes shape from overhead, ribbons of emerald green running through the brown, unirrigated rough that was once Pebble's norm. It's a striking image, this blast from the past – the dung browns and verdant greens looking more like a helicopter shot over today's Scottsdale or Palm Springs than Monterey.

Wearing a black blazer stamped with a Shell insignia the size of a grapefruit, Jones turns next to his color man, "the legendary Gene Sarazen," who is ruddy of complexion and bedecked in scarlet tie, powder blue sweater vest, beige blazer, and matching plus fours. It looks like ol' red-faced Gene just walked right out of the players' lounge after a highball with Bobby Jones. "Well, George, I've traveled all over the world," the Squire says on cue, "and I think this is the finest seaside course I've ever seen. It's tops with me and I've been coming here since 1923."

The gallery of locals—pillboxed and fedoraed and horn-rimmed—looks strangely formal and erudite. They line the first tee one- or two-deep, casually interested, as if a match between the young gun soon to become the greatest golfer of all time and the winningest golfer of all time, Sam Snead, happens every day in Monterey. Someone's rust-colored retriever runs onto the fairway as Nicklaus addresses his 3-wood, though the disturbance doesn't seem to flap the unflappable Jack. He's right down the middle, while Snead blocks it into the pine straw and the group's scorekeeper—the spitting image of Jackie O.—looks on. "The greens look beautiful this morning," Sarazen enthuses.

Snead Versus Nicklaus Revisited amounts to an invaluable visual archive—preserving Pebble as it looked not long after the first NBC broadcast of the Crosby in 1958 and just a couple of years after Pebble's first Major, the 1961 U.S. Amateur captured by Jack Nicklaus with Monterey's own Didi Gonzalez on the bag. Here in full color is the era Casey Boyns, Bobby Clampett, Tom Watson, Robert Boerner, Tim Berg, and others have described to me, a time when the world was just beginning to catch wind of the windy, winsome links and a young Berg could ditch a business conference in Berkeley in 1962 and play his first-ever round on the largely undiscovered, roughly conditioned gem for a mere $10.

After my titillating Snead v. Nicklaus DVD arrived in my Carmel P.O. box wrapped in a brown paper bag, I'd called Al Barkow in San

Francisco to ask about the contest between the two golfing heavy-weights. Barkow, who golfed on Roosevelt University's NAI National Champion team in 1959 and wrote for *Shell's Wonderful World of Golf* in the 1960s, recalled, "I remember Sam was kept waiting by Jack. Snead was pretty teed off about that. He was a legend and Jack was just a young guy."

I'd asked him how the producers decided on the courses where the matches would be played. Some of them, he'd said, like St. Andrews, were selected by Sarazen. Other times, he'd recalled, "We did the shows in places where they [Shell] had business interests and had gas stations, or where they wanted to develop oil."

A half-century later, Pebble and commercial TV are still in bed together. Jim Nantz is a passionate supporter of Pebble, so when he pipes up, in a lull in the coverage, to say, "Folks, you got to get out here and see it in U.S. Open shape," I know he's doing a favor to Pebble's marketing department, which has been urging reporters this week every chance it gets to remind our readers that: a) Pebble's open for play in the lead-up to the Open, and b) it's still possible to score a ticket.

Nantz broke into the broadcasting biz with CBS at Pebble in 1986, and he's fallen so thoroughly in love with the place he's let it be known in multiple interviews that he wants one day to live in the Dukedom. He begins each day at the AT&T National Pro-Am at dawn, with a jog on the course out to Arrowhead Point, meditating at seven tee before running back to The Lodge. He likes to eat an omelet at Katy's Place in Carmel before chatting up the pros on the Pebble putting green pre-broadcast. Nantz, who played on the golf team and shared a room with Fred Couples at the University of Houston, once described to *Pebble Beach Magazine's* Marcia Smith his "deep spiritual connection" to a place where his "senses go into overdrive": "I love what Pebble Beach stands for—excellence. It's the Rolls-Royce, the Rolex watch of real estate. It is managed perfection. It exudes pure class. As you get older and wiser, you know what you want and where you want it to be. And Pebble Beach is that place for me."

Like no other course in the world, the story here every February—and more so since the advent of high def—is the course itself. Indeed, in the first half hour of CBS airtime it's the stadium, strangely, that merits more attention than the athletes. Amplified by Snoopy-blimp views of the eighth and deep shots from the on-course cameras that penetrate the sea mist as far as the pedestrian frolics underway on Carmel Beach, on-course commentator Ian Baker-Finch effuses, "The golf course is absolutely superb, as is the golf, as is the area. Spectacular!" Minutes later the usually cynical Gary McCord, praising the "great galleries this week," asks rhetorically, "Why wouldn't you want to walk around this cathedral of golf?" The CBS control rooms plays a pre-recorded interview with Goydos in which he offers a Homeric ode to the coliseum where today he'll vie for golfing supremacy, saying, "God's gift to golf was Pebble Beach."

It's the dulcet Aussie Baker-Finch, though, who seems to be the designated bard du jour, waxing poetic in the segue to each and every station break as the cameras take in the turquoise waves and acrobatic gulls. "What a glorious day," he gushes on one lead-in to commercial. "Absolutely spectacular." Then, after a pregnant pause so the viewers at home can drink in the made-for-TV image, he purrs, "Wish you were." And the fawning doesn't stop there. Even snarky David Feherty opines to Nantz, "I don't remember two days like this here, Jimmy." Not to be outdone, Finchie one-ups his fellow on-course commentators by calling it a "golfing heaven," "one of the most beautiful places in the world of golf," and a "real gem of American architecture."

The sublimity of this week's conditions stirs even my dad from his wine-dark slumber in the Sunshine State, where he's watching the broadcast in high def from an RV park in Naples. On Friday he'd written, out of the blue: "I've spent the entire day in veg mode watching the AT&T between the coverages of the Golf Channel and CBS. As you are well aware, I have watched this tournament since before you were born, and I have never seen Pebble more magnificent than it is today. I remain awed that you are actually there somewhere!"

Dad's words makes me feel proud and guilty all at once. In them I hear the bewitchment Michael Murphy first spoke about six months ago in our lunch at Sausalito, the seduction fair Pebble possesses in abundance. When Dad writes that the links look "more magnificent than ever," I hear the voice of a man paying compliments to a beautiful woman, the kind you expect to be followed by a kiss of an outstretched hand, a bowed head, a whispered, "Enchantée, mademoiselle." Pebble seems weirdly better with age, not the way a good merlot does but as if nature itself has been defied and the clock turned back, as if, in the ultimate male fantasy, the wizened wife has transformed back into the coquette.

Like Dad, I've been positively spellbound these last few days, more by the place itself than by the golf. On air, Nantz tries to bait Faldo—who's prone to long lapses of silence unbecoming a color commentator—into sharing some of his Pebble experiences. Back in his playing days, did he ever got distracted by the scenery here? Sir Nick replies with his usual dry wit, "I did glance on the odd occasion just to make sure I wasn't playing St. Andrews." Nantz and Faldo proceed to crack about Faldo's renowned "blinders"—the single-minded focus that made him a six-time major championship winner—but the subject is allowed to drop until, out of the blue, Faldo picks up the thread a few commercial breaks later. "It's mesmerizing, isn't it," he waxes. "What I love here is the repetition of the waves. They come in stacks of six or seven and their color . . . *pearlescent.*"

On the heels of Faldo's poetry, CBS cameras find Dustin Johnson and Paul Goydos on the eighth green, Johnson one up at 19 under par. The TV talking heads commence to setting up the kind of storyline only TV folks can: the "long-hitting, strapping" Johnson versus the guy who McCord dubs the "plodder."

But when Johnson double bogeys nine and "the Plodder" suddenly becomes your leader, we realize we've got a tournament on and the back nine at Pebble is beginning to do what only Augusta National can do as well: completely reshuffle the deck. Though he's leading and playing inspired golf as he charges onto the back nine, Goydos, with his slouched shoulders, love handles, and herky-jerky, Kenny Perry swing is the recipient of more passive-aggressive comments than your average mother-in-law. "He's waiting to see if all these show ponies come up and do something," McCord wryly observes.

The effect on poor Goydos is emasculating but it makes for pro-vocative TV. Driving statistics are trotted out for both Goydos—256 yards a poke—and Johnson—305 a bomb—to further dramatize the diff. The boys at CBS have lucked into a bevy of archetypal narratives: short guy versus tall guy, old guy versus young guy, wild guy versus straight guy (in the golfing sense, mind), nervous guy versus unflappable guy, veteran versus upstart. Every time Goydos strikes an iron, the number on its face and the distance to the hole is reported with a droll sense of incredulity, an implied raised eyebrow, as when the Plodder pulls a 7-iron from 133 on the treacherous par-5 fourteenth and still leaves it *short*. As the surreality of a Goydos lead sinks in with the press, it's like waiting for a wreck at a NASCAR race . . . like waiting for the Spirit to move at a gathering of Quakers. No one believes for a minute that Goydos could be the Chosen One.

By the time the lovable Plodder's wheels have come off, I've hustled back to the cordoned-off press area, where word spreads that Goydos has taken *a quad* after blasting it over the back of fourteen, a position even we reporters know means death. Meanwhile, over on CBS, the Muppets in the balcony are having a field day with the self-destruct button Goydos has just pushed. Faldo rips the veteran for his "negative visualization" from the fourteenth fairway, where he'd chatted with Johnson about the terrors of the tiny green while both of them watched Bryce Molder make a 9 by pinballing his pearl back and forth over what Faldo calls the "smallest landing area in all of golf." Staggering off the fourteenth duly chastened, Goydos had tracked down on-course commentator Peter Kostis to do something stranger and more self-effacing still: remind the viewing audience he'd suffered a

9 in a final round earlier in the year. Now, having notched a second 9, they should call him Gretzky, Goydos wryly points out, to match the Great One's jersey number.

I take advantage of the temporary denouement to chase down Chuck Schwab — philanthropist, altruist, corporate baron — who, as I watch, signs more kid autographs shoved at him through the iron cattle gates than any other AT&T participant bar Phil Mickelson and Bill Murray. It's Chuck, short, powerful, well-tanned, resplendent in pastel sweaterage Chuck, and a gaggle of prepubescents crying out for his John Hancock. It's a weirdly archaic sight — like something out of Dickens or *Annie* — this giant of industry surrounded by enough pink-skinned, enthusiastic innocents to make even the most hardened cynic shake his head and say, "Only in America." How do these kids, these young Republicans, know who the hell Chuck Schwab is, anyway?

To my surprise, Schwab agrees to gift me with a quick comment or two en route to the scorer's tent. I lead off with the need-to-know: Is that really his house off the eighteenth fairway? "Yeah," he says in a voice so laid back it's well-nigh tranquilized. "The one to the south. The white one." It sounds like he's giving directions to a little bungalow on Maple Street in Middle America, but the white one he's talking about is, in fact, a great white whale . . . a low-slung, coldly geometric affair of polished stone and floor-to-ceiling glass that might be Ayn Rand's sexy architectural fantasy. Its lines are straighter than Clay Aiken and more muscular than the Governator. Since the AT&T kicked off on Thursday, the usually deserted hacienda has been party central, stuffed to the gills with young guns in crisp collared shirts working on their tans, martinis in hand. Each time I've passed, a new genre of music has blasted forth from the kick-ass surround system. Clearly, the mice have been monkeying with the tunes while the cat's been away stalking birdies.

The slimmest of hedgerows separates Schwab's dream house from America's dream links. The casa — a mixture of an Egyptian step tomb and a French expressionist's wet dream — commands the right side of the fairway at a 60-degree angle from the preferred drive line off the eighteenth.

I ask its billion-dollar owner what made him hang his hat here. "The serenity," Schwab replies, breathing deep. "When you come to Pebble Beach it gets you out of the busy zone of the business world. It brings a certain amount of calm and gets you re-fired . . . regenerated to go back and fight the battles."

Schwab's voice is gravelly and molasses drip all at once—a freak accident in the audio editing room that mixed James Earl Jones with Owen Wilson. I find it hard to believe the uber-mellow, slow-talking tycoon has ever had his cage rattled. "We've probably been here nearly twenty years," Schwab adds. "We try to make it six or seven times a year. It's fabulous to come down here and visit."

Sensing he'll indulge me one more question, I head right for the jugular, for you, my golf reader, *mon semblable, mon frère.* I want to know: Has some hack ever busted out one of his floor-to-ceiling windows with a wicked cut? "No, of course not," he says. "They put the tee up close this week."

How about the amateurs during resort time? I follow up. Do they rain Titleists down upon him? Suddenly, I'm Barbara Goddamned Golfing Walters. "Maybe a few. But never a window," Schwab insists. "Sometimes I find a few balls over in the high grass," he says, chuckling.

And then he's off, Chuck is, hopefully home to put the kibosh on whatever jackass has commandoed the ghetto blaster. C'mon, boys, what do you think this is, the frickin' Waste Management Open?

As the tournament leaders begin to come in, the lazy reporters who've heretofore watched the action on the pressroom boob tube surround the scorer's trailer like flatulent wildebeests around a watering hole. The Johnny-come-latelies are usually the slower, older guys sporting bellies and specs and mustaches, the guys who would have long ago been culled from the herd in an alternate savannas but who have some-how defied Darwinism and risen to the level of alpha males among golf-writing Homo sapiens. Often they'll be finishing a sandwich or something when the pro starts to talk, a little dab of mayonnaise still stuck to the 'stache.

I stick around just long enough to hear Prince Phil wax nostalgic about David Duval's game: "He struck it so flush and pure with such a penetrating ball flight," Lefty says, recalling the scary-good skill of today's surprise contender, the Ghost of Golfing Past. Double D's coming up the last fairway just 1 shot back.

The Mystery of Phil's Shiny Pants and Other Tales will have to wait for another time, as I opt to hotfoot it out to seventeen tee, where the Johnson group arrives with the swift, serious purpose of a Mongol horde. D. J. plays quickly all the time, but in the last group, with the heat on, he's shifted into warp speed. He barely breaks stride as he pulls a short iron from the bag and yanks it long and left into the back bunker—jail . . . certain damnation, possible playoff! Meanwhile, over on eighteen fairway, Duval is on his hands and knees examining a Monterey mud ball.

After Duval and J. B. Holmes both miss legit birdie rolls and Johnson makes the expected bog from the kitty litter, Johnson marches to the eighteenth tee needing a bird to win. While just about anyone else on Tour would pull a fairway metal, the Carolina Kid with ice in his veins rips a driver left of the cypress trees bisecting the fairway . . . 300 yards out, easy, and no more than 10 paces from where the Pacific takes a McGruff-sized bite out of the short grass. For his second shot the kid pulls a 3-iron, dumping it into the front bunker, where he'll have an up and down to slam the door on Duval and Holmes. A blast from the sand and a 4-foot birdie putt later, Johnson's your repeat champ, and it's over, just like that, this most legendary of pro-ams.

The finish to a major golf tournament, like the ending of siege or a cricket match, shocks the system, as staggering as last call. People who've been out here on the links for four days solid, faithful as Mohammedans, all of a sudden look at one another and blink, as if to say, *It's really over?*

A guy in front of me — a big Hoss with a lobster burn — celebrates tourney's end and four days of cell phone abstinence by taking golf's post-coitus of calls. The guy on the other end tries to tell him something — insert Charlie Brown phone voice — but all Hoss wants to know is if his buddy can see him on TV. Hoss mentions that the camera's already caught him talking to then-leader Goydos on the thirteenth. Apparently Goydos had asked Hoss what delicious elixir Hoss happened at that moment to be drinking.

"A screwdriver," Hoss reports he'd said to the man of the hour.

"Those aren't usually any good," Goydos had said.

"They are when they're made with fresh-squeezed orange juice," our man had said.

"That's the only way I'll ever have 'em," Hoss says Goydos had said while allegedly peering into Hoss's cup. Our hero had then told Goydos to sink his birdie on thirteen, and damned if he didn't do just that.

"Next thing you know he gets a frickin' quadruple bogey on fourteen," Hoss hollers into his phone. The dude's got some serious pipes.

Then, as we wait for Johnson to tell us what we want to hear so we can all go home, Hoss proceeds to narrate his day from beginning to end, from the shrimp omelets he inhaled at breakfast at the party house off the fourteenth fairway to the complementary Bloody Marys he has, by the look of him, been sucking down ever since.

For the last five minutes Hoss has been the recipient of countless are-you-for-real looks. Even the twenty-something, cell phone–slinging divas are offended. Finally a middle-aged woman in a sunhat who can stand it no longer breaks into unsuppressed laughter. "Tell me I'm on *Candid Camera*," she roars. Peninsulans — and I'd be willing to bet you Padraig Harrington's Lucky Charms she is one — don't truck with obnoxiousness. They're a refined, fine-spirited people, sensitive types who, while they know how to get down, typically get down with a little class. This guy . . . this guy is Mike Ditka and Chris Farley and your most obnoxious uncle put together.

Finally, when we long-suffering, unwilling eavesdroppers are about to commit hari-kari for the collateral cell phone violence we've suffered, Ollie Nutt comes out to briefly warm up the crowd and stave off a rebellion. Nutt is the CEO of the Monterey Peninsula Foundation, which puts on this shindig. He is about the most jolly, jovial guy you'd ever want to meet, and actually looks a cross between the mayor of Munchkin Land and a beardless Santa Claus. Hoss has ended his call, thank God, but has moved on to unsolicited running commentary of the afterglow events now unfolding while his wife, a head shorter than he is, cringes.

"Ollie Nutt. I can't stand this guy. He's here every year," Hoss whines. Not only is the honorable Nutt in the house, much to our man's chagrin, but Nutt's flanked by a veritable Who's Who of Monterey Peninsula golf: Pebble's chairman and CEO of business affairs, Ron Spears; Bill Perocchi, the CEO of the Pebble Beach Corporation; and a certain Academy Award–winning actor-director-mayor with an enigmatic grin almost as famous as the Mona Lisa's. To top it all off we've got Carmel's favorite son, Bobby Clampett, as emcee. Suck on that, Waste Management Open.

Beside me, Hoss hoots in ironic basso profundo, "Oll-lee!" Meanwhile, Clampett's expertly building up to the man that we're really all hanging around to catch a glimpse of. "And the chairman of the Monterey Peninsula Foundation, Mr. Mayor, Clint Eastwood!" The crowd reserves its loudest applause yet for the prince whose benevolent overwatch has filled the coffers of 220 charities to the tune of nearly $7 million this week and $85 million over the tourney's fêted run . . . the legend, the apparition, "the Big Man," as Robin Williams calls him whenever he celebrity roasts his friend in Monterey.

Clint's wearing beige slacks, a navy blue blazer, and bright white tennis shoes. He looks more David Letterman than director. In his eighties now and enviably trim, Dirty Harry's still a wiry, rail-thin bullwhip of a man. Head down, Eastwood mumbles through his ultra-short speech. It's the same raspy, whiskey-on-the-rocks voice we all know and love, but it's a pitch higher than I'd been expecting. "The real winners this week will be the folks who came out in this beautiful weather to watch this great golf," he says. Not exactly Oscar-worthy.

Hoss is apoplectic. "A man of few words," he hoots. Before us, Eastwood, the Count of Monte Peninsula, looks down at the ground demurely.

Another seldom-heard man speaks next when Clampett puts the mike in front of him. "I don't think we could have had a better start," Bill Perocchi says, pronouncing "staaaaart" just like JFK. Pebble's prez's Brahmin accent startles here on the Left Coast, meriting polite applause. Perocchi steps back into the lineup of venerable suits, and Eastwood and Ron Spears manhandle the Waterford trophy, Clampett cautioning, "It's in two pieces, fellas. Careful."

As Johnson at lasts hoists the hardware, Clampett addresses the champ: "Do you know some of the names of some of the people who've won this back-to-back?"

"How about Jack Nicklaus?" Clampett asks after a dramatic pause.

"Yaaaaaaa," Hoss bellows.

"How about Tom Watson?"

"Ya-uh," Hoss goes, lowering his big moosie call still another octave.

"You now, my man, are the fifth. You enter the history books here at Pebble Beach!" Clampett enthuses.

At last Johnson is free to make his own comments, minus the golf pop quiz. "First of all, I want to say happy Valentine's Day to everyone." The crowd sighs at the champ's overture—the she-voices and the he-voices emoting in a perfect harmonic chorus.

"Yeah, Valentine's Day," Hoss soccer-holligans in my eardrum.

After an unexpectedly poised Q and A at the trophy ceremony, Johnson is hauled up to The Lodge to give the obligatory champion's interview to the couple dozen scribblers that aren't next door in the pressroom desperately pecking out a story on deadline. D. J.'s a bit Eddie Haskell, charming in a thin-lipped, long-limbed, big-eyed Jude Law sort of way. But with his cap pulled down over his eyes, his Carolina drawl and smirk make it difficult to tell whether he's humoring you or just plain ridiculing you. Regardless, he's played some admirably kick-ass golf this week.

I ask Johnson whether his wishing the crowd a happy Valentine's Day had been premeditated. He looks at me blankly, and I hasten to add that since the U.S. Open typically concludes on Father's Day, the event has become synonymous with tributes to dads. Had today's occasion been on his mind prior to holing out at the last?

It's an out-of-left-field question, and purposefully so. The champ regards me with those deep, Dorian Gray eyes of his and says, "Obviously, you know, it being Valentine's Day, Amanda, my girlfriend, she had to leave early." He pauses, cocks his head, his lips twisting into what just might be—what no doubt is—a supercilious smirk. "But happy Valentine's Day to you."

The crowd of sportswriters erupts in a high school locker room guffaw. I've thrown myself to the wolves and, while I know it's totally adolescent, I need to make some overt, hetero show of masculinity. And as I can't very well ask the champ to step outside—he'd have that Holmes versus Tyson reach advantage on me anyway—I stomp out of the pressroom, ostensibly aggrieved. I want my candy-ass colleagues to realize I'm properly pissed, that only the folding table with its flimsy Velcro skirt prevents me from getting in the face of this talent-laden Carolina punk ten years my junior, this hotshot phenom with his three-million-a-year income to my pathetic TIAA-CREF, his hot girlfriend waiting for him back in Myrtle Beach to my rent-a-cat stretched out and shedding for me at my Carmel bungalow.

Back in the pressroom I check the malaprop-prone interview transcripts the PGA Tour produces and, sure enough, appended at the end of my trial balloon is a simple, chagrining notation of what followed Johnson's reply: *[Laughter].*

Press conference now in the books, the newsroom clears out quickly. The few representatives of the few outlets still sufficiently recession-proof to support a full-time golf writer—among others, *Golf Digest,*

Golf, and the Japanese, who seem to have an infinite yen (pardon the pun) to cover their golf—say, "See ya in Phoenix," where the Tour moves next and commence to loading up their rental cars outside The Lodge for the next stop in the magical mystery tour.

The Japanese man next to me, who's hasn't said boo to me in days but who has become my personal Pat Moriaty, bows, and says in broken English to my tablemate and me, "Hope to see you at U.S. Open," then disappears—back to Tokyo, I presume, or to Phoenix, or to some Shinto heaven. The local journalists who yesterday made plans for beers at Brophie's in Carmel slink away, eyes averted, saying they need to get home to their wives. When, predictably, they're razzed for their diligence, they say if they don't go home now there won't be a home to go home to, leaving the instigators to nod sympathetically and back off.

For four days we've been a band of brothers brought together by the thing that makes us feel young, that keeps us from becoming thoroughgoing middle-aged cynics. At times this week I have hated us—me and my ilk—with an intensity I typically reserve for *American Idol*—hated us for our ridiculous subservience, or needless genuflecting, our delight when tossed the most egregious clichés. I've hated us for the very fact that we're all too willing to piss away endless bookish hours immersed in golf trivia, searching for the last person to eagle Pebble's eighth hole in competition. I've loathed us for the masturbatory rhythm with which we too eagerly strike our keys, getting into our pathetically pseudo-athletic "zone" as deadline approaches, hated us the more for the puffed-up, self-satisfied way we strut around the newsroom once our stories are complete.

But now, as the tournament wraps, I'm unaccountably overcome with admiration for my fellow scribes—these underpaid and under-trusted, freelanced and outsourced liberal arts majors trying to string together a few decent syllables before going home to teenage kids who probably think their dads are dweebs, to wives who put up with a job that knows no regular hours and pays no respect to the quaint and sustaining domesticities that keep ordinary souls betrothed. These are good guys, and in a better world—Poland, maybe, where they're daft enough to elect writers to high office—these guys could be, as they say in the world of sport, "difference-makers." They could be go-to dads.

Outside the pressroom, amateurs who've played side by side all week clap one another on the back and say heartfelt good-byes while lifelong friendships get cemented over farewell beers in the Tap Room. It's a moment of auld lang syne before the Rolex strikes midnight and Pebble turns back not into a pumpkin but into America's number-one resort course chasing the expense account dollar, offering Bubba T. Flubba from Terre Haute, Indiana, his only legitimate shot at playing a truly timeless, open-to-the-public U.S. Open venue.

The media shuttle driver duped into carting my sorry, already Anchor Steamed ass back to the fairy-tale village-by-the-sea whistles appreciatively as we roll into town: "Carmel is poppin'." Dropped at Carmel Plaza, I double back down Ocean Avenue, strolling aimlessly until I merge with the small but purposeful Valentine's Day throng gathered in front of the Carmel Bakery and Coffee Co. display window to witness the heart-shaped window-dressing cookies showcased like they're baby Jesus. I beat the slobbering horde inside and grab the last corner table, directly behind the smudged-up dessert cases, settling in for some hot chai. Over the next half hour spent Toulouse Lautrecing the joint I'll see Jack and Jill arrive by the baker's dozen, each asking sweetly for the gooey Valentine's novelties.

Brian Wilson and I agree on one thing: California girls really are the cutest girls in the world, and Carmel-by-the-Sea, AT&T week, is at the top of the Cali heap. The cutie pies tonight, Cupid's night, are, without exception, younger and hotter than their male escorts. Exhibit A is seated directly in front of me: a Stephen Hawking look-alike feeding cream puffs to his comely dark-haired lover in the most gratuitously sexual way; Exhibit B is the middle-aged cougar with the thigh-rise leather boots and long lashes who I overhear (Scout's honor) say to her exquisitely dumpy beau, "Maybe I should just start stripping right here." Exhibit C, prima facie, is a couple of Euro-lookers doing the palm-to-palm, gaze-into-the-eyes thing, the move where you put your palms up flat against your sweetie's. Even to a dateless jaded guy like me returned from the sausage party of a PGA Tour pressroom, these love-gestures strike me sweet.

At the Carmel Coffee House on the other side of Ocean, where I move for a change of scenery, a variant of the same stream of honeys queue up for gelato and whipped drinks. Here, too, wait a bevy of erotic sweetmeats behind glass: heart-shaped cookies with Hershey's Kisses pressed in their sweet spots, sugar cookies shaped and frosted like plumped-up Rolling Stones logos or come-hither Angelina Jolie lips. Sinatra's croony version of "Love and Marriage" smacks over the stereo system.

On the wall hang movie posters for *The Good, the Bad, and the Ugly*, and *Pale Rider*. From where I'm hiding behind my laptop (the way guys used to hide behind broadsheets in film noirs), I'm heartened that at least one cowboy, Clint of the grizzled visage, won't be buying a caramel macchiato on this femme-driven, Flying Lady of a holiday.

Oh, Carmel-by-the-Sea, shall I compare you to the PGA? Thou art more sweet, and more temperate.

16

The Boy Wonder, the
Bündchen-Brady, the Bathetic Mex,
the Bra-Bearer, and the Boomer

Celebrity Rounds at
Carmel-by-the-Sea-and-Be-Seen

Living in Carmel-by-the-Sea is a bit like living at the foot of Mount Olympus . . . only here the mountaintop Valhalla is Tehama Golf Resort, and that's not Zeus hurling a thunderbolt, it's Clint Eastwood dusting his gold-plated Oscar. We in the shadow of the mount sometimes hear the sounds of ambrosia being chugged, amphoras being clinked, and nymphs being mussed, but all we really know of our benevolent overlords is the occasional low rumble and celestial lightshow from on high. It's sort of Grinch-like. A few times a year our patron/pariah eccentrics descend from their Mount Crumpets to carve the roast beast with we wee Whos down in Whoville.

February's especially plum for close encounters of the celebrity kind, the Pro-Am bringing home to roost some of the American idols who pick up their mail here. It's winter, after all, and though these may be stars, they're still subject to the bouts of cabin fever and where's-my-public angst we mortals experience. Some bigwigs I meet only in passing—Kenny G., for instance, who, like Huey Lewis and a whole bunch of other folks in these parts, goes by a nom de plume, or nom de sax. When I run into the curly haired, Grammy-winning horn-blower at Spyglass Hill, I can't help but float a question.

G., nee Kenneth Bruce Gorelick, looks a little long in the tooth in the Spy graylight, some salt mixed in with his pepper. He's got that lean, alley cat look. Add a baby blue cap and a pony swinging out back, and he doesn't look a lick like a golfer let alone one who's scratch. Like so many others who call the Peninsula home away from home, it's hard to tell from his voice where "the world's most renowned saxophonist," as his website describes him, hails from. Turns out he's from Seattle. He's so Space Needle, in fact, he happens to be one of the original investors in Starbucks. Naturally, I ask G. why he digs the Monterey P.

"Everybody's into golf. They're interested . . . It's like everybody cares about what's going on, so when you're in a tournament, people go, 'Hey, have a good round.' It's not like playing in a city, when you go out to dinner and nobody knows what's going on. It's like you're part of the scene. I like that."

The beautiful and the saxy—pardon the pun—have been drawn to Pebble's benighted shores since Sam Morse hung up his Yale pigskin uniform and began rubbing shoulders with stars instead of linemen. Since then it's been considered Good Sam, not to mention savvy biz, to protect the peace and privacy of the stars. A case in point is the Beatles, who *Pebble Beach Magazine* reported, once arrived here incognito in June of 1968 to engage in an unthinkably bourgeoisie pastime: horse-back riding. "Staying at the Lodge under a prearranged anonymity that was so efficient no one learned the names of their wives, the two couples played a round of unhampered golf at Pebble Beach," reads the article.

Historically, when Beatles-caliber deities fly in from San Fran or L.A., Carmel-by-the-Sea and Pebble Beach play congenial hosts, keeping things rollicking, upbeat, discrete. Stars aren't so much fussed over here as they are aided and abetted. Whereas celeb-starved Anywhere,

U.S.A., would mob a star of Eastwood's magnitude—literally slobber all over him—Peninsulans are spoiled by such a feast of VIPs that the most evolved among them have come to project cool disinterest, especially where idols are concerned. Those that haven't yet learned to play it cool in the presence of immortals instead inherit a natural, almost maternal instinct toward protecting the privacy of their natural aristocracy, combining midwifery and "bodyguardery" to ensure nobody hassles the stars of greatest magnitude. Peninsulans, then as now, are well-practiced at the social graces of distraction and polite obfuscation in the service of discretion—the cocktail party swerve, the look-away pass.

Carmel Magazine keeps its eyes peeled for celebs passing through in its "C-notes" section. The past few months alone, C-notes tells us, we unhip Whos have missed Jerry Seinfeld in his baby blue 1970 Porsche, CIA director Leon Panetta, with his fistful of Jefferson-Lincoln awards, and *The Godfather's* Academy Award–nominated James Caan, who was spotted scarfing down lunch in the Tap Room after a casual round on the links.

Life in my adopted hometown of cause célèbres proves tailor-made for do-overs; folks come here to start fresh, turning over a new leaf after a divorce or a death or a downsizing or a corporate indictment, taking on a new name or simply a show-biz alias like "Bing" (née Harry Lillis) or Kenny G. In fact, in the first few weeks after setting up shop two blocks off Ocean Ave., I'd met one golf professional enjoying his first legal name change and a middle-aged artist enjoying her second. When I'd called a local mailbox store to inquire about gettin' one of those nifty, spinning lockboxes, the manager at the newish, full-service shipping center had told me he expects to sell out of his surfeit in less than a year. If I wanted a box, he'd said, I'd first need to prove I was who I said I was. Lots of people, he'd said—"Of course, sir, I know you're not one of them"—want to set up an alternate P.O. here for all "the wrong reasons"—that is, namely and paradoxically, to avoid certain kinds of mail. Couple the desire to avoid exes and court summonses and the like with the glut of small business startups and a rainbow coalition of not-for-profits and, well, a burg like this needs a whole hell of a lot of numbered cubbies. In sum, more celeb-friendly confines could not be found outside the French Riviera—beauty, privacy, tomfoolery, and charity as charitably mixed here as the perfect martini, not to mention the abject unaffordability for the peasants priced out of the proximity necessary to pester you.

S.F.B. Morse recognized the Mediterranean appeal of the place from the beginning, penning a piece for the August 1928 issue of his own magazine, *Game and Gossip*, in which he wrote, "I do not intend to dwell on the great beauty and charm of southern France, of the Riviera, and of Spain . . . California need not bow to them." In the beginning, Morse wined and dined silver screen icons and designated Beautiful People Mary Pickford and Douglas Fairbanks, convincing them to put a glam-bug in their fellow actors' ears that some Errol Flynn–worthy, Zeus-ready recreating was happening just upcoast of Hollywood. In the Roaring Twenties, Morse cranked up *Game and Gossip*—a peculiar periodical best described as the lovechild of a ménage à trois involving *People*, *Harper's Bazaar*, and *Golf Digest*. Every so often it dished on what the big shots were up to vis-à-vis golf, tennis, equestrianism, and sport shooting, until, in the 1950s, it stopped to congratulate itself, running an ad that read, "Over more than fifty years Del Monte has entertained virtually every important visitor and celebrity that has come to California." In a sidebar entitled "Glancing through the Guest List," Morse and Co. listed some three dozen visiting luminaries "picked at random," among them Andrew Carnegie, Amelia Earhart, the Duke of Kent, William Randolph Hearst, Charlie Chaplin, Charles Lindbergh, Rockfellers Sr. and Jr., Will Rogers, and, oddly enough, Gertrude Stein and the maharaja of Indore.

Ever since, Pebble's happily been in bed with celebs to the tune of what my Internet movie database numbers as almost two hundred movies shot in Monterey County. The iconic links was used as a set for Mickey Rooney's and Liz Taylor's *National Velvet* and Ben Hogan's bio,

Follow the Sun, while Doris Day wanders in and out of Pebble's Lodge and Beach Club in her 1956 flick *Julie* and Alan Ladd does likewise in *The Deep Six*, from 1958. In 1978, 20th Century Fox Film Corporation bought, fittingly enough, Pebble's glam links, coughing up the cash it made from *Star Wars*. In 1999 another Hollywood legend, Eastwood, bought a piece of the dream course from a subsidiary of the Japanese Taiheiyo Club Inc., the Lone Cypress Company. Decades after Morse first courted Pickford and Fairbanks as unofficial celebrity reps, Pebble still publishes its own saucy self-titled glossy, still courts Hollywood icons who'll talk it up in Tinseltown, and still attracts a steady enough stream of silver screeners that even a duff like me can occasionally suck their essence.

THE BOY WONDER

In February I bat cave away a few minutes with Chris O'Donnell—Robin, to you and me. In the hasty prep I'm afforded before our impromptu interview at Monterey Peninsula Country Club, I'm amused to learn he beat out Leonardo DiCaprio for the role of Boy Wonder only after producers asked a group of preteen pipsqueaks at a comic book convention who of the two would win in a fistfight. The punks chose wisely.

Like Phil Mickelson, O'Donnell is impossible not to like. He bristles with boyish energy and clear-eyed intelligence. He's an easy, eager interview, too, offering all the extroversion of a Chicago native (if you count the mean streets of Winnetka as Chicago) and the hip, upbeat enlightenment of a Californian. Basically he's about as boy-next-door as anyone since Jimmy Stewart. In fact, O'Donnell married and has five kids with his college sweetheart, Caroline Fentress. He golfs well and stylishly, but not well enough to make you jealous. He lives right across the street from Riviera Country Club, but you don't smell it on his breath.

"I grew up in Chicago and love Los Angeles. But it's like Groundhog Day there," O'Donnell tells me after a round. "It's the same way every day. I come up here and the air feels better. Everyone loves the golf here . . . I have no reason to be up here because my work is in L.A., but any chance I get I jump at it.

"The first time I played at Pebble it was fifteen or twenty years ago. I went left of seventeen green, went right to the spot, dropped the ball and tried to hit the shot. There's so many memories. It's kind of like why people enjoy watching the Masters so much. Because they feel like they know the course and know every hole. I feel like I knew Pebble pretty well before I ever played it."

I ask him if the golfers on Sunset Boulevard know one another, if they kvetch. "I'm working with LL Cool J right now," he says, "and he's not much of a golfer, so we're not trading too many golf tips." O'Donnell's home club, as it is for many of the So Cal glitterati, is Bel-Air Country Club. "The truth is, most of the golf I play is with my regular buddies who aren't in the business," he tells me. "Right now, the work schedule is so extensive, on the weekends I can't bail on my kids and play golf."

O'Donnell, who adores Carmel, actually claims he still gets goose bumps driving down Ocean Avenue. In parting, he confesses that with five kids he can't just pick up and leave to go golfing, but he does choose his spots, and one of those spots is the AT&T Clambake. "When we started this new show on CBS, the first thing I said was, 'Come February, I'm going to Pebble, so you're going to have to work around it.'"

THE BÜNDCHEN-BRADY

While it's true that Carmel isn't exactly a mecca for the young-famous—it's something short of Fergalicious—for a week or two in February it's possible to get close with a hunky NFL quarterback or two.

Before me and a small gaggle of reporters stands the 6'4", 225-pound, dimple-chinned father of Gisele Bündchen's bambino. Everything about three-time Super Bowl champion signal-caller Thomas Edward Brady Jr. screams either quarterback or Superman or both. A San Mateo, California, native who grew up idolizing Joe Montana, the first words out of Brady's mouth when I meet him do not concern Bill Belichick's hoodies or Bündchen's bikinis, but the benefits of breathing in his home state: "I love this Northern California air," he tells a small group of us reporters. Brady's partner in the Pro-Am is Steve Marino, but the Pro Bowler's groovin' on Vijay Singh, who, at 6'4" himself, is virtually the only pro in the field this week who can look Brady in the eye. "He hits the crap out of the ball," Brady whistles. "You watch 'em swing, and you think it'll help you with the tempo . . . But they just play at a ridiculous level. It's definitely something to appreciate."

I'd followed the heavy-hitting Brady and Singh for a few holes on their back nine, so I ask the two-time Super Bowl MVP if he out-sticked the Fijian on any holes. He laughs. "I had the tees up a little bit. I think head to head he's still gonna blow it by me, as all these guys are gonna. Golf for a tall guy like that is tough. There's not a lot of tall golfers. Most of the guys are more medium-sized."

It's my turn to laugh when the future Hall of Famer uses the term "medium-sized"—as if he's ordering a Coke at the McDonald's drive-thru—to refer to the average Lilliputian pro golfer, which must make me "pint-sized." So why have so many quarterbacks—John Elway and Steve Young, to name a couple—been such good golfers? "We're athletes. It's an athletic game. It takes an athletic swing. We don't have so much muscle. You've got to be able to turn. You've got to have some finesse. This is not really a muscular sport. You've got to be long and lean, like Vijay. Big and bulky isn't good for golf."

And what's it like being a professional athlete playing your second- or your third-best sport in front of crowds? "There's a lot of intensity the pros bring to this," Brady says, "but I think we amateurs are just trying to come out here and not kill anybody off the tee or embarrass ourselves around the greens."

I may not be able to relate to Brady's designer stubble, or his cover photos, or his perfect chin-dimple, but this . . . . this killing people off the tee . . . this, I can relate to.

THE BATHETIC

George Lopez is one of the rare down-to-earth celebs you might just see someday at the Pebble practice green or up at the Pebble Beach Market, grabbing a bottle of vino. While most of the stars that hang their hats in America's golf mecca come home once a quarter at best, Lopez runs amuck in the Del Monte Forest enough to have real neighbor jokes to tell. When I'd encountered him for the first time behind the eighteenth green at Pebble back in September, I'd asked him what he liked best about his home away from home.

"What I love about it is that it's not what people think it is. They think it's like this pretentious, stuffy, Pebble Manner place. People couldn't be nicer, more accommodating, more welcoming. It's a destination. One of the greatest places on earth. You know Scotland has St. Andrews. America has Pebble Beach. Pine Valley is rated number one, but it doesn't have what this has."

"It's tranquility," he'd gushed. "There's never a bad day. Even when it's overcast and rainy and drizzling, it's still one of those places that's weatherproof. You might not be able to golf, but you can still sit around the fire." Lopez was the first and most forthright celeb I'd met on the Peninsula, and so his lavish praise for the links, coming from a kid who grew up poor in San Fernando, stuck with me.

When I meet him again after his water-logged round at the Monterey Peninsula Country Club in February, I'm curious to see if he'll use similar language to explain why he chooses to play his golf here.

"Because I'll be home in fifteen minutes," he quips, adding that he's in the process of trying to join Monterey Peninsula Country Club. "I ran into a dude on the committee today," he tells me, all exited.

"They're probably doing a background check on you right now," I say.

"I better get in quick then," he jokes, adding that the funniest thing he saw on the course was a five-million-dollar party house too cheap to afford anything other than plastic patio chairs.

I mention to him that I'm pretty sure Dirty Harry is already a member at MPCC, as he is at Cypress Point. "I think he's a member everywhere," Lopez jokes. "Wherever he goes, he's a member."

The Lopez meter is ticking, and ticking fast, I realize, so I ask the funnyman what's funny about golf—something I'd meant to ask him the first time we met, but lacked the balls.

"The funny thing about golf is that it tortures you no matter what your economic or social status," he says, getting serious. "It doesn't discriminate. There's a lot of bias in this world. Golf has no bias. It'll torture you whether you're Donald Trump, or George Lopez, or Vijay Singh."

And how does Monterey Peninsula Country Club, where he played today, compare to Pebble Beach? "Pebble just hangs on the earth," Lopez says, soft as a sea breeze and not the least bit silly.

THE BRA-BEARER

Brandi Chastain is to soccer what Woody Austin, a.k.a. "Aquaman," is to golf. She's universally identifiable not only because of her successful career on the pitch but because of something she did in the heat of competition that was slightly more provocative than windmilling into a lake during President's Cup play in 2007 (sorry, Woody). Chastain's "bra-bearing" after scoring the winning penalty kick against China in the 1999 World Cup follows her to this day. Tell Google to go fetch and it brings back such memorable Chastain hits as—"12 Best Nude-Athlete Pictorials of All-Time" from an outfit called nerve.com, a Brandi Chastain "breast biography," and Chinese pornographic solicitations of the San Jose soccer great too saucy to repeat.

When I meet up with Chastain and ESPN's Chris "Boomer" Berman, the other celebrity member of her foursome, behind the eighteenth green at Pebble after their round at the AT&T, the bra-bearer's answering a TV reporter's questions and her pro playing partner, Ricky Barnes, needs a friend as another TV raven-hair pitches him some high heat: Why is Chastain the only woman in this year's Pro-Am?

Barnes furrows his brow and says, "That's a great question. I don't

know. A lot of celebrities and athletes in the world are noticeable men."
Noticeable men? The gaff sounds so Public Speaking 101, my heart
goes out to the sincerely likeable Californian. "Maybe sometimes it's
nerves," he adds, digging himself deeper. "I notice she gets nervous
out here. But even the men do, too . . . If I had the answer for you, I'd
tell you, but I don't."

Calling herself a "total amateur with a capital A," Chastain finds
herself addressing the same gender question, again, for the couple
of Bay Area newsies who've joined me. "There's a lot of women out
there," Chastain reminds us. "I've seen them along the ropes. There's
a slight responsibility, because if I do a good job perhaps they'll add
more women to this tournament . . . It gives more women a chance
if I do well and if they enjoy my company."

If I do well, and if they enjoy my company? I'm no Betty Friedan, but
let it be said that none of the dudes in the nation's top star-studded
pro-am are sweating next year's invite over their social graces. In fact,
if you're a celebrity stud, the more entertainingly boorish you are on
the course, in some ways the better. "The nice thing about tradition is
that it keeps people coming back, but the game is changing," Chastain
tells us. "They're more females playing golf than ever before. There's
some unbelievable golfers out there on the LPGA that I admire as much
as I admire these gentlemen . . . There's no reason that any young girl
who's out there right now . . . shouldn't aspire to participate at the
professional level or even be invited to play at this tournament."

I squint into the late-afternoon sun reflecting off the bay and ask
the soccer great the question that interests me most: What are the San
Jose native's memories of Pebble Beach?

She smiles. "My grandfather brought me to this tournament when
I was eight or nine. He loved golf. Jack Nicklaus was second to God
to him. He wore the same light yellow sweaters and plaid pants. We
would literally line up along this fairway, and we would sit down and
eat strawberry shortcake. He loved golf and I loved my grandfather,
so I would come with him."

"My mother's claim to fame was that Kevin Costner hit his ball toward her, it rolled up on her magazine, and he came face to face with her. I have really great memories, too . . . and I look forward to sharing them with my son for years and years to come."

Barely into her forties, Chastain finds herself already living her mother's dream: not so much inviting Costner over for casserole as much as routinely playing the course where a star once rendered her mom speechless. "I've had the luxury of playing Pebble quite a few times . . . Anytime anybody brings it up . . . 'Hey you want to play Pebble for this that and the other?' I immediately say yes."

A reporter from the *San Francisco Chronicle* rejoins our little scrum, asking facetiously if his headline should read: "Brandi Rips AT&T for Sexism."

"Oh no! Brandy loves AT&T." Chastain hastens to make amends. "Can you make that the headline in big bold print?" Humor aside, she's serious in her eagerness to make nice with this week's sponsor, and serious in her advocacy for more and better gender representation. "I would love for people like Carol Bartz, the president of Yahoo, to play . . . She's a good golfer," Chastain adds.

And, really, it's the tourney's admirable track record of inclusivity—a tradition begun when tournament founder Bing Crosby invited Willie Mays and other prominent African Americans to his Clambake long before it was politically expedient to do so—that has saddled Chastain and, to a lesser extent, minority stars like Don Cheadle, with an important responsibility that sometimes feels like a burden.

THE BOOMER

"I've been singing that one-hit wonder by Looking Glass for two days," ESPN's Chris "Boomer" Berman says of playing with Chastain. "You know, 'Brandy, you're a fine girl . . .' She's on the tee, and I'm thinking, 'Do-do-do-do . . . Do-do-do-do.'"

Berman's fresh off a round where, hobbled by bum knees and hips, he looked like he was laboring just to get to the house but for a few putts sunk courtesy of some playful advice dispensed by the soccer goddess:

Think penalty kick against China. No one's in the goal. Boomer's eager to purge himself of the eighteenth hole nightmare just now suffered, which found him duffing a series of shots from the right rough directly in front of the boozed-up fans in the corporate tent. Finally, Boom had managed to hack his ball out of the spinach up to the green to a chorus of cheers. "The first time I ever played here I made birdie on eighteen for an eagle with Jeff Sluman to make the cut," he remembers. "This is the getting even part. 'You've had your memory at eighteen. You're finished,' said God . . . I was heartbroken coming up eighteen today. I was like, 'Really, you're going to do this now?'"

A Connecticut Yankee in S.F.B. Morse's court, Berman's staying at The Lodge this week with wife, Kathy, at what he tells me is one of his "favorite places on earth." He's fresh from the coveted emcee gig at the traditional Wednesday night Pro-Am volunteers' dinner, where he warmed up the crowd by describing Pebble as "the place where God waits for tee times." While the Bermans have been coming here since 1983, Pebble's virtues have yet to grow old. "If I give myself a present, we stay here. I deserve it at the end of the Super Bowl," Boomer tells me.

ESPN's mainstay majored in American history in the Ivy League, and one of the many things that keeps him dropping anchor at Stillwater Cove is the golfing lore buried on this broad sweep of Carmel Bay. "I've given myself in the past a little pep talk on seventeen or eighteen," he confesses. "Today I stood on seventeen, I looked to the left for a minute and said, 'There was Watson.' I shanked a 5-iron, and it was like, 'No! You wait your life for this?'"

Berman plays at an 18-handicap but, having followed him as he "carved up" Pebble's back nine, I'd say he's closer to a 28. The multitalented SportsCenter anchor—a virtuoso who's belted out tunes with Huey Lewis before—tells me, by way of explanation, that he didn't start playing golf until his mid-twenties. "I watched the Clambake as a kid," he recalls. "I don't come from a golfing family. The point is, I would watch this. It was cool. Golf equaled fun. And way back then there wasn't a lot of those subliminal messages . . . golf didn't equal fun."

Does the consummate showman among sportscasters think an event like this one, in a place like the Monterey Peninsula, thrives because it allows people to be themselves? "Personality is okay if it is real," Boom intimates, talking close. "Personality is not okay if it's, 'I have come with gags in my bag.' I'm not knocking Lee Trevino. I'm not knocking that . . . that was him . . . It wouldn't hurt golf to have people who are themselves." Berman's legacy at Pebble rests in exactly this kind of comment—honest assessment delivered from the ESPN tower, from whence he's been covering the U.S. Open since 1986. It's the historical perspective he offers—and the useful comparative data it reveals—that makes Boomer such a keeper, and why fans clamor to have the semiretired broadcaster suit up to call the biggest events.

Thinking with his broadcaster's cap on, Berman loves the idea of the U.S. Opens staged on the West Coast, where Pacific Time means primetime golf out East. "I remember in the 1992 U.S. Open [at Pebble], it was me, a producer, and a cameraman covering the whole golf course. And Andy Dillard came up in the second-to-last group in the dark, but they wanted to finish . . . We had to, like, shine a flashlight on the green. ABC begged us for the footage because everyone else had been off the air for hours. We were the only ones . . . It was like our little secret, you know. None of the papers had it in the East in the morning . . . You know, that 'second round still in-progress' sort of thing."

Boomer snaps himself out of the reverie induced by memories of that long-ago U.S. Open, recalling the question. Why does he feel permitted to be so much himself here, and what is it about the old Crosby Clambake that conjures free spirits like a jinni? "Huey [Lewis] calls me The Jack Lemmon of This Generation," he says. "But I'm not trying to be Bill Murray. I'm not a comedian. I'm just trying to be human."

Behind and below us, one of the week's many hapless amateurs has air-mailed the eighteenth. The few people around us in the press area gawking at the ballsy, impossible, off-the-sandstone recovery shot-in-progress halfheartedly shush Boomer's running commentary, but Boom, bless him, keeps right on booming at a volume and frequency surely registered by migrating whales.

All mischief now, Boom looks over at me, and, raising an eyebrow, commences to heckle the hack on the rocks below: *"Really . . . ?! That's why God invented sleeves of balls!"*

17

Hard, Brown, and Out of Control

U.S. Open Performance Anxiety and
Premature Tony Jacklination

The balcony at The Lodge positively overflows with Pebble Beach underlings, the housekeepers and bellhops and service staff, the indispensable invisibles without whom Pebble could not function, the real VIPs, the ones without a prayer of landing tickets to golf's glam event on golf's glam links. They've gathered to see the stigmata, to witness the wound. Below, on the first tee, director of the USGA regional affairs, west region, and U.S. Open starter for twenty-five years, Ron Read, clears his throat to announce the second coming: "Now on the tee, from Windemere, Florida, Tiger Woods."

Before us stands Jesus Christ Superstar, the martyr-villain, the Spaghetti western black hat and white hat rolled into well-muscled one, the cowboy who hasn't saddled up for a competitive round at Pebble Beach since 2002, marking the longest-ever divorce between Woods, the world's number one golfer, and what just might be its number one course. It's a mother and Tiger reunion, and it's only an Open away.

When former Peninsula resident and golf addict Huey Lewis botches a ditty on tour, he says he bogeyed it. If a Grammy-winners' logic applies to a plebe like me, it's fair to say I've quadruple-bogeyed life these last two months, leaking oil as I come down the home stretch of my U.S. Open year.

My boss back home, a mostly kindly man, has threatened to invoke my contractual obligations unless I get my ass back, forthwith, from my golfing pilgrimage. At work, unfounded rumors beget in my absence range from an alleged personal "meltdown" to a scintillating romance—ironic considering I've lived a monk's existence during my Open year, wrapping my loving hands only around my niblick. Mostly, I find the gossip amusing in a Bonnie Raitt, let's-give-'em-something-to-talk-about way, knowing full well that in the Protestant Midwest, "meltdown" and "personal crisis" are roughly synonymous with "gone to California." The most noticeable symptoms of the malady are shaggy hair, a steep increase in the consumption of organic produce, and a sudden tendency to address one's superiors as "dude." Apparently I'm exhibiting all three.

Any one of these professional setbacks, taken on its own, might constitute a bog. But the snowman hit when the haunt I'd felt that August day on Carmel Beach concerning my father—the man who always said golf was a paradigm for life—inscribed itself on my score-card, unavoidable and unerasable as an "X."

It happened quickly. In February, Dad had emailed exuberant notes from Florida, waxing rhapsodic during the AT&T about Pebble's made-for-TV beauty, contemplating a trip to see Freddie Couples make his Champions Tour debut in Naples, even intimating he might replace the Tommy Armours he bequeathed me pre-Peninsula pilgrimage with a new set of Chinese knockoffs off the rack. Now, as U.S. Open month begins, I find myself booking a trip to stare into his dying eyes, he who brought me to this game, he who now stands on the threshold of leaving it to me.

June, as Paul Simon crooned, will change your tune. When I arrive at Dad's bedside, he holds my head roughly between his palms like the rough thing I am, the thing he made, and when he tells me his round is soon to end, I weep like a child for this, the moment I've feared. I had hoped my U.S. Open year would end on a fantasy note: my father, my partner and right-hand man, with me beside the healing waters of Carmel Bay. In the fantasy, his youthful self strides alongside, twirling a 7-iron, all shoulder-length jet-black hair, all piss and vinegar, as we scramble to get a view of one of Watson's ageless escapes from the rough.

Instead, my pre-Open dreams have turned dark and anxious. In one I am attempting to play a shot through the west wall of our old farmhouse, which has been blown open to reveal a blinding sun. A well-tanned and quaffed Pebble Beach corporate exec lounges in a recliner while talking shop with a local sportswriter. Around me the walls close in, and I am left to try to engineer my ball's impossible exit via the windows through which Dad and I once watched the sun set over Foxbriar G.C. In another, Pebble, fast and brown as a drought, grafts itself onto the topography of the farm, the landscape of my memory. Its greens are baked hard, banked crazy, backed up against my grandparents' dream house like treacherously elliptical tilt-a-whirls.

In his biography with Ken Bowden, *Jack Nicklaus: My Story*, the Golden Bear recalls the nightmare that beset him on the eve of his ultimately victorious final round in Pebble's inaugural Open, a phantasm that had him running golf's demonic version of a treadmill, damned if he did and damned if he didn't. In this nocturnal hallucination all Jack could do, leading by 2 on eighteen, was "hit the tee shot either into the ocean on the left or out of bounds on the right." The dream was "just awful" enough to cause him to leap out of bed and wake Barbara.

Now, as I crouch beneath the ropes to witness Tiger on the first tee—the great maestro, the great Houdini, and, according to some this week, the great Satan—I am aware of another dream-moment sweeping me away at waltz rhythm, slow and quick, now and forever, past and present, vortices I can only vaguely name merging the way they do only in the planet's most enchanted places. On bended knee I am my father watching Watson in his prime, and I am the son I don't yet have, watching the next Great One, the one I won't live to see play a game I hardly recognize, but, still, down deep, somehow know.

After several days at my father's bedside, hours in which I interact only with family at the still center of the circling of wagons that forever attends the terminally ill, the madding crowds of U.S. Open come as a shock. I let the multitudes wash over me, immersing myself in what Pebble's R. J. Harper had called back at the U.S. Open breakfast "The People's Open." To me the 2010 edition unfolding before me seems more crowded, because it *is* more crowded. "In terms of scale," Harper, chairman of this year's Open told Tim Sweeney of *Pebble Beach Magazine*, "the U.S. Open is probably 50 percent bigger than it was in 2000. The size of each component has grown considerably over the past decade."

For the next four days, sellout crowds of 37,500 will ruminate on what was once a seaside meadow grazed on the hoof, gazing upon the passing trains of Phil and Tiger. We are thirty-odd thousand ex-pectorating, excreting, sneezing, jostling browsers huddled up for an opening round so brisk it may as well be sponsored by The North Face. In toto we make up roughly 6 million pounds of 5.92-inch-tall adult American man-flesh projected to consume 55,000 pounds of beef in a single week. The hotdogs, domestic beer, and port-a-john ghettos smack of demos, but the $6 dogs, $7 draws, $9 cheeseburgers (in paradise), and $34 to $45 hats put the Duke back in the Duke of Del Monte. Another difference in this year's Open: Pebble will call the shots and name the prices in the merchandise tent and, friend, that's bad news for you and your mad money. Each day I leave the house with $40 in cash earmarked for only essential on-course feeding and watering, and each night I return home with chump change. It's the cost of doing business.

Because the majority of U.S. Open ticket holders are of the dude persuasion, the tourney features plenty of cigar-smoking, beer-swilling, dirty-joke-making boys-will-be-boys behavior resident of the x-y chromosome. The U.S. Open's tradition as a high-end debauch may be little publicized but it is long-standing. Back in June 1972, circa Pebble's first Open, *Monterey Herald* staff writer Jon Herald suggested, tongue only partly in cheek, that perspective U.S. Open gallery members be screened for, shall we say, desirable traits. "The ideal galleryite," he wrote, "is about 5-foot-6, around 115 pounds, long hair, flashing eyes and, say, 36-23-36. Some variations in this allowed (Hiya, Racquel)." Adding insult to injury, Fitzgerald added, "She should also know a water hazard from a Scotch on the rocks, and be able to shut up when Jack is putting or Arnie is frowning."

This very afternoon, as I have dutifully scribbled in my notepad, plans have been made around me to layover at the last all-nude strip club in Silicon Valley on the way back to the Bay Area. Binoculars have been deployed to examine cross-fairway cleavage—a dangerous game, considering most of the trophy blondes hiding behind Versace shades also come with "Player's Guest" credentials. The beer-fueled machismo is so thick in pockets that female members of the press corps are jocularly accused of checking their Match.com accounts anytime they surf the Net on their Androids. Imagine, played out in real time, the over-the-top scenes mimed in the sexual harassment training videos that HR forces you to watch at work, and you'll come close in the yardage book.

The best behaved among us are invariably the many fathers and sons in attendance this Father's Day weekend. The sheer number of shared genes trekking the links this week make for arresting, downright uncanny viewing, making the old adage that the nut doesn't fall far from the tree—the cone from the cypress—a living truth here. It's positively weird to walk among the generations, to see creator and created side by side, like that freaky investment commercial where the early middle-aged business traveler encounters his retired, wise, salt-and-pepper self on an airplane. The U.S. Open is all about the looking glass, the future written on our genetic scorecards, and it can't help but put you in mind of your own father, the seminal influence, progenitor, the *pater familias.*

Perhaps because of this long-view, chip-off-the-ol'-block, flesh-of-my-flesh vibe, the sometimes bawdy Open crowd also produces countless acts of paternal kindness. Wide-eyed juniors are collectively and charitably smuggled into front-row seats; hand-held TVs, available this week exclusively to American Express card members, are passed around like peace pipes; citizen mechanics hit the brakes to help elder galleryites troubleshoot the high-tech, motorized vehicles the USGA makes available to the disabled. In sum, you and me, the people in the People's Open, no matter how bovine, are good folk, the kind of people that'd stop to help fix a flat on a dark road.

More than 9,000 golfers with a USGA handicap index of 1.4 or better attempted to qualify for the 156-man field in this year's Open. The best among them advance to sectional qualifying, a penultimate stage this year reached by Dallas QB-playboy Tony Romo, who made it all the way to sectionals only to have his hopes of reaching the Double-Bogey-by-the-Sea derailed by the unholy combination of a Texas weather delay and the Cowboys' brutal summer practice schedule. Of the field of 156, 79 of the planet's best are exempt by virtue of previous performance, while a chosen few are gifted with what the USGA calls a "special exemption." This year's class of "specials" is headlined by Vijay Singh and young Tom Watson. So beloved is Watson that the granting of an admittedly symbolic exemption to a sixty-year-old, semiretired legend has caused no waves. Watson's fêted, fated participation in this, the 110th U.S. Open, makes him the only player to tee it up in all five U.S. Opens at Pebble. Justifying the granting of golf's ultimate hall pass, USGA president Jim Hyler explained, "We certainly would like to congratulate Tom and recognize his terrific record at the Open and also his recent success. And, obviously, last year at the Open Championship at Turnberry, Tom had an incredible performance, an inspirational performance, and was 8 feet away from gaining a five-year exemption into the U.S. Open."

Who says close only counts in horseshoes?

Watson may be here by the grace of the golf gods, but the rest of us hacks are here by virtue of having ponied up the $110-per-day face value of the tics to experience not just the felicitous meeting of land and sea but also the flatulent meeting of 95,000 hotdogs and 180,000 cups of brewski. Round One of the People's Open represents all that's best and worst in cramming the equivalent of a small cornfed city into a slip of coastal acreage. Naturally, it's the Open first-timers who are the most vocal, those whose carpe diem called them to see Rock City but whose pocketbooks aren't sufficiently deep to see it on the weekend. Thus are the magi-for-a-day overcome with the unchecked narrative instinct eager dads fall victim to on maiden voyages to America's other national treasures: the Grand Canyon, say, or Fenway.

In today's opening frame, boilerplate conversation among the jacket-clad, baseball-capped, don't-tread-on-me dad denizens of the state boasting the world's fifth largest economy mostly concerns, in no particular order:

> That lucky s.o.b. who smuggled his iPhone through security
> What "big dudes" Jim Furyk, "Bones" Mackay, and Ernie Els are up close
> What we'd shoot if we teed it up on Pebble (between 114 and 118, if the last two amateurs to tee it up in the *Golf Digest* U.S. Open challenges are any barometer)
> Vittles
> Where to go next (because the Open offers smorgasbord choice of the world's best and most appallingly dressed golfers, and because most spectators have a buddy, spouse, sig fig, or kid in tow, the where-to-go, who-to-see question becomes golf's version of North v. South, severing kin from kin)
> Hot chicks
> Phil's tits

What's up with Tiger Woods
What's up with Tiger Woods

Take the average guy, pour a couple of Buds down his pie-hole, give him a trusted buddy to run his mouth off to, and parade before his discerning eye an assembly line of cookie-cutter, tight-ass golfers, and the resulting humor is pretty much pro forma, even for boobus Americanus who, among the international crowd at the Open, is definitely the quickest to the quip, beating the Germans, Italians, Englishmen, and Japanese hands down and nosing out even the Irish by a cup. Still, the Open of the new millennium makes it difficult for Joe Q. Gallery to generate his best material, unlike the more wit-friendly 1972, for instance, when, after excoriating Pebble in the press and turning in two tortured rounds in the eighties, pro Frank Beard walked to the cliff edge on eighteen and some wit in the crowd called out, "Don't jump, Frank!" Or Lee Trevino's one-liner, also in '72, when, coming up the home hole in the final pairing to find Vietnam protestors had locked themselves to the Monterey pine that then stood in the middle of the home hole, the Merry Mex turned to playing partner Jack Nicklaus and said, "Put a match to that tree, and the key will appear mighty fast."

Fast forward to 2010, when what we spectators are allowed to see is so controlled, so distanced, so sanitized of personality beyond the individualistic swings of the privileged golfers, that even America's secret weapon—good humor—is reduced to cracks about who's "taking a leak" (this when the pros take a quick, unscripted piss in one of the porta-potties cordoned off for their exclusive use) to who's wearing what loud outfit, to who's munching what brand-name nutrition bar.

This year's action is played out almost entirely between the ropes, meaning the British Open–esque scramble to encircle the pros when they yank a tee ball into the heather is mostly a dinosaur. Plentiful grandstands, ample elbow room on the back nine especially, and Pebble's naturally fine amphitheater setting have pushed the throngs back from the fairway, thereby increasing the area of lush, irrigated rough and speeding up play. Just once in a week of Open viewing will

I personally witness the marshals drop the ropes and move the fans back on account of an errant shot. Unlike, say, at a matinee at Wrigley Field, we Open fans do not purchase omniscience with the cost of our ticket. We can't see the field and the players from on high and we're not privy, as we would be watching from the comfort of our La-Z-Boys, to the miked conversations whispered between golfers and caddy, or between golfers and anyone else, for that matter.

What we're left with is high school minus the text messaging—who's wearing what, who's hot, who's drunk, who's evil. The standby joke goes something like this: Famous caddy (select from among "Bones" Mackay, Steve Williams, or Fluff Cowan) walks to the tee ahead of his man, who's trailing behind eating a Red Delicious or shooting the shit with his playing partner du jour, at which time Joe Q. Gallery huzzahs to the early-arriving caddy, "Go get 'em, Bones!" or "Good work, Stevie!" or simply "Fluff!" at which point the crowd erupts in merriment at the idea that a mere sidekick would merit such a cheer. It's our way of asserting our humanity and our inanity, roped in as we are, stripped of telecommunications dignity, summarily shushed.

Perhaps as an attempt to shake off our USGA-imposed straightjackets, I hear more F-bombs dropped in a single afternoon at the Open than I do in 180 days of facetime with college sophomores. I hear enough beer-fueled innuendo involving "balls," "woods," and "nuts" to last me until my proverbial last lecture. This year, thank heavens, the scatological humor is tempered by the presence of a newly tragic hero for our Greek Chorus to bewail: Tiger Woods. We claim we're so over him, but, OMG, do we follow him.

Our abundant love-fear makes us wholly schizo. Teeing off on one, Tiger is Lazarus, as signaled by the dude in the grandstand who taunts Woods's playing partner, Lee Westwood, with a reminder of the margin by which the then-twenty-four-year-old American Achilles lapped the field in the 2000 Open. "Fifteen shots, Lee!" he needles from safe needling distance. On nine tee, the most angelic of female voices rises above the roar, "We love you Tiger!" Right of ten, supplicants crowd

Carmel Beach like members of some bare-footed, khaki-shorts cult waiting for the rapture or a sale at Gap for Men. A Monterey County cop stands alongside, hands in pockets, apparently guarding against an attack of idolatry by sea.

And yet our resurgent love affair is fickle, lasting only as long as Tiger's on-course performance conforms to our established expectations. On the eighteenth green, after 3-putting for a lackluster opening round of 74, Woods tosses his club in disgust, causing the woman beside me to announce, with convincing finality, "I'm done with Tiger." The mediocrity of his 2010 Open debut now a matter of record, there are whisperings of the desperate and disenchanted sort made when a high-dollar slugger falls into a faith-shaking slump. "It's almost like he's afraid to hit the ball," one guy tells me, shaking his head like his kid just went 0 of 5 in a Little League tilt. At his postround press conference, Black Hat Woods will irk USGA Executive Director David Fay by doing what no one but Tiger has the huevos to do: criticize Pebble. Rising up to defend the seemingly unassailable integrity of the links in the wake of the Woods/Standard and Poor's downgrading of its greens to "awful," Fay insists, "These putting surfaces have never been better," adding Phil to the fire in saying, "I think two players used the word 'awful' . . . Phil said he putted awful. Tiger said the greens were awful."

Phil we adore. Phil is all soft fades and sandy ringlets and pink ribbons. Phil we love but don't fear. Phil's a walk in the park; Tiger's a 1-iron held aloft in a lightening storm. And yet it's Tiger, not Lefty, who wields ultimate power over our psyches. He's the dark prince, the outlaw, the Johnny Cash, the wizard with the scar. We love-hate him. We want-fear him, and we regard him with all the trepidation and anger and awe of a god, not less this U.S. Open year after his fall from grace, but more.

Still, Tiger and Phil mania pales in comparison to the week's real star, the one who's elicited more prose and punditry and second-guessing than golf's two brightest stars combined; the one who's gotten sneaky long while Tiger's tee-bombs have been tamped down; the one who's gotten tighter over the last six months than Phil's pecs; the one who's really wearing the polyester pants in golf's family: Pebble Beach. It's Pebble we newsies itch to discuss; Pebble whose tighter, longer, meaner look since the last Open held here trumps Tiger's tortured transformations by far. Even Tiger's talking about it. "This is a completely different design, a complete redo from when we played," Woods tells the media after round one, and he's right: Pebble's always new, the USGA and the Pebble Beach Co. insuring that it is so. If it's not, there's no escalation, and if there's no escalation, no illusion of progress, no golf equivalent of crack cocaine to snort, there's minimal buzz, minimal hype. In 2000 the stir was the new fifth hole and the new sand in all 87 traps; in 1992 it was the Jack Nicklaus–directed bunker renovations, the revamped green complexes on four, five, and seven, and the War Against Kikuyu; in 1982 it was former USGA president Sandy Tatum's proposed changes to the traps on sixteen and four; in 1972 it was the knee-high rye, which local sportswriter Al Perez called "that fiendish rough which those devils from the USGA created." About that still-resonant Open, Dan Jenkins of *Sports Illustrated* wrote, "Pebble Beach, in fact, almost played too great a role. For a while it appeared that the winner wasn't going to be a man, but the course. Pebble—good old monstrous Pebble . . . won every battle, one-on-one, even with Nicklaus."

Throughout the winter, the point man for the controversy surrounding the championship-inspired renovations has a single face: the USGA's senior director of rules and competitions, its "setup man" since the early 2000s, Mike Davis. After the last Open at Pebble, Davis took the reigns from his somewhat less warm and fuzzy predecessor, Tom Meeks, who once so pissed off Payne Stewart with his diabolical Open setups that Stewart called him "crazy" and "impossible" to his face. By comparison, Davis's reign has been less controversial but no less noteworthy.

As former major champions filtered through Pebble during the winter, I'd made a point of asking each about the USGA's man behind the machine. "I really give Mike Davis a lot of credit," Jim Furyk told me. "He's done a great job setting up the courses the last four or five years. The scores have been high and difficult but you haven't heard a lot of players complaining."

As Furyk knows, every USGA setup man dreads crossing the line by which an exquisite course turns into an exquisite corpse. By his own admission to *Golf Digest* in 2004, Meeks walked the plank in trying out a dicey back-left pin on the eighteenth hole at San Francisco's Olympic Club in 1998. He recalled, "Later that day Payne Stewart 3-putted from 8 feet and wound up losing by 1. Tom Lehman 4-putted. I [had] crossed the line," he admitted. "It was a terrible mistake on my part and made the whole USGA look bad. There aren't a lot of highs and lows in my job, but this was a huge low. I still think about it." Then-USGA Chairman of the Championship Committee Sandy Tatum—the man largely responsible for bringing the first Open to Pebble—likewise took some serious heat for the stern test he set players at Winged Foot in 1974 when, he recalls, he famously defended his mandate by saying, "We're not trying to embarrass the best players in the world. We're trying to identify them."

When I'd asked him, Padraig Harrington intimated similar concerns about Pebble becoming a monster its makers hadn't reckoned on, especially on the shortgrass. "They can't get them [the greens] too quick with the slope that's in them," he said. "The ball would move on them. I had a ball move here the last time I was here."

Like Harrington, Mike Weir gives props to Davis's deft touch. "They've just done an incredible job setting up the golf courses in the last few U.S. Opens," he told me. "If you hit a real wayward shot, that's the deepest rough, when in years past that happened to be maybe trampled down. The graduated rough is really good."

If Davis's setup of Pebble does "cross the line," it will happen on nine and ten, where Harrington tells me he fears a well-hit drive on a firm, running fairway could bound down over the edge of the cliff, or on the fourth, eighth, or thirteenth greens, which dry out first in the wind and which could easily turn to farce in the absence of what the USGA euphemistically calls "corrective watering."

The historical odds that Pebble will get fast, brown, and out-of-control this week are better than good. In 1972, the Year of the Golden Bear and the 1-iron, Nicklaus, after receiving a congratulatory call from Tricky Dick, marched into the pressroom and said, "I can't ever recall seeing a day when we were almost not playing golf. Skill was practically eliminated. Half the greens were almost dead." The gruesome sequel continued ten years later in '82, when eventual winner Watson opined after a practice round, "The greens are difficult to putt . . . mostly [they're] *poa annua* and that's a weed. The footprints don't leave quickly, so they get bumps . . . They are treacherous." In 1992, a victorious but nevertheless spooked Tom Kite observed, "The greens were turning blue out there today. They really were. There were some that were very, very scary." In 2000, Pebble Beach Head Superintendent and Director of Agronomy Mark Michaud declared, "Greens will be as fast as humanly possible without killing them." For the 2010 edition of the U.S. Open, Tom Watson, in his Friday media center interview, made the most colorful comment yet to describe Pebble's singular moss: "You get a bunch of crowns out there," he observed. "They look like the backs of turtles. You're putting over backs of turtles."

The notion of Pebble as a monster course, the diabolical creation of a demented USGA, stretches all the way back to the days of hot pants and butterfly colors, well beyond the early 1990s when pro Richard Zokol compared eighteen holes at Pebble to "going eighteen rounds with Godzilla." The enduring mythos largely stems from Pebble's inaugural Open in 1972, a year in which the USGA, expecting becalmed winds, let the fescue rough reach knee-length on the then-6,815-yard links while simultaneously shaving the greens to within $\frac{3}{32}$ of an inch of their life. Average scores for the first several rounds hovered around 78, heading northward on Sunday with the introduction of gale-force winds that prompted small-craft warnings up and down the coast and caused pro George Archer such great consternation that he intentionally hit his tee shot on eighteen into Carmel Bay to post an insult-to-injury 87. In that '72 Open, *Los Angeles Times* sportswriter Jim Murray called Pebble a "hellship," a pirate conceit he repeated in his columns about the '92 Open, in which he wrote, "I've always said if Pebble Beach were human, it'd have a dagger in its teeth, murder in its heart, a patch over its eye, a price on its head, and the British Navy would be looking for it to hang it from the highest yardarm in the fleet." In the pirate course's defense, USGA president Lynford Lardner Jr. invoked the mollifying phraseology used by the powers-that-be at every Pebble Open since: "The course," he said, "is a hard and fair test."

Nearly forty years later, a kindler, gentler USGA has evolved to become more customer-friendly. Still, some pros admit to being less than 100 percent satisfied with Davis's handling of Pebble's natural endowments. At the Callaway Invitational, Champions Tour pro John Cook had argued to me that the course "would defend itself," adding, "Hopefully the USGA doesn't get too silly and try to embarrass people."

PGA Tour veteran Steve Flesch had agreed, telling me, "Sometimes making holes longer doesn't make them better, it just makes them longer . . . Pebble's not a long golf course, but I think the severity of the greens is enough. If he [Davis] gets the greens firm and fast like they always do, and they have the rough high enough . . . it's going to be hard enough."

A few days before polling the pros, I'd received an invitation to attend the renovated Pebble's coming out party, a media reception cum debutante ball billed as a preview of the 2010 Open. Drifting through the door of Pebble's Gallery Café, I'm greeted by a gratis glass of merlot and the sudden realization that all the king's men are in attendance: Pebble CEO Bill Perocchi, President and Chief Operating Officer Cody Plott, Executive V.P. of Brand Management David Stiver, Head Professional and Host Professional for the U.S. Open Chuck Dunbar,

Course Superintendant Chris Dalhamer, and, last but not least, good ol' Ollie Nutt, president and CEO of the Monterey Peninsula Foundation. Emceeing the generous, open-bar event is Pebble's senior vice president for golf, R. J. Harper.

In the twin hotseats arranged on either side of the U.S. Open replica trophy and staged Pebble backdrop are Mike Davis and two-time Open champ and indefatigable Pebble Beach booster Johnny Miller, whose victories on this, the holy of holies, span an incredible five decades. In 1968 Miller won the California Amateur at Pebble with a crazy-good score of 28 under par, a tally he would later tell *Pebble Beach Magazine* showed not only that he could play Pebble but that he could "kick its rear."

Harper leads off with a canned question: Why did the USGA choose to come back for a record fifth Open even though the links is the second shortest in the rota? On cue, Davis points out that while the 7,040-yard Pebble is shorter than all but Merion, it compensates with "the smallest putting greens you see for any Open." He then proceeds to remind we reporters that while Tiger ripped Pebble a new one at 12-under in 2000, TW's nearest competitor that year managed only +3.

We newsies throw a couple of heavies Davis's way concerning the extreme lengthening of three holes—nine, ten, and thirteen—in reply to which our "special guest" continues an expert, summary argument: "In the case of nine and ten, we really wanted to put drivers back in their hands," Davis tells us. "The thing you have to remember is that those holes should play straight downwind to a very firm fairway, and both holes play slightly downhill. In the case of the tenth, it brings the bunkering back into play . . . And in the case of the ninth, a driver can still put them over the hill . . . In the case of thirteen, I think it's going to be incredibly exciting that if we do get a couple-club wind into their face, it puts that cross bunkering, which was originally very much in play in the 1920s and 1930s, into play."

"Ten has more slope than any at Pebble," Davis continues, adding, "but it's widened compared to resort play. And we moved the teeing ground to the right so you're hitting more into the slope . . . In the case of nine, if you watched past U.S. Opens when it was firm . . . when you got it over the hill, a well-struck drive would roll into the rough . . . Now if you hit the right kind of drive . . . you can literally hit it down to the bottom and have an eight, nine, or wedge into it. However, if you really hit a strong drive there . . . you can knock it in the ocean, which you could never do before. The idea then is that you've got some risk-reward."

By this point the outspoken Miller, who's either been sedated or been purposefully biting his tongue to prove he can, can resist no longer. "A couple of the holes that will make a pretty big difference are the blind holes," he interjects, throwing his hat firmly into the ring. "Eight is a blind shot. The fairway's been moved over near the cliff, and you've got to know your new sightline, which is 15 yards farther right than it's ever been . . . And of course eleven is a blind tee shot and that fairway now has been moved over to the right, and everything pushes it there anyway. And then you've got another blind shot into fifteen . . . I don't want to say anything negative, but that's sort of an awkward tee shot."

"There's been a lot of changes that you might notice and might not," Miller continues. "Like six. That big tree is gone now that Tiger went over with a 7-iron from 210 or 220. Those bunkers at the top of the hill are way bigger than they used to be . . . The second hole to me is just really hard now with that bunkering on the left."

Miller hasn't made a living in the broadcast booth by pulling punches, and now that he's given Davis plenty of carrot, he's ready to whack him with a stick. "There are a lot of good changes at Pebble, but I keep telling Mike this: I don't believe in super-hard fairways. I don't like it when . . . you get the fairways running 50, 60, 70 yards, like Shinnecock Hills. Then good drives end up in bad spots."

"Mike keeps talking about this nice downwind on eight, nine, and ten, but I've seen it about six times my life, and I've been coming here since I was seven years old . . . Those holes are sort of going to make or break the championship. The guy who wins the U.S. Open is probably going to play those holes reasonably well. If you go through seven thinking this course is not too tough, you better hang onto your underwear for the next hour."

Grinning at his own digression, Miller belatedly returns to the Q in the media Q & A. "To answer the question about the most underrated hole, I really believe it's fourteen . . . Now it actually has a wiggle to it, and it's very narrow. That hole is absolutely going to be a terror in the Open for a 5-par."

"The most underrated part of Pebble," Miller says, picking back up on the theme, "is the sidehill lies on the shots into the green, and also how much tilt there is on the greens, especially from the mountain down to the water. Historically, guys on the front-right of eight, nine, and ten will never get that putt to the hole . . . You just have to continually remind yourself, where's the mountain and where's the water." He pauses. "There's a of local knowledge out on Pebble. That's why I love it."

If Miller were tasked with tricking out Pebble for the national championship, he tells us, he'd be punishing, but selectively. "When you get a hole, say six or eight or nine or ten, and the guys are nervous about the ocean and the cliff, that's where you want to put some good rough for the guy that's too chicken to play the shot. You don't want to reward the guy for totally bailing on the really good design features."

As the reception sprawls into evening, it's Miller who gradually steals the show, offering the perspective of a veteran from the trenches in lieu of the theories of the technician, though Davis is no slouch as a player, having won the Pennsylvania Junior and having later played college golf at Georgia Southern. Miller's waxing nostalgic, and getting a little misty-eyed — maybe it's just the wine — about the significance of golf's national championship. "Growing up, the British Open was just gaining popularity and the Masters was, as Tony Lema put it, 'fun at the top.' The U.S. Open was *the championship* . . . For me, that was the one I always wanted to win. My game was always geared to win an Open . . . My whole career really revolves around what happened at Oakmont."

Miller remains in awe not just of his own blistering 63 in the final round of that 1973 Open, but Tiger's record-breaking 12-under final tally at the 2000 Open at Pebble, where, Miller reminds, Tiger never once lipped out a putt. "It was the greatest putting performance I've ever seen. He was at the top of his game. That was like a Bobby Jones year . . . you could just feel it watching Tiger. His clubhead speed was probably eight miles an hour faster than it is now. If Tiger Woods hit the new equipment now, he would be leading the Tour stats by 30 yards a drive. He had a 131 miles an hour clubhead speed. The fastest guy now is like 122 . . . That was the greatest performance in the history of the modern game."

Even though he lapped the field by 15 Tiger swipes, Woods triple bogeyed his nemesis, Pebble's third hole, on that historic final round—a blemish that, to Miller's way of thinking, only made TW's mental toughness more apparent. "It [the Open] usually goes to really strong-willed guys . . . Nicklaus, Hogan . . . the guys that are just so tough mentally . . . Tiger picked up that percentage golf from Jack, but he's more aggressive with the lead than Jack was. Jack actually told me he didn't like to win by several strokes. It just wasn't as interesting to him."

"Nicklaus was the greatest out of the rough. Els was one of the greatest out of the rough. Watson. Tiger. Those guys are able to muscle it out of the heavy stuff, and still get it on or around the green . . . The precision players are pretty much gone."

Before the Pebble cotillion ends, I ask Davis if it's hard on him being golf's equivalent of a tough prof—a C-grade giver when, by analogy, when the fraternity of Waste Management Open setup guys hand out easy As. "When you set up a golf course it's incredibly subjective," Davis admits. "The USGA absolutely, positively wants a very stern, difficult championship . . . I know no one believes me, but we're not fixated on par winning this thing."

A month or so after our U.S. Open media soiree, I call Davis up at his office in Far Hills, New Jersey, with some nagging questions. After listening to all the strategical, tactical, logistical smack he and Miller talked, I want to know how this thoughtful, articulate man *feels* about Pebble, if he feels for it at all. "The first time you're there you're almost bowled over with how pretty it is," Davis confides, recalling the first time he set foot on the sacred turf in 1990. "You see it on television, but until you experience it in person, until you experience hitting that second shot over the canyon on the eighth hole . . . or the tee shot on seven . . . really, it's just magical. As much as anything, what's hard about a place like Pebble Beach is that it's almost easy to overlook the architecture of the course because of the sheer beauty of the place."

In preparation for that long-ago Open, Davis rented a bungalow in Carmel-by-the-Sea, recalling that he was "spoiled" for months and that he can still find the house from whence he jogged daily to the ocean. "I'm not sure there's really a town like Carmel anywhere in the country . . . where you've got these wonderful little houses with all kinds of architectural interest to them. Some almost look like gingerbread houses. It's just a wonderful downtown with great shopping and great restaurants."

Trip down memory lane dead-ended, we return to the question at hand, the one Harper had led off with at the media reception, only this time I'm after more substance: Why has the USGA come back to Pebble, with the mania of a jilted lover, when so many longer, newer, courses are deserving of golf's major prize? The answer, as it turns out, has less to do with mystery than it does predictability—the hard facts of agronomy, weather, and television time zones, the latter of which allows Left Coast weekend rounds at the Open to be seen in primetime out East.

"Unless you go to coastal California with the U.S. Open," Davis explains, putting his tactician's hat back on, "there's really nowhere we can dial in the firmness. There we can dial it in because it just won't rain that time of year. That means we can prep the golf course exactly like we want. We can put down as much water as we need to put down. That's tremendously exciting."

"Once you get past ten or eleven in the morning, you can pretty much count on one club of wind," he explains, breaking it down now to hours and minutes and knots. "It's when you get up to two or three clubs of wind that it changes things dramatically . . . It certainly happened on the fourth day in 1992, when it just howled," he reminds me, citing the four- to five-club gale that caused Tom Kite to resort to a 6-iron on the 107-yard seventh, a club he yanked 20 yards left only to sink the come-back pitch for an unlikely bird.

"Pebble is so special, you just get it set up properly and then just let Pebble be Pebble . . . Even though we moved some fairways closer to the ocean and built three new teeing grounds on nine, ten, and thirteen, at the end of the day we really haven't done much to Pebble, because you really don't need to do much to Pebble . . . It's such a special place. Of all the U.S. Open courses it's the one that people know best."

Thursday night finds Davis, USGA President Jim Hyler, and chairman of the USGA championship committee, Tom O'Toole, breathing a sigh of relief. Aside from Tiger's inflammatory comments about the putting surfaces and the potluck draw of a gray, brooding Monterey day not well-suited to the tube, all is going according to plan. The winds blow from the northwest, giving the longest hitters a wedge into ten and a short iron into nine, just as Davis had promised. The new setup has indeed put the driver back in the hands of the leaders, inducing even bombers like Dustin Johnson to pull the Big Dog as many as seven times in their rounds. Day one, only nine players beat par; bogeys outnumber birdies two to one. In his press conference, Mickelson calls the greens "fair," adding, "I think Mike Davis has a good grasp on the golf course . . . He's not looking to make 10- or 12-over win. He has a good understanding of what a fair test is, without going over the line."

However, Murphy's Law dictates that because all went swimmingly among the pros on the links, things cannot be entirely hunky-dory among the galleryites. Thursday evening finds us, smug in our wisdom to "let the crowds die down" before attempting to board our shuttle bus, clomping merrily along, expecting quick, efficient transport back to our Japanese automobiles. We climb the new, temporary overpass (built for our convenience) over 17-Mile Drive, cordially chatting and jostling en route, and descend to cross the Peter Hay par-3 golf course, which has been turned into a main entrance featuring banner pictures of former Open championships, copious potted flowers and ornamental grasses staged to look as if they'd always been there, and merchandise tents up the wazoo; these include the Palmer's Place concession stand, the Trophy Club, the Lexus Performance Drive title sponsor tent, the big top–sized main merchandise tent, and, my favorite, Missing Persons/Lost and Found.

Exiting the tent city built atop Pebble's Pompeii of par-3 courses, we quietly anticipate a repeat of 1972, when shuttle buses and traffic patterns, wrote Monterey sportswriter Al Perez, "were so astutely planned that the old excitement of traffic jams, dented fenders, tow-away trucks, misplaced autos, bruised pedestrians, and crippled dogs was missing." But Pebble pride goeth before the fall, and just as we golf-satiated ruminants contemplate how we'll conclude a near-perfect day grazing the grassy links, our unimpeded stampede to return to the ranch in time to watch the tail end of the NBA finals is stopped at Stevenson Drive by a Monterey County mountie. Fifteen minutes later, with the mounting sense of dread one imagines cows must feel on their way to becoming ground chuck, we realize we are merely pre-boarding—waiting for the line of people themselves waiting to board the promised one hundred shuttle buses that are supposed to deposit us back to the California State Monterey Bay University stockyards.

Confronted now with the specter of what appears to be an endless, un-American queue, the four golfing buddies chomping at the bit behind me, who awoke at the butt-crack of dawn to make the drive down to the Peninsula, begin laying down bets on how long it will take us to reach the slaughtering house. The most cynical among them puts his cash on ninety minutes—nine o'clock PBST, Pebble Beach Standard Time. But something is rotten in Denmark, and Pebble CEO Bill

Perocchi's pledge in this week's *Pine Cone*, that "every detail has been addressed; every contingency has been accounted for," now sounds like laughable irony.

We inch through the football field–length chutes of cattle gates at an agonizing rate of about one 100-yard run of the maze per hour. The sun goes down and the moon comes up over the spooky pines of the Del Monte Forest, and still we languish hours away from the terminus of the convoluted, impossibly large intestine we have been swallowed by. The already clear chilly day, topping out at 60 degrees, turns into a cold, damp night. And a low rumble of dissent builds among we bovines.

The good-time guy-group behind, one of whom has to catch a red-eye to New Jersey, makes an attempt at levity, periodically raising the ironic chant, "Let's go, Warriors!" in honor of both the in-progress NBA Championship, whose viewing we're forgoing, and in mock celebration of Golden State's hapless pumpkin-pushers.

But what was laugh-out-loud funny during the first hour of our queue-for-slaughter is no laughing matter by the second. As we wait, one woman reads a copy of *The New York Times* best-seller *A Reliable Wife* cover to cover, finishing by the light of the generator-powered Sho-lights being forklifted in at a frenzied clip.

After the third hour of zombie-like immobility in bone-chilling, hug-your-honey high school football weather, the thoroughly sardonic crowd begins to cheer every time a single coach arrives to carry off a load. To pass time, the ringleader of the dudes behind me crafts a mock CNN headline: "Golf fans riot at U.S. Open"—the "funny" in it being that we fans of the royal and ancient game really are the most forgiving, most docile, most orderly in all of major sportdom. The faux headline's amusing, too, because, this being Pebble, we know our woes won't get reported as they would if passengers were trapped aboard an aircraft on the tarmac without food or water or phones for an equivalent number of hours.

By ten p.m. the Monterey fuzz has begun to assemble en masse, either fearing a riot or wanting to stave off the Del Monte Forest version of a humanitarian crisis. The atmosphere is actually tense. Among us there are children, pregnant women, disabled persons, and still the line is barely moving. Finally, a cop fires up a portable mike and broadcasts a call to the several thousand waiting Israelites to raise their hand if they are "in need of water." When too many hands to count go up in the far-off convolutions of the steel-gated maze we're trapped in, Monterey's finest, having no other access point to the interiors of the maze, begin lobbing 20-ounce bottles of Dasani into the crowd. Another cop rips open a box of Doritos and spreads the bags among the kids along the edges who are clamoring for sustenance.

At ten-thirty, three chilly hours after our involuntary stand-in began, a raggedy-ass bus pulls up to our bay, the nonsensical sign above the windshield reading "American League." The foursome of dudes behind me raise their hands in jubilation, like they've just seen Jesus. "We are delivered! We are the chosen ones!" they ballyhoo. For the past hour they have been composing aloud, at some small comedic relief, complaint letters they will never write: "Dear *Chronicle* Editor," one would begin, while another would clear his throat, Thomas Jefferson–style, and intone, "Dear Sirs . . . "

As we board the bus bound for the abandoned military complex of Fort Ord, where our wheels wait somewhere amid the pitch-black sixteen thousand parking spots and graffitied warehouses with busted-out windows, the most ironic among them, the one with the flight to catch a few short hours from now, deadpans, "Congratulations, USGA, on a successful pickup." When an hour later I arrive at Natalie's house—where I, golf-crazed and celibate, will be sleeping on the couch for the U.S. Open week—it's well-nigh the witching hour. Beneath our feet as we embrace, Nat's roommate's little daschund, Allie, wets the carpet she's so thoroughly over-stimulated by our late-night reunion.

And I thought it was just me.

18

May U.S. Open Winds
Be Always at Your Back,
May 17-Mile Drive Lay at Your Feet,
May Pebble Rise to Meet You

By the end of Day Two I have established a revised M.O., prompted by a much-feared repeat of the Thursday eve shuttle debacle. Each night at the conclusion of play I eschew the cattle-mover and leave the links instead on foot, through the Carmel Gate, musing en route at the intricate, post-party, sorority girl–esque preening it takes Chris Dalhamer and his expanded U.S. Open grounds crew to erase the grand old lady's worry lines. The most ingenious makeup method resorted to is the leaf blowers employed to stand up the matted rye grass rough until it's as spiked as Ian Poulter's hair. (In past Opens, feet, not blowers, were tasked with manually standing up the spinach.) No cosmetic detail is spared for the big date; as part of Pebble's pretty-up for the Open, course superintendent Dalhamer told me, the sand in Pebble's traps had been color matched with the sands on the Carmel Beach, to avoid jarring overhead shots from the blimp.

After Dalhamer and his crew have put the course to bed each night and after I've cooed sweet nothings into my adopted dachshund's ears each and every slumbertime, I return every fair morn to my village-by-the-sea and, whilst nibbling on nuked quiche and sipping java at the Carmel Coffee House, I read a new section of the blissfully free *Carmel Pine Cone*. Nice work if you can get it.

The village's venerable newspaper is arguably the best window into the sublimely contradictory *vita loca* here, especially during the U.S. Open, when the burg's weird eclecticism reaches fever pitch. On any given week the *Pine Cone* can be counted on to contain a pleasing mixology of stories concerning dogs, crime, land use, fraud and abuse, charity, and golf, listed here roughly in order of importance. This week's edition, for instance, features the full range of headline-grabbing dog-gery, including the page 2 "Sandy Claws" feature introducing "Hula Pie Schellhous, 13," a Jack Russell/Chihuahua mix who is "crazy about road trips to Tahoe and loves chicken breast poached in salt-free broth." In the bleeds-it-leads category of dogdom, or doggerel, this week's rag covers the untimely death at sixty-six of the "Dog Lady from Monterey," and offers an update on the ongoing legal battle over KCBA and KION TV anchorwoman Olga Ospina's mauled Maltese, Lulu, whose attack at the hands of a Labrador has already earned Ospina approximately fifty grand in pain and suffering and lost wages. Puréed with coverage of a doggie dining fundraiser is macabre reportage concern-. ing a twenty-three-year-old man who committed suicide this week by throwing himself off the iconic Bixby Bridge on coast-hugging Highway 1, and local stories of rape and husband abuse. These cautionary bylines reside in close proximity to a full-color, half-page lingerie ad with a semi-nude she-lynx provocatively she-handling a club (BTW, her grip's a little weak) to welcome we U.S. Open fans. Adverts peddling backyard putting greens ("Your own personal version of luxury") and offering a $250 off U.S. Open Special complete the only-in-Carmel mix.

Upholding my OCD U.S. Open routine means I must next leave the *Pine Cone* behind at my corner table and emerge onto Ocean Avenue, fully caffeinated, to unexpectedly commerce-challenged streets. I had fancied seeing, I'll admit, bottomless shopping bags and deep wallets, but what I have found is bustle slightly below par for the AT&T Pro-Am and on par with the average shopping weekend at the height of the Carmel-by-the-Sea tourist season. The shops here in the commercial district have done their part, Lord knows—golf paraphernalia populates the window displays from coffee shops to markets to bars; a sign outside Friar Tuck's proclaims "Welcome U.S. Open fans! Breakfast and Bloody Mary's all day until . . . "—the dot-dot-dot pretty much signifying until the cows come home. Eastwood's old place, the Hog's Breath Inn, is slinging its crowd-pleasin' Dirty Harry sirloin dinners and the decidedly un–Dirty Harry, totally pansy, Dirty Harry portobello burgers.

Carmel, bless its dignified soul, is on the hustle, is showing its wares, is shaking its money maker, but, thus far, and by analogy, the hoped-for level of grab-ass has not materialized. Instead we're in a capitalistic holding pattern. The woman in the window of Augustine's on Ocean repositions the same pair of women's saddle shoes over and over, hoping one pose will loosen the wallet of a passerby more than another, while the town's token case of Turrets wanders up and down Sixth Avenue muttering, "It's not about Bob. It's about *power*. Beaker . . . Beaker . . . Beaker."

This may be the anomalous, once-per-decade week of golf windfall, but ego-strong Carmel is suffering no identity crisis over it. It's still litigation-minded, with its cover-its-ass earthquake warnings plastered on the plate glass storefront of the Carmel Camera Center—"This is an unreinforced masonry building. You may not be safe inside or near unreinforced masonry building during an earthquake." And it's still not about to fall completely prey to crass commercialism, no more than it was eighty-five years ago, when Carmel writer Daisy Bostick penned of Carmel shopkeepers, "To do some business each day is all right, but to pursue more of it eagerly would be liable to brand one a worshipper of the Golden Calf." Still, the town that time forgot is doing its best to let its ringlets down. The code requiring a permit for high heels is flagrantly flaunted as the she-galleryites exit Pebble via the Carmel Gate each night to clip-clop the uneven streets en route to sushi or swordfish.

One night, as I wait to catch the bus post-round, I am agog at the sight of two kids, a boy and a girl, playing Wiffle ball in Devendorf Park, ironically right behind a sign that reads, "Bicycles, Skateboarding, Dogs, Frisbee Playing, and Ball-type games prohibited." Laub's Country Store has added some Chinese-made, screen printed t-shirts to its usual window mix, ones bearing thematically apropos slogans like "There's more to life than golfing . . . Let me know when you find it," and "Pebble Beach . . . When the going gets tough, the tough go golfing." Aside from a ticket-happy meter maid or two working the parking-prohibited side streets, I am pleased to report no gig-harshing, spoilsport police presence.

In fact, Carmel, as Carmel goes, has bent over backward for this here People's Open. Fresh from her reelection in April, Mayor Sue McCloud, in partnership with the Pebble Beach Company, has constructed the promised rustic, pleasingly sinuous walkway (emphatically not a sidewalk) of finely crushed gravel and fragrant, rough-cut pickets meandering its way to Pebble's lower entrance, just beyond the Carmel Gate. Many businesses are staying open late despite their incredulity; the clerk at the Carmel Coffee Company who typically brews my dark roast tells me she's doubtful customers will do anything après golf but head straight to their high-end dinners. But she's staying open for desserts anyway, because, as she puts it, "It only happens once every ten years."

Mostly the denizens of Carmel, whose homes sport just 50 percent occupancy rates even during ordinary weeks, have left their fair city to the multitudes. McCloud had intimated as much when she'd mentioned in the fall that, "people sort of hunker down and wait until it [the U.S. Open] is over," while acknowledging that it's a "a big shot in the arm" for the city's revenue. There's brisk walk-in traffic at the realty offices up and down Ocean Ave., where the Pebble Beach siren song appears to be charting Billboard Top 40. Recently on the market, and the subject of considerable speculation this week among its passersby on the links, is the casa called *Out a Bounds,* ideally located between Pebble's fifteenth fairway and fourth green. The listing alone has us duffers hot and bothered: "Constructed of clear-heart redwood and walls of glass, the home, built on a slight arch, surrounds the sunny patios and terraces. With a landscaped 1.5-acre parcel, a spa and detached guest house, a total of four bedrooms, three and a half baths, and an attached three-car garage, the home is within walking distance to The Beach Club, Casa Palmero Spa, and The Lodge. Or, if you just feel like staying home, you can even order in room service from The Lodge." *Out a Bounds* exemplifies the fine Carmel art of home-naming, whose linguistic recipe, not unlike the christening of a yacht or sailboat, consists of two parts double entendre, one part elitism, and one part overt sentimentality. On my walk to the Carmel Gate I will pass hovels with such nudge-nudge, wink-wink sobriquets as *Someday Came, By Coastal, C'est La View, 1st Love,* and, naturally, *2nd Love.*

U.S. Open week ethos in Carmel-by-the-Sea and Pebble Beach is totally open house. For the golf-crazed public, the art galleries have thrown open their Dutch doors, tops and bottoms both, among them the elfin den of the village's most famous artist, Thomas Kinkade, who could use a mulligan about now. In an event that made national news late last week, Carmel's world-renowned "Painter of Light" was arrested by the Monterey County sheriff's deputy for a missing front plate and subsequent suspicion of drunken driving after an officer spotted Kinkade's Mercedes leaving Clint Eastwood's Mission Ranch. Kinkade, whose website claims him to be "America's most collected living artist," was booked in the Monterey County jail after he failed a field sobriety test for balance, coordination, and the ability to multitask—a test most men, including me, would bomb sober. I drop into Kinkade's Garden Gallery thinking I might express my sympathies to the Painter of Light in person, but the master is not in his shop, though his painting, "Pinocchio Wishes Upon on a Star," gets props in the front window. In the pic's foreground, the long-nosed boy-liar stands wide-eyed and enthralled atop a hill overlooking a magical seaside village of steeply pitched Swiss chalet-styled roofs. It's Carmel-by-the-Sea to a tee.

Though at the chamber of commerce breakfast Pebble's R. J. Harper had talked up the incremental business generated by the Open for local eateries and hotels especially, trumpeting what was, even then, a 90 percent occupancy rate, on the ground it's hard to see the Pebble-projected $150 million being spent by U.S. Open–goers at area hotels, restaurants, retail stores, movie theaters, and the like. The vacancy signs hanging out front of some of Carmel-by-the-Sea's most venerable and conveniently located inns, including the Normandy Inn and the Village Inn, are a mystery. It's possible that Pebble Beach and the USGA have unwittingly shot host city Carmel in the foot with repeated suggestions that street parking will be as rare as hen's teeth. (It isn't, if you are willing to walk a dozen steeply pitched blocks.) Much like at the AT&T Pro-Am, tourney transportation logistics now make it possible to bypass Carmel entirely, arriving by shuttle bus from a remote lot as far away as Marina, where the *Pine Cone* quotes mayor Bruce Delgado as saying his burg's eateries are "humming," thanks to his city's sixteen thousand satellite parking spaces. Marina's hotels, Mr. Mayor reports, are 80 to 100 percent full—a range commensurate with the costlier lodgings in Carmel-by-the-Sea.

The United States Open may not be the Waste Management Open, but this year it just might be the Economy Open.

Like many of the natives, my host for the week, the saintly, raven-haired, ruby-red-bathrobed Natalie, has timed her summer vacation with her new beau to coincide with the Open week hustle and bustle, leaving me, for a few extra rupees, much gratitude, and an I.O.U. for a piece of Rosine's yellow cake, in care of Nat's simple, stucco bungalow in Seaside, inclusive of a neurotic wiener dog to feed and water. Even with the dachshund it's an exceptionally rad deal, with the craigslist going rate for two- to three-bedroom rent-a-homes in Carmel hovering around five grand for the week, and comparably hospitable digs in Monterey fetching around two Grover Clevelands.

My U.S. Open week marching orders, taped to the front door, are simple enough for a Neanderthal: 1) Leave sliding door open for wiener to come and go according to wiener's whims; 2) Collect mail; 3) Leave key when through. Because Allie the dachshund belongs to Nat's roommate and because Allie and Natalie, the two women of the house, are prone to shrill, alpha she-male struggles, Natalie assures me that if I should accidentally kill the pooch, as would happen in a *Brady Bunch* episode, she would grant me Nixon-esque pardon. Given Allie's habit of spontaneous urination when overstimulated, I am asked to limit my interactions with the hound to those that could reasonably take place atop the easy-clean kitchen linoleum. Sage advice, I figure, for any new relationship.

After the trauma of Thursday night's U.S. Open cattle haul, my tournament days fall into the comfortable rhythm of a totally tubular house-sit. Each evening I return from America's number one public course pleasantly fatigued, flop down on the couch, channel surf to SportsCenter, and wait for Allie to make overtures, which I duly yet sensitively rebuff and which she takes hard, returning to her crate, all hangdog. It's eerily like a relationship.

Mornings I wake up, sweet-talk the wiener from her crate-bound pout, feed her half a cup of Super Premium Bil Jac dogfood, brew the day's joe in Nat's super-cool, super-Swedish Keurig coffeemaker, then commence to showering with my absent hostess's Touch of Happiness body wash that foams to decadence without pouf. There, amid the surfeit of sweet-smelling, cruelty-free exfoliants and ointments, I contemplate my strategic navigation of the links. Après full-body cleanse, I have but a four-block walk amid the tacquerias and mercados and liquor stores and uniform shops and vacant lots and chain-link fences to be the sole Anglo, to say nothing of U.S. Open ticket holder, audacious enough to board the bus, whose principal raison d'être is to deposit the Peninsula underclass from Monterey and Seaside to do the dirty work of the two million well-to-do folks who annually visit the hamlet in the forest. It's a tale of two buses: the U.S. Open shuttle with its upbeat, russet-cheeked, exquisitely orthodontiaed, deep-pocketed golfers, and the Edgewood Route #11, a.k.a. the Carmel Express, with its generally wordless, almond-eyed, thoroughly humble, mostly impoverished riders.

Unlike the urban melting pot U.S. Opens held at places like Torrey Pines, where spectators of all stripes board the light rail to and from satellite lots, the Monterey Peninsula makes it possible, for better and for worse, to experience the tourney in its entirety without once leaving the Del Monte Forest or, indeed, ever laying eyes on a single soul who doesn't share your income tax bracket. If you dig this particular appeal of a Pebble Beach Open, you have former USGA president, Rhodes Scholar, and Tom Watson buddy Frank "Sandy" Tatum to thank, as Tatum helped convince the USGA circa 1970 that a remote confederation of quaint coastal villages 120 miles south of San Francisco could host a kick-ass, world-class championship. Back then the USGA was so dubious about the prospect of staging such a far-flung Open that Pebble's owner, Del Monte Properties, had to sweeten the pot with a $250,000 guarantee and the tacit agreement that golf's governing body could prep the course as they saw fit.

With a total population of around 150,000 for the entire Peninsula, staging the Open at Pebble was, and is, something akin to plunking America's tourney down among a half-dozen scattered coastal towns whose total population doesn't quite equal Des Moines and to do so without the benefit of an international airport. Pebble's R. J. Harper once astutely pointed out to *Pebble Beach Magazine*'s Tim Sweeny that, "most of the major metropolitan areas that host major championships—whether it's Winged Foot or Oakmont or Baltusrol—are all in luxury residential private areas. The roads are not four-lane highways.

Pebble Beach is no different." The upside of the Peninsula's unique transportation situation is the rare prospect of attending a week of top-drawer golf without need of a car. By exiting the course on hoof at the lower spectator gate beside the eleventh tee, and meandering a mere few blocks to town, Joe and Suzy Q. Gallery enjoy a town-and-gown, links-and-minks proximity available only in the world's other great golfing mecca: St. Andrews. And, with Pebble's tenth green and eleventh tee backing up practically onto the Carmel commercial district, it's as weirdly time efficient to take an intermission break in town for some noontime tilapia as it is to queue for an overpriced Nathan's Famous hotdog at the Open concession stand.

The pleasures born of Pebble's proximity to Carmel are surreal when you think about it: imagine a village, and a week, where a fair citizen of fair Carmel could, drawn by the distant roars wafting through the Monterey pine canopy to the doorstep of his bungalow, decide that he is, after all, interested in seeing that golfer everyone's talking so much about these days . . . that Tiger Woods . . . and, wandering down San Antonio Street, buy a scalped ticket and, a minute later, sashay onto the links on foot, easy-breezy. Imagine a place where, during Open week, it is all but ordained that even the most casual, clueless fan shall be treated to the most phenomenal golf.

And phenomenal golf it has been. After a Thursday round in which Mickelson failed to birdie a hole—any hole—for the first time in a competitive round in three years, Lefty comes out firing on Friday after a text message and cell phone brush-up with short-game coach Dave Pelz. After St. Mick cards a 5-under par 66, playing partner Padraig Harrington professes he has never seen Phil play better, and ESPN's analyst and two-time Open champ Andy North will, conjuring his inner Joe Biden, call it the "cleanest" round he's ever seen Phil play.

On Saturday it's the alter ego's turn to go low: Tiger catches fire on Pebble's decidedly more difficult back nine to post his best-ever U.S. Open nine, a 31 that has crowds jamming seventeen and eighteen for a look at the Tiger of Yore. Their roars, when Tiger sinks his birdie putt on seventeen and threads the eye of the fairway cypresses to reach the eighteenth in 2, can be heard at the farthest reaches of Abalone Corner. At round's end, when Woods's kick-in bird leaves him under par for the tourney and in sole possession of third, an exuberant media proclaims Tiger's return to form, with Rick Reilly deeming the fist pump officially "out of storage."

Woods is upbeat at his born-again press conference, every bit a man once lost, now found: "What I've been working on is building. It's getting better," he intimates. "I was getting better and better. But I just hadn't had long enough . . . Today I hit a lot of good ones."

Through three rounds, the 2010 U.S. Open at Pebble has lived up to its storybook predecessors—Jack's fabled, pin-seeking finish in 1972, Watson's chip-in, and flippant, I-told-you-so finger point at caddy Bruce Edwards in 1982, and Tiger's record-setting, 15-shot dismantling of the field to ring in the new millennium in 2000. Now, heading into the final round, horses-for-courses favorite Dustin Johnson, he of two straight AT&T Pro-Am victories, stands atop the leaderboard at a generous 6-under, with steady-as-she-goes Irishman Graeme McDowell at 3-under, Tiger at minus 1, Phil and Ernie at plus 1, and the week's dark horse Frenchman, the Jean Van de Velde du jour, 391-ranked Gregory Havret, in the mix at even.

A glance at the scoreboard at the end of Day Three, though, reveals the real leaders in the clubhouse are the Pebble Beach Company and the USGA, which find themselves gifted with a logjam featuring the world's top two players—America's most promising up-and-comer in Johnson, a likeable Irishman in McDowell, a no-name Frenchman in Havret, and a beloved, postcolonial veteran in Els—all thick as thieves. Better still, Old Man Par, the USGA's perennial favorite, has been bested by just three men.

The smart money among the press corps is on Johnson, who's averaging more than 310 yards per drive for the week and whose touch around Pebble's undersized greens has been soft as a teardrop. The unspoken hope, though, is for a duel between contemporary golf's

Big Three: Woods, Mickelson, and Els. If anything, Team DJ may be overconfident, as Johnson caddy Bobby Brown, a former Pebble Beach looper, had boasted to the USGA's Thomas Bonk earlier in the week, "Dude, whoever says winning at Pebble Beach before is not a factor is full of it. He [Johnson] sees things here. He sees the greens and he knows how to miss it. He's not missing much . . . Dude, there's a vibe here. I can feel it and Dustin can feel it, too."

But nothing ices a young, anxious golfer more than a late tee time, and because the powers-that-be are eager to go primetime, Sunday's x-factor is that the leaders don't tee off until well-nigh teatime. On Friday, Mickelson had said of the TV-minded late weekend starts, "At Augusta I thought it was late at three. I mean, four o'clock, I'm . . . driving home, getting the kids ready for doing their homework, and getting ready for bed."

Whether it's the late tee time or early nerves at work, Johnson un-expectedly implodes on the second hole of his Sunday round, losing 5 shots to par in the first three holes. DJ's Waterloo means the wreck-waiters have been satiated as well as the Tiger–Phil–Big Easy boost-ers. True to form, as the day wears on it's the course that emerges, inexorably, as the victor. One by one the top competitors lose strokes to par until, by hole ten, only McDowell is left in red, Els's hopes hav-ing died in the cliffside hay right of ten, where, above us, a low-flying plane towed a sign that read, "Tiger, are you my daddy?"

It's Father's Day. And no one is laughing.

It's at hole twelve that the surreality of the day's happenings sets in, a feeling reinforced by an eerie atmospheric calm that descends after a week of freshening winds. As the crowds leave McDowell to follow Tiger, who at 4-over through thirteen holes is, for all practical purposes, out of the tournament, the Irishmen behind me, apparently wounded by the defection of my countryman, asks me, "Are you kid-din' me? He [McDowell's] the leader of your championship."

Among the fatalistic Irishmen who've found themselves joining Mc-Dowell's gallery when they'd assumed they'd be cheering on Harrington or Rory McIlroy late in the day on Sunday, it's not yet *Ole Ole* time. Their exhortations as McDowell leaves the twelfth with par are almost English in their reserve: "C'mon Graeme, 3 shots would be a lovely cushion." Meanwhile, the U.S. Open winner-in-waiting—the very precision player that Johnny Miller had claimed was all but extinct—moves among crowds that are, all along the rope line, a mere one or two spectators deep, as if the throng cannot admit to itself that the winner of the national championship could be this middle-roader—not a superstar nor a dark horse Jack Fleck, but a solid, steady-as-she goes, top-40 ranked thirty-year-old sporting a painter's cap and sponsored by Bushnell's Whiskey.

By hole fourteen Mike Davis and USGA president Jim Hyler, inconspicuous in baseball caps and khakis, have joined the McDowell-Johnson group, their presence all but making the coronation official. And when, sporting a good-for-any-occasion navy blazer, Pebble part-owner and former MLB commissioner Peter Ueberroth joins the march to the sea coming down the home stretch, we know it is all but in the bag, despite the red-herring hustle and bustle out front with Mickelson, Els, and Tiger.

When McDowell comes through with his easy, 2-putt par on eighteen to best the Frenchman Havret by a shot, what started out as the impossible and grew into the inevitable has become the unbelievable: the first European since Tony Jacklin in 1970 has won America's Open. Behind me, the orange-haired Irishman with the caterpillar eyebrows shouts, "A bottle of Bush for you t'night, m'boy!" As McDowell stands before us on the green, disbelieving, the requisite scrum of song-ready, flag-draped Irishmen make their way to the grandstand, where they will raise their voices in a long-suppressed "Ole! Ole! Ole! Ole!" As the serenade begins, members of the USGA executive committee ring the green where Hyler hands the best golfer of the week the championship trophy and an I.O.U. for the $1.35 million winner's check.

In the pressroom the Ulsterman is humble before the course that he has, at even par, not brought to its knees so much as endured. "To win at Pebble Beach, to join the names, Jack Nicklaus, Tom Watson, Tom Kite, Tiger Woods, me . . . wow. I'm not quite sure if I belong in that list, but, hey, I'm there now," he says.

"To win the U.S. Open here at Pebble Beach is a special feeling," G-Mac, as his countrymen call him, continues. "I came here, I think, in 2001. I was a college player over in Birmingham in Alabama, and we were playing a golf tournament locally, and we came here to have a look around. We were in awe of the place . . . It reminded me of home quite a lot, the coastline and the ocean and just the beauty of it all."

True to pattern, the highlight reels and headlines of the evening to come will be as much about Pebble as about McDowell. Blood-and-guts headlines range from "Pebble Fights Back" to "Carnage," as, in the end, only six players better par on Sunday, and the Big Three—Woods, Mickelson, and Els—tally a combined 8-over in their respective final rounds. For the week, scores on the links' homeward nine will average nearly 39 strokes, the eighteen-hole average approaching 75. Notable train wrecks include a 49 on Friday's back nine by defending PGA Championship winner and Tiger-slayer Y. E. Yang, and a final-round front nine of 42 for defending AT&T champ Johnson. Scores on just two holes, the drivable par-4 fourth and the reachable par-5 sixth average under par, while totals for others, most notably fourteen and seventeen, play nearly a half-stroke above their par. To the delight of the USGA and golf purists everywhere, McDowell's winning score lands right at even par, 12 shots tougher than Tiger's thrashing of the links in 2000, 3 shots higher than Tom Kite's tally in the blustery 1992 Open, and a full 6 shots more rigorous than Watson's 6-under, Reagan-era number. And while skeptics of Pebble's Open-inspired course lengthening have longed claimed that Pebble favored the bombers to begin with—Nicklaus in 1972, Woods in 2000, Johnson each and every AT&T—the week's number one and two finishers turn out to be the shorter-hitting McDowell and Havret, the latter of whom Johnson out-drove, on average, by more than 20 yards a tug.

In victory, McDowell is effusive about the USGA's setup man, telling the press, "I thought Mike Davis did a great job with the golf course this week. It rewarded good golf and punished aggressive golf." But not everyone is as pleased as the Ulsterman. When asked postround what made Pebble so difficult on Sunday, Mickelson stops himself short, saying, "I'm not really sure. I kind of know, but I would rather not get into it. It just doesn't sound good." Lefty's not-so-veiled reference is almost certainly to the bumpy *poa annua* greens, the very surfaces Tiger lambasted on Thursday only to have St. Mick rush to their defense.

In his after-comments Woods blunts the tone of his earlier criticism, making only passing mention of the course "playing too hard, too fast." Asked why a marquee name didn't end up on top, the World Number One takes the most subtle of swipes at the man who is widely seen as having "Tiger-proofed" Pebble: "He [Davis] has given more guys the chance to win the golf tournament. It's more open now. With the graduated rough, being firm and fast like this, it brings a lot more players into play who have a chance to win," Woods says.

Meanwhile, the Golf Channel's outspoken Brandel Chamblee calls Davis's setup of the fourth hole "too short," adding that it "should not be driveable." Colleague Frank Nobilo agrees, calling it "way too short," while singling out the postage stamp–sized, 92-yard seventh hole as the only "weakness" of the course. Alex Miceli goes his fellow commentators one better, accusing the USGA of "manipulating one of the best courses in the country" in its desire to pander to television dramatics.

After finishing his Sunday round, pro Ryan Moore, a past winner of the USGA's U.S. Amateur and U.S. Public Links, launches into what the *Los Angles Times* calls an eight-minute, anti-USGA "rant" that finds him saying, "I feel like instead of difficulty, they just go for trickiness." Moore saves his heaviest artillery for the par-3 seventeenth, where in the final round less than 10 percent of the world's best golfers hit the shallow, canted green with a short iron, and the par-5 fourteenth, the hole where Paul Goydos had shot himself out of contention in the

AT&T with a 9 and where, this week, Zach Johnson made a 9, and Paul Casey, Yang, and Poulter each suffered a snowman. Watching his wedge bound over the dried-out green on seven on Saturday, the ever-political Poulter made his case directly to the worldwide viewing audience, turning to the camera to pose the rhetorical question, "How on earth are you supposed to play to *that*?"

"It wouldn't take much to make that green at least halfway reasonable, and they [the USGA] refuse to do it," Moore tells the *Times* about hole fourteen. "I think they go for a spectacle; they want some hole to draw attention and make everybody look stupid, I guess. It doesn't reward good golf shots like Augusta [National] does, and I don't understand why you'd have a tournament that doesn't reward good golf shots."

When all is said and done, it's not the layout or course setup that makes the 2010 Open such a memorable one, but the human drama it touches on. Today, Father's Day, the highly emotional storyline is all about dads. In a sense, it's been the overriding theme of a U.S. Open year that's been more topsy-turvy in the world of golf than anyone could have ever imagined, a year when the People's Open played in the country the founding fathers made in the name of We-the-People returned to the "granddaddy" of Monterey golf courses, a course conceived by the visionary Samuel Morse, father of Monterey golf—a year punctuated by two sharply contrasting models of father, husband, and golfer: Phil Mickelson and Tiger Woods.

Sunday at the U.S. Open, the culmination of that year-long drama, includes tears, as Tom Watson putts through saline for what is likely to be his last major tournament at Pebble; it includes dark comedy, as a rent-a-plane circles over Pebble's Cliffs of Doom, trailing a banner that reads, "Tiger, are you my daddy?"; and it includes ecstatic hugs exchanged between champion son Graeme and devoted father Kenny, who retired to follow his son's career. "I said, 'You're something, kid,'" Kenny McDowell reports when the media ask him what words he shared with his number one son. "And he said, 'Happy Father's Day, Dad.'"

Fittingly, it is father and local boy Tom Watson—whose brother Ridge lives on the Peninsula, whose father played in the Crosby and adored Pebble Beach—whose story best captures all that Pebble is and all that it has been in the five U.S. Opens here in which Young Tom has teed it up. Among its calculated, hand-picked pairings this week, for the first two rounds the USGA chose to pair golf's Father Time with golf's two most notable rising stars, Rory McIlroy, age twenty-one, and Ryo Ishikawa, age eighteen. "I started adding up the ages," Watson joked with the media on the eve of his first round. "I think their combined age is what, thirty-eight? thirty-nine? I've got them by twenty-one years."

Today, after his final round, Watson can't help but wax philosophic. "It was overwhelming today coming up the eighteenth hole," he says. "Just after I hit my 3-wood into the bunker, it started to hit me. It's Father's Day, with your son on the bag . . . And the memories started to hit me again, and it's just a wonderful feeling to be here at Pebble Beach. I owe a lot—probably most of what I have—to my dad, as far as my ability to play golf. My love for the game, my passion for the game, my ability to play the game; that came from my dad."

After the trophy has been hoisted and duly swaddled, after the obligatory jokes about swilling Guinness from the claret jug have been put to rest, after the scoreboard operators have tossed aside the now-meaningless numbered tiles that once inscribed the sacred birdies and bogeys of Tiger, Phil, Ernie, I set out across the links in the Peninsula gloaming, heading toward the flickering, fairy-tale lights of my home away from home, the village-by-the-sea. It's a walk I can make in my sleep.

At the fourth and fifth greens I meet the stalwart, red-jacketed marshals still standing guard in their soft-soled tennis shoes over Pebble's sacred *poa annua*, shooing away the smattering of fans who approach with a powerful desire to lay hands on the holy of holies.

I understand too well: assets need to be protected. Image must be considered. Soon, USGA section agronomist Pat Gross will be enlisted to reassure the TV audience that the "mottled, spotty, discolored greens that would be alarming and perhaps unacceptable to many super-intendents and golfers" are a natural part of the various "biotypes" that make up Pebble's one-of-a-kind native turf. Gross will go on to tacitly assure would-be bookers of post-Open tee times that, "They [the greens] . . . will continue to provide outstanding enjoyment for golfers who want to see how their game holds up on one of golf's greatest courses."

Tomorrow, Pebble Beach will return to its bread and butter resort play, and leveraging its Open exposure, will run its online banner ad urging this week's new crop of converts to "Play the course of the 2010 U.S. Open!" Rumor has it that Pebble will get $1,000 per round from the hard-cores wanting to play the beauty and the beast fresh on the heels of the world's best pros.

And then there's the rest of this week's impeccably timed news to consider: Pebble will host the 2019 U.S. Open and the 2018 U.S. Ama-teur. "There's a wonderful symmetry for the 2019 U.S. Open," Tom O'Toole said. "Pebble Beach hosted our one-hundredth U.S. Open in 2000. Now, we return to celebrate their centennial with our national championships." Pebble CEO Bill Perocchi seconded the motion, add-ing, "Pebble Beach and the U.S. Open have become synonymous."

Out beyond holes four and five, on the wind-buffeted Arrowhead Point, the marshals have abandoned their posts and in their stead a few dozen of us penitents move in, gently, almost reverently, tiptoe-ing the fringe of a handful of the world's most famous dance floors, crouching low to run our palms across the frog's hair as if stroking the fragile, wispy dome of our firstborn.

Alone in the rock-hard eighth fairway, a father and son hazard the red line marking the Cliffs of Doom. The son, Matthew, peers into the oceanic abyss below with a mixture of fear and wonder and awe while Dad, hovering close, cautions him over and over to stay away from the edge. Further down the hole, on the eighth green, a salty gray-beard in a bright blue knit hat crouches on the kidney-shaped green charading, with crazy arms, the way Watson's putt moved in '82. Beside him, two twenty-somethings stand rapt.

I follow the boy, Matthew, along the rim of the ravine, not for any journalistic purpose but because we share, I think, the youthful instinct to get to edge of things, to the shore of wonder. We want to touch the periphery of the thing we've dreamed, the way you do, eyes closed, hands working, before a tremendous gift. Halfway down nine fairway, and suddenly desirous of the low road, I part ways with the kid, clambering down the sandstone and granite cliff to the beach from whose vantage I regard him now from the worm's eye, his Gap hoodie and U.S. Open lid silhouetted against the robin's egg blue that has infused the sky from Santa Cruz. Above me, he is an idol, an Icarus, a boy Hermes, as free and full of wonder as God made him.

Beneath ten fairway, near the far, southernmost edge of the course that has become part of me during this U.S. Open year, some inspired hands have painstakingly spelled out "Go Phil" in strands of dark seaweed meant to be read from above and, farther down the beach, re-spelled the same blessing, this time in firewood. On the sandstone bank opposite me now, in the mysterious little inlets and coves where wildflowers and kikuyu grow, where unseen water from America's most majestic course trickles down to the sea through unknown fissures, I stop to examine the long-ago love notes etched in porous stone. Almost on cue, a couple tumbles down the cliff onto the beach, arm in arm, Jack and Jill, their U.S. Open badges still swinging at their belt loops.

Mercifully, I leave them, as lovers are meant to be left to their peace, moving to a point further down the beach that affords a view of the yachts and sailboats leaving Stillwater Cove for points unknown. I find myself in the exact spot where, nearly a year ago, I arrived after four days of pilgrimage across burning sands, towering pines, and sky-scraping mountains to bury my feet in Carmel's sugary sands and azure surf; the spot where, one midnight thereafter, I struck two shots: one into the ocean, for sacrifice, and one onto the links above for Dad, for forever.

My U.S. Open year in America's golf mecca has not turned me into a scratch golfer, a Latin lover, a flawless son or brother. I have not joined the ranks of the rich and famous, have not achieved the ageless power and grace of these beautiful blue-green waters. But I have found a home away from home. I have experienced a national treasure that just happens to be a golf course, a golf course that, despite the many imperfections of its guardians, is carefully, unselfishly, even reverently kept.

In 2019, when next the Open is held on these shores, I will be pushing fifty. With any luck I will share the moment with my own son or daughter. I will speak of their grandfather, of Watson and Tiger, of the legendary course and the fairy-tale village that, once upon a time, enchanted me.

I turn back toward the links that dress the ancient cliffs like a garland, back toward the couple who, seizing their moment, have finally and deeply embraced, fingers moving up and down spines, memorizing the topography of the other, storing the feel in the far-off place we reserve for the holy.

And as the sun sets and the granite and grass of Pebble Beach at last yield to shadows, I fall in love all over again.

Acknowledgments

Profoundest thanks to Michael Murphy and Steve Cohen, Jeff Sluman and Bill Murray, Bobby Clampett and Casey Boyns, Ray March and Doug Acton, Kristen Hunter and Ed Vyeda, James Raia and Jerry Stewart, Mayor Sue McCloud and Carmel-by-the-Sea, Robert Boerner and Tim Berg, and all who enlightened my stay on the enlightening Monterey Peninsula; to the many good souls and great swings of the PGA and Champions Tours; to Chris Dalhamer, R. J. Harper, Laird Small, and Aven Wright-McIntosh, for yearly welcoming golf writers to experience America's greatest public course. My esteem belongs to Neal Hotelling, whose fine history *Pebble Beach Golf Links* served as stimulating background reading. Gratitude likewise goes to the good folks at the WorldGolf Network who supported me in my love of Pebble and who were kind enough to publish some of the news stories and interviews resulting from the ecstatic wanderings of my U.S. Open year. Heartfelt thanks to Amber and Nat, especially, for their immaculate hosting, and to Mira, who, though she hardly knew it, kept the manna coffee and good vibes coming.